More Than Painting

Exploring the Wonders of Art in Preschool and Kindergarten

by
Sally Moomaw
and
Brenda Hieronymus

Redleaf Press

Published by: Redleaf Press
a division of Resources for Child Caring
450 North Syndicate, Suite 5
St. Paul, MN 55104-4125

Distributed by: Gryphon House
Mailing Address:
P.O. Box 207
Beltsville, MD 20704-0207

Library of Congress Cataloging-in-Publication Data
Moomaw, Sally, 1948-
More than painting : exploring the wonders of art in preschool and kindergarten / by Sally Moomaw and Brenda Hieronymus.
p. cm.
ISBN 1-884834-67-1
1. Art--Study and teaching (Preschool) 2. Education, Preschool--Activity programs. 3. Kindergarten--Activity programs.
I. Hieronymus, Brenda, 1945- . II. Title.
LB1140.5.A7M66 1999
372.5'044--dc21 99-35321
CIP

To the children, families, and staff of the
Arlitt Child and Family Research and Education Center,
University of Cincinnati

Acknowledgments

As always, we thank the Arlitt Child and Family Research and Education Center for its continued support. Our colleagues continue to inspire us, and the children are our greatest teachers. In particular, we thank Peg Elgas for her insights and support involving group projects.

We are indebted to Charles Moomaw for his extensive computer support in the preparation of this manuscript. We also thank David C. Baxter and PhotoGraphic Services at the University of Cincinnati for once again enthusiastically and patiently working on the photographs for this large project.

We would like to express our appreciation to artist David Kelly, of the Chicago Commons Social Service Agency, and Greg Watton, of the Fort Hayes Metro Education Center, Columbus, Ohio, for their informative workshops on wire and clay. They are very helpful in guiding teachers in the use of these expressive art media with children.

We especially thank the children who participated in the photo sessions: Dominique, Sijia, Wesley, Alex, Alexander, Amadou, Andrew, Andy, Baxter, Becca, Benjamin, Ciara, Dana, Davell, Elias, Elizabeth, Fumi, Haoming, Jack, Jalen, Karen, Katy, Lilly, Maria, Molly, Nikhil, Quentin, Safira, Sharon, Sjaya, Stephanie, Stephen, Steve, TiChina, and Will.

We also thank Napoleon for his willingness to pose as a teacher in some of the photographs in chapter 8.

Contents

Chapter 4 Collage 87

Chapter 5 Painting & Printing 129

Preface

Art is one of the early symbol systems of young children. It is also an important tool for learning about their world, expressing their ideas and feelings, communicating with their friends and families, and exploring their own creative ideas. In order to fully support children's explorations with art, early childhood classrooms must provide a variety of interesting, open-ended materials and large blocks of time for children to explore them. For this reason, the art curriculum is centered around an open art area in the classroom, where children can explore art materials every day, and special activities that focus on particular art materials and techniques. Chapter 2 details a large variety of art area designs, from simple art centers with basic materials for the beginning of the year to more complex and varied areas as the year progresses. Specific suggestions for displaying a wide range of materials are included. Chapters 3 through 7 focus on specific types of art experiences that teachers may plan as special activities: drawing, gluing, painting, printing, sewing, stringing, modeling, and working with three-dimensional materials. Chapter 8 discusses the opportunities for exploring art outdoors.

Children must first construct knowledge about art materials before they can use them creatively. This requires many experiences with basic art media. In order to provide children with the necessary experiences to develop skills and construct relationships about how materials respond to their actions, teachers need to plan many variations on standard activities. Slight changes in activities help maintain children's interest as they fully explore these materials. Repeated experiences with fundamental art materials are far more valuable to children than cute crafts devised by the teacher. Therefore, the chapters on drawing, collages, and painting present basic art experiences with many interesting variations.

Teachers often wonder about the best ways to talk to children about their art. In an effort to be positive and supportive, they frequently respond with comments that are perfunctory and unrelated to the specific artwork. "That's nice" or "how pretty" are typical. In order to help teachers develop skills in commenting on specific artistic elements or the process involved in the art experience, each activity includes suggested comments and questions. Teachers can use these as examples of alternative ways to discuss art with children.

Teachers need some basic information about children's stages of development in the art area before they can successfully plan an extensive art curriculum. Chapter 1 includes information about children's stages in artistic development and relates them to specific classroom planning. Designing an art-rich environment, supporting children's creative development, and the role of the teacher are discussed.

Art is an important vehicle for supporting both individual and group work. Teachers interested in emergent curriculum and group projects often use art to support children's explorations of a topic. Group art projects allow children to express their individual creativity while contributing to a group effort. They have the opportunity to discuss ideas with their peers and observe a variety of ways to artistically explore a topic. For this reason, group art activities are interspersed throughout the book. Class books, group murals, several types of class quilts, group sewing and weaving projects, and collaborative efforts in outdoor activities are included.

More Than Painting follows the familiar format of the other books in the *More Than* series. Each chapter begins with questions teachers often pose related to specific types of art experiences. Each activity includes a photograph that clearly shows the materials and how to present them aesthetically. Clear directions for making or assembling the materials, guidelines for the most appropriate age levels, a list of specific materials, suggestions for what to expect as children use the materials, comments and questions to extend thinking, and modifications or variations are also included with each activity. Where appropriate, activities also include integrated curriculum ideas.

More Than Painting contains over 100 ideas for art experiences. Each activity focuses on the process of creating while emphasizing artistic elements. The book is designed not only to support teachers who are learning how to design and extend basic art experiences, but also to provide ideas for more unusual art media and explorations for teachers looking for new directions and possibilities. All of the art activities have been field-tested in early childhood classrooms. It is our hope that this book will provide an extensive resource for a wide range of early childhood teachers, parents, and caregivers.

The Art-Rich Classroom

The early childhood classroom hums with life. Throughout the environment, children interact with art on many levels:

In the art area, three children draw with markers and add selected collage materials to their creations. Stories emerge as they describe the ongoing action in their pictures.

At the special activity table, a group of children press clay into a variety of shapes. One child exclaims that he has placed a bird nest on the top of his tower.

In the reading area, a child marvels at the beautiful illustrations in the book that a parent volunteer is reading to her. She asks if she can use the same colors of paint at the easel.

At the easel, a child paints streaks with brushes of varying widths. He carefully watches the lines created by each brush.

A small group of children cluster around a painting by a Native American artist that was recently added to their classroom. They eagerly discuss the shapes and colors they see in the painting while their teacher records their observations.

Through a large window, a child watches as another class uses feather dusters to paint a large mural stretched across the fence of the outside area. He asks if his class will get a chance to paint with the feather dusters when they go outside.

Art is an important tool for exploration and expression for young children. It helps frame their perceptions of their world. Through their artwork, children can explore complex ideas and emotions at a manageable level:

> *A family portrait sometimes includes or excludes a new baby.*
> *A scary monster seen on TV is fatally stabbed by a young boy.*
> *Giant buildings are reduced to people-size.*
> *A desired pet is drawn over and over again.*

Children naturally gravitate toward art as a way to explore new materials and experiment with an ongoing creative process. In art-rich classrooms, opportunities for art exploration are woven throughout the curriculum.

Why are art explorations so important for young children? Why do children spend so much time with art materials?

- ▲ Art is one of the early ***symbol systems*** of young children. While children initially have no concept of drawing something specific, during the preschool years they increasingly attempt to represent objects, actions, and ideas through their art, and their artwork becomes both more realistic and more imaginative.[1]
- ▲ Manipulating art materials helps children develop ***fine-motor skills***. Painting, drawing, cutting, and modeling with clay and playdough all utilize muscle groups in slightly different ways and contribute to overall strength and dexterity in the fine motor area.
- ▲ Experimenting with art materials encourages the construction of ***physical knowledge***. Children learn that paint and glue have different properties when they are wet and dry. Colors can combine to produce new colors. Some materials have properties of adhesion and others do not. Paint drips on a vertical surface but not on a horizontal one. The type of painting or drawing tool used affects the mark on the paper. These are just a few of the many physical-knowledge concepts constructed by children as they explore art media.
- ▲ Art fosters ***creativity***. As children acquire information about the properties of art materials, they can then utilize the materials to create representations of their own experiences and imaginings.
- ▲ Art encourages ***cultural sharing***. Since most cultures have some form of art, opportunities to experience the art of many cultures encourages children to understand similarities among diverse peoples; however, since art materials, techniques, and styles vary among cultures, exploring the cultural aspects of art also helps children understand differences.

- ▲ Art experiences aid ***cognitive development***. As children experiment with various aspects of art materials and the creative process, they develop more complex reasoning. They learn cause-and-effect relationships and utilize the symbolic properties of art to further their thinking.
- ▲ Art assists in ***language development***. Research, supported by ongoing teacher observations, shows that children converse and socialize as they create with art materials. They describe to one another what is happening in their pictures, evaluate and comment on one another's work, and create elaborate stories to expand upon the action shown in their pictures. Children often "piggyback" off one another and add aspects of each other's language to their own descriptions.[2]
- ▲ Art provides ***emotional release***. Children may use art materials to express difficult feelings. One child painted only in black and dark gray for several weeks following the death of his grandmother.
- ▲ Art experiences foster ***art appreciation***. Children learn to look more carefully at their environment and at art representations. They explore texture, perspective, shading, design, balance, and form. Their own experiences aid them in understanding and appreciating the artwork of others.

Art and the Young Child

For young children, art is much more a process than a product. Their excitement and enjoyment come from interacting with the materials and experiencing the result. Initially, children don't know what to expect. What happened to the red when they put the yellow on top? Why doesn't the glitter sparkle after they smear glue over it? Where did the white glue on their picture go, and what is that clear hard stuff that's there now? Why does the silly putty ooze off the tray? The playdough never did that. What will it feel like if they spread the paint with their hands?

To adults, it may look like children are just playing or making a mess. It certainly does not look like art. However, children are going through an important process. They are learning about the properties of art materials and are storing the information for future use. After children have had many experiences with art media, they begin to use that information to create. Art becomes more than an experience; it evolves into a means for expression and communication, whether it be just for themselves or to share with others. For example, the child who initially just cut slits with the scissors now uses them to cut out a circle. Because she understands the properties of glue, she uses it to adhere the circle to a piece of paper. She draws eyes and cheeks with a wide-tip marker and a smiling mouth with a fine-tip marker. Next she cuts pieces of yarn and staples them to the top of the circle to produce hair that bounces. She uses both her knowledge of the materials and her own imagination to create a unique representation of herself.

As children explore art materials, they progress through predictable and sequential stages of artistic development. The two broad stages, scribbling and representational, also contain progressive substages within them. While all children pass through the same stages, the ages and rates of development vary widely depending on experience and individual characteristics. **Table 1** is a summary of the stages of artistic development along with implications for planning art experiences.[3] Note that there is some overlap of stages.

Art and the Early Childhood Teacher

Early childhood teachers play a crucial role in guiding children's development of creative expression through art. The teacher's role includes:

- guiding children in the exploration of a wide variety of art materials
- helping children visualize what they want to represent, while avoiding creating models
- commenting appropriately about children's artwork
- documenting children's progress in the use of art materials

Teachers who encourage children's free exploration of art materials create an environment that supports the development of children's creativity. By commenting on the process involved in art experiences, teachers help guide children in understanding the properties of art media and how their actions affect the materials. Carefully formulated questions may direct children's attention toward aspects of the experience that they may not have previously noticed. For this reason, each activity in this book includes suggested comments and questions for teachers to facilitate children's construction of knowledge when exploring art materials.

While teachers may sometimes teach techniques in using art materials, such as coiling with clay, it is important to avoid creating product models. This stifles children's creativity since it encourages them to copy the model rather than to create their own representation. Modeled art also frustrates many young children, who can seldom create a copy that is as perfect as the adult model. Thus, modeled art tends to discourage children's interest in art rather than to encourage and nurture it.

Table 1
Relationship of Stages of Children's Artistic Development to Art Experiences

Stage	Phase	Characteristics	Art Experiences
Scribbling Stage 1½ to 4 years	*Random Scribbling*	• use large arm movements • show interest in process • make no attempt at representation • take pleasure in tactile experiences • produce accidental, random marks • hold marking tools with whole hand	• need large paper (at least 8 by 10 inches) • may need to have paper taped to the table • can hold chubby crayons and brushes • explore art materials tactilely • need close adult supervision to keep hands and art materials out of their mouths
	Controlled Scribbling	• use wrist movements rather than large arm movements • make smaller marks on paper • produce a variety of lines • pay close attention to the marks they are producing • stay within the confines of the paper • may place scribbles in particular areas of the paper	• still need large paper • continue to explore art materials tactilely • can hold chubby crayons, markers, and brushes • may continue to need close adult supervision so that they do not put art materials in their mouths
	Named Scribbling	• give names to scribbles • do not plan specific forms to draw ahead of time • may change names of scribbles while drawing • hold marking tools with fingers • show better fine motor control • spend more time drawing	• may prefer marking implements that are smaller in diameter, such as thinner pencils or crayons • can use paper in a variety of sizes and shapes • can utilize a wider variety of drawing implements, including pencils, markers, crayons, and chalk • may benefit from special activities related to specific topics, such as a class book related to a song or book
Representational Stage 4 to 7 years	*Design Phase*	• make first representations • draw recognizable geometric shapes • elaborate on drawn shapes to create symbolic representations	• use a variety of drawing implements • may wish to combine drawing tools • may combine drawing implements with collage materials
	Almost Pictures	• draw what they know, not what they see • may focus on drawing people • adults may still not recognize the objects drawn by the child	• may wish to add dictation to accompany drawings • may desire opportunities to practice drawing the same thing over and over • continue to need open-ended experiences
	Pictures	• draw different objects in different pictures rather than repeating the same forms • draw pictures that tell stories • combine different art materials in one picture • demonstrate spacing and balance	• may have a stronger desire to dictate stories to go with their pictures • may write their own captions for pictures • enjoy drawing and conversing with other children • may utilize art to further play, such as creating puppets or costumes • get ideas from one another, which they incorporate into their artwork

While many teachers would not think of introducing modeled art, they may be lured into it by children who ask them to draw particular objects. Rather than succumbing to a child's request to draw a particular form, such as an elephant, the teacher might ask leading questions to guide the child. Does an elephant have a head? What do the ears look like? How many legs does an elephant have? This breaks the project into manageable segments rather than the overwhelming task of drawing a whole elephant. If the child has trouble remembering what an elephant looks like, the teacher can serve as a resource and supply books or photographs of elephants to assist the child. In this way, the teacher facilitates the child's artistic development, rather than ignoring the issues posed by the child, yet avoids solving the problem by drawing the elephant for the child.

Teachers often wonder what to say when children show them their artwork. Some teachers fall into the habit of always saying, "That's nice," or "It's pretty." Such comments, though positive, are judgmental. They are also frequently fake, and children readily perceive this. Instead, teachers might focus on a particular aspect of the picture and comment on that. For example:

> *"This person looks happy. I see a big smile. That makes me feel happy, too."*
> *"You put a circle inside of each one of your squares."*
> *"You covered up all of the white on the paper with paint."*

The teacher might also comment about the process used in creating the picture:

> *"I see a lot of purple on your picture, but I don't see any jars of purple paint. How did you make purple?"*
> *"Some of your lines are wide, and some are thin. What did you use to make the thick lines?"*

Art activities provide excellent examples of children's development in the fine motor and creative areas. Many teachers include selected examples of each child's work in a portfolio to share with parents at various times during the year.

Art and the Early Childhood Classroom

Art in the early childhood classroom emerges in four ways:

1. through child-designed activities in an open art area
2. during specially planned activities

3. through work on group projects
4. incidentally, throughout the day, and in various areas of the classroom

Art areas provide children with a wide variety of materials and tools to fuel the creative art process. Although the art area is a permanent part of the classroom, teachers can regularly change the materials to reflect long-range goals, the overall classroom curriculum, and input from the children. The art area allows children extended periods of time to fully explore materials, experiment with combining media, engage in the creative process, and converse with other children about ongoing creations. Chapter 2 provides specific information about setting up art areas, as well as many examples.

Special activities allow children to experiment with specific art media or tools that may need more adult supervision than materials in the art area. For example, while finger paint might be too messy to include in an open art area, children can explore it fully at a special activity table with an adult to facilitate. A special activity table also allows teachers to highlight particular activities that they wish to explore with children. Typically, the special activity table is located near the art area but separate from it. This helps children distinguish highlighted activities from art center materials. The table usually seats three or four children. Materials are attractively displayed, often with a tray for each child to hold the materials needed for the activity. Painting, sewing, gluing, modeling with clay, drawing, or stringing are some of the many art experiences that might be presented as a special activity.

Many teachers are interested in facilitating group projects with young children. Often these projects include representations or experiments with art materials. Projects allow children to express their individual ideas within the context of a group exploration. Art is often the medium chosen by children to interpret their ideas. Teachers may encourage children to explore various aspects of a project through a variety of art materials in order to increase the thinking and creativity of the children.

Art is one of the many languages of children.[4] As such, children often utilize art throughout the day to extend play opportunities, communicate their ideas to one another, or record new discoveries. Art is not limited to particular areas of the classroom, but rather extends throughout the curriculum. For example, children in the dramatic play area might decide to make party invitations with fanciful decorations on them. In the block area, children might create maps to reach hidden treasure or draw representations of favorite block structures in order to remember how they were built. In the science area, a child might trace leaves and copy their colors and lines. Teachers can encourage children throughout the day and across the curriculum to extend their ideas through art.

Goals

As teachers, parents, and caregivers reflect upon the importance of art in the development of young children, particular goals emerge:

- ▲ provide opportunities for children to explore a wide variety of art materials
- ▲ nurture the creative process
- ▲ expose children to the art of many cultures
- ▲ encourage the construction of knowledge through carefully planned activities
- ▲ enjoy art with children, and encourage their appreciation of art
- ▲ provide opportunities for group participation in art creations
- ▲ explore many forms of art with children, including painting, drawing, gluing, sculpting, and creating with multimedia

These goals allow for the individual needs and interests of young children, encourage active participation in the creative process, and facilitate the construction of knowledge. They also encourage collaboration among children as they work together and communicate their thoughts, both verbally and through the medium of art.

Endnotes

1. Barry J. Wadsworth, *Piaget's Theory of Cognitive and Affective Development*, 4th ed. (New York: Longman, 1989), 61.
2. Anne Haas Dyson, "Symbol Makers, Symbol Weavers: How Children Link Play, Pictures, and Print." *Young Children*, 1990, 45(2):50–57.
3. Information on children's stages of drawing compiled from Viktor Lowenfeld and W. Lambert Brittain, *Creative and Mental Growth*, 8th ed. (New York: MacMillan, 1987), 474–5; and E. Anne Eddowes, "Drawing in Early Childhood: Predictable Stages." *Dimensions of Early Childhood*, Fall, 1995:16–17.
4. Carol Edwards, Lella Gandini, and George Forman, *The Hundred Languages of Children* (Norwood, NJ: Ablex, 1996), 119.

Art Areas

Samudra moved directly to the art area as his class entered the classroom from the outside area. He surveyed the art shelves and selected several pieces of green construction paper, scissors, markers, and a stapler. He sat down at a nearby table with his materials and was soon busy cutting out a variety of shapes from the paper. As Samudra worked, he chatted with several other children also working at the art table. "I'm making a man, and he'll be able to run and jump." As his project proceeded, Samudra stapled the shapes together to form a human body with head, body, arms, and legs. He then drew a face on his creation and showed everyone at the table the moving parts on his man.

▲ ▲ ▲

The art area allows children extended periods of time to explore a wide variety of art materials. Children first experiment with the materials to discover their physical properties and then use them to create. An open art area as part of the early childhood classroom enables children to return again and again to fully explore the creative potential of the materials. They develop fine motor skills as they learn to manipulate tools such as scissors, hole punches, staplers, and markers. The art area also provides a rich setting for children to converse and create stories as they share their artistic endeavors with one another.

Teachers' Questions

Why is it important to have art areas in early childhood classrooms?

Art areas enable children to explore a wide variety of materials over extended periods of time; experiment with art tools, such as scissors, staplers, and hole punches; and combine materials in many creative ways. Children need long periods of time and repeated experiences in order to construct knowledge about the physical properties of art materials. Their skill at using art implements also develops over time. It is only after children have had extensive opportunities to experiment with art media that they are able to use their knowledge and skill to begin to create. Art areas afford children the time needed to explore materials, experience the creative process, and communicate ideas with one another.

How should an art area be set up?

Art materials and equipment should be neatly displayed on low shelves so that children have ready access to the materials. A table next to the art shelves provides a space for children to work with the art materials. Art materials should be aesthetically displayed so that they are inviting to children. Divided trays for collage materials, baskets or holders for markers and scissors, and special trays or shelf sections for paper enable children to clearly see all of the materials and consider various possibilities for their use. When an art area becomes cluttered and the materials jumbled, children are less motivated to use the area. Children are also less likely to respect the materials and use them appropriately when the area looks "junky." Many teachers apply labels to the various sections of the art shelves so that children can readily return materials to their proper places when they are finished using them.

What materials should be included in an art area?

The art area should include standard art tools, such as markers, scissors, and glue; paper; and a variety of supplemental materials, such as collage pieces, that can be changed periodically to encourage continued interest in the area. Some items are typically included in the art center throughout the year. Glue, markers, and scissors might fall into this category. However, teachers may vary these materials slightly over time in order to extend children's experiences with familiar materials. For example, the glue might occasionally be colored with food coloring, double-line markers might temporarily replace standard markers, and scissors that cut jagged or curved lines might sometimes be substituted for some of the regular scissors. Changes in standard tools should be made sparingly so that children can have many opportunities to create with art implements that they expect to find in the art area.

Accessory materials in the art area are usually changed more regularly to foster ongoing interest in the area. Size and type of paper, collage materials, and various types of drawing materials rotate in and out of the art area depending on the interest of the children, the overall curriculum, and the teacher's long-range goals. Additional items, such as materials for stringing or stamp pads, may sometimes be added.

What types of activities are appropriate for an art area?

Drawing, gluing, and cutting activities are commonly available in art areas. Additional activities, such as stringing pasta or beads, paint-

ing with sponge-top bottles, or punching out shapes with design hole punches, might also be included periodically. A main concern when supplying an art center is including materials that do not necessitate a large amount of adult supervision. Activities that need adult monitoring, such as fingerpainting or drawing with crayons on warming trays, can be planned as special activities so that an adult can always be present. Of course, children's abilities to independently handle materials vary with age, experience, and development. Sometimes a teacher might plan an activity first as a special activity and later transfer it to the art area after children have had experience manipulating the materials. Designs for art areas and art area activities are included in the activity section of this chapter. **Table 2** suggests materials and activities that might always be present in an art area as well as additional materials or activities to add on occasion.

Table 2
Materials & Activities to Include in Art Areas

Standard Materials	Additional Materials
• 3 or 4 sets of markers	• collage materials, such as:
• 3 or 4 glue jars	colored pasta
• 3 or 4 pairs of scissors	small pieces of colored paper
• 3 or 4 pencils	fabric scraps
• inexpensive white paper	glitter
• construction paper	natural materials (leaves, nuts, shells, etc.)
• stapler	colored cotton balls
• hole punch	ribbon pieces
• masking tape	• design hole punches
• cellophane tape	• crayons
• recycling box	• colored pencils
	• stamp pads
	• stringing materials, such as:
	colored rigatoni
	pasta wheels
	straws cut in pieces
	pony beads
	• chalk
	• colored glue
	• design scissors
	• roll-top paint bottles
	• sponge-top paint bottles
	• corrugated paper
	• foil
	• doilies

Note: These materials are recommended for older preschool or kindergarten classrooms. Teachers should make selections based on the age and development of the children in their own classrooms.

How often are accessory materials changed?

The length of time that accessory materials remain in the art area depends on the interest of the children. Two to three weeks is typical, with slight changes or modifications occurring as needed. Changes are often made gradually. For example, if children are very interested in colored cotton balls, they might remain on the shelf while other materials that have lost their appeal are changed. Teachers sometimes introduce new materials gradually so that children are not initially overwhelmed. For example, the teacher might start with one type of pasta on the art shelf for stringing. Later, when children are adept at cutting the plastic stringing cord and manipulating the pasta, the teacher might introduce a variety of other sizes and shapes of pasta.

How does an open art area encourage creativity?

An open art area allows children to combine materials in a limitless variety of ways. While special activities are typically designed with a particular technique or type of material in mind, the manner in which materials in an art area are used or combined is controlled by each child's imagination and desire to experiment. Thus, in the opening anecdote of this chapter, Samudra was able to use the stapler in a unique way that enabled him to move the body parts of the man he created. Such imaginative applications of materials occur often in open art areas.

What concepts do children construct when working in art areas?

Children construct knowledge about the function of art implements and how their actions with these tools affect various art media. For example, children discover that if they use the side of a crayon instead of the tip, the crayon makes a very different mark. If they press down hard with the crayon, the mark is darker. If they color too many times over the same spot, they may wear a hole in the paper.

Children also learn about the unique characteristics of various art materials. Paint and glue start out wet, but later dry. Glitter sticks to their paper if they sprinkle it over glue but does not stick to marker. Glue changes from white to clear when it dries, but paint maintains its color. Yellow and blue paint combine to make green, and so do yellow and blue cellophane. The list of children's discoveries in the art area is endless.

How do art areas differ depending on the age of the children?

Art areas for older children usually have a greater variety of materials and tools. Since older children have typically had more experience with art materials than younger children, they are often ready for tools and materials that are more difficult to manipulate. For example, older preschoolers can usually handle scissors, staplers, and small pasta for stringing without much adult facilitation. Younger children, on the other hand, might need an adult to hold the paper while they cut, help them press on the stapler, and monitor the pasta so that they do not put it in their mouths. Thus, the teacher might wait until her class is older and more experienced before adding such items to the art shelf.

Art areas for younger children often have several containers of the same material. Young preschool children, who are typically in the developmental stage of parallel play, are often just learning to share materials. Having duplicates of art materials allows children to work next to each other without having to argue over materials. As children become more mature, they learn to share materials, wait for turns, and negotiate trades. Activity 2.3 provides an example of an art area for young preschoolers, while activities 2.4 and 2.5 are designed for older preschool and kindergarten children respectively.

How do art areas change from the beginning to the end of the year?

Many teachers start the year with basic materials attractively arranged. As the year progresses, more materials are added and the activities become more complex. Starting with a limited amount of basic materials minimizes management concerns as children "learn the ropes." Markers, paper, glue, and a single type of collage material might provide a good beginning for some classrooms. Later, as children learn how to manipulate more materials and art tools, the amount and complexity of available materials increases. As children become more accustomed to classroom routines, they are able to assume responsibility for putting away an increasing variety of materials in the art center. Activity 2.1 describes an art area for the beginning of the year, while activity 2.2 includes changes for later in the year.

Are works by artists ever displayed in art areas?

Children may be stimulated to think creatively about their own art through exposure to the work of established artists. Therefore, prints of art from various cultures, as well as artwork in other media, may sometimes be displayed to broaden the artistic experiences of children. Exposing children to quality art is very different from encouraging children to copy teacher-created models. From the work of acknowledged artists, children may observe detail, shading, spacing, form, and the use of color. Such exposure may inspire them to experiment with these dimensions in their own art. This is very different from the conformity that often results from teacher-created models.

What is the teacher's role?

The teacher plans materials and activities for the art area based on the developmental levels of the children, their interests, the overall classroom curriculum, and long-range goals for artistic development. As children mature and have more experience with art materials, their changing development is reflected in the teacher's plans for the area.

Often teachers include items in the art area to support the interests of the children. For example, when a class became interested in spaceships, one teacher provided a variety of knobs, gadgets, springs, and wire, which the children then used to design flying saucers, spaceships, and space stations. Sometimes children bring materials of interest from home, such as pebbles or stickers, to include in the art area.

Teachers sometimes correlate materials on the art shelves with the overall classroom curriculum. For example, fabric squares, wallpaper cut into geometric shapes, and fabric to draw on might be included in the art area for a class working on a quilt project. Ideas for art centers based on seasonal changes, sea life, dance, valentines, quilts, and babies are included in this chapter.

Teachers also consider long-range art goals when designing art areas. Therefore, a variety of materials and art implements may be introduced throughout the year. For example, in order to encourage children to experiment with shading, crayons might be substituted for the ever-popular markers since children can shade with crayons but not with markers. Teachers might also alter traditional paper shapes in order to spark renewed creativity. Ideas for an art center based on circular shapes are included in activity 2.10.

Teachers assist children in learning to use materials by encouraging them to experiment. For young children, the creative process is often more important than the outcome. Teachers can encourage children to try a variety of activities and comment on the process so that children more closely observe the relationship between the way they use a tool and the result. For example, the teacher might comment:

> *"Look. This marker made two lines at the same time. I wonder why."*
> *"The glitter fell off this part of the paper, but it's sticking over here."*
> *"Look what happened when your red cellophane overlapped the blue."*

How can teachers avoid clean-up problems with art areas?

Teachers can start with fewer materials, label the shelves, and foster clean-up as an ongoing part of daily classroom routines. Children are less overwhelmed by clean-up when there are fewer items to put away, so limiting the number of materials on the art shelves in the beginning of the year really helps. Clear labels for the materials on the art shelves assist children in remembering where they belong. Pictures to accompany the words on the labels help children independently follow the signs. Routines are an important part of classroom management, so stressing clean-up as the final step in the use of all areas of the classroom establishes clear expectations for children.

How can teachers assess children's use of art areas?

Teachers can include descriptions of each child's use of art materials in ongoing anecdotal records. They can also save examples or photocopies of children's work for portfolio assessments. Anecdotal records should be as detailed as possible. For example, if a child drew with markers, the teacher might include the way the child held the markers, which hand was used, what the child said about the drawing, how much time was spent in the area, and the stage of drawing represented. Samples of children's work are invaluable. Paper snipped or cut with scissors, examples of drawing, and photographs of more complex projects all show aspects of a child's continued development in the fine motor and creative domains. Some teachers keep a folder or notebook for each child to hold examples of their work; other teachers divide a loose-leaf notebook into sections for each child with pocket holders to contain work samples. Some teachers include art samples in a scrapbook compiled for each family at the end of the year.

Art Area Activities

2.1 The Basic Art Area

Starting the Year

Description

This standard art area is designed to provide children with clear and easy access to art materials. The materials each have a specific place on the shelves that is clearly labeled. Materials are contained in attractive baskets, trays, or holders so that they are aesthetically pleasing. Standard tools for drawing, gluing, and cutting are included.

Helpful Hints

Put the glue in containers with brushes or plastic spreaders. Children will quickly squeeze all of the glue out of bottles.

Art Experiences

- ▲ drawing
- ▲ gluing
- ▲ cutting

Materials

- ▲ 3 sets of markers
- ▲ 3 glue containers, with spreaders
- ▲ 4 pairs of children's scissors
- ▲ 3 colors of construction paper
- ▲ 2 divided trays, with colored crepe paper pieces for collage

Child's Level

This basic art area is appropriate for young preschool children or older preschool and kindergarten children at the beginning of the school year.

What to Look For

Children will experiment with the materials.

Some children will put collage materials on top of the glue and then pull them off. They do not yet realize that glue can be used to adhere materials after it dries.

Some children will not realize that the glue has to go under the collage pieces. At first, they may put the glue on top.

Children may display different stages of drawing, from scribbling to representation.

Some children will make snips with the scissors, while others will cut across the paper. Some children may not know how to hold the scissors.

Modifications

Add another type of collage material, such as colored pasta, after the children have had some initial experiences with glue.

Reduce the number of markers in each set to three or four for very young preschoolers.

Comments & Questions to Extend Thinking

What happens when you put the crepe paper on top of the glue?

Let's leave the crepe paper on top of the glue and see what happens by the end of school.

What can you do with these colors of markers?

Would you like to try the scissors?

Do you want me to hold the paper while you cut?

Integrated Curriculum Activities

Take photographs of the children using art materials. Children can describe their experiences as they look at the photos.

Include books about the start-up of school, such as *Betsy's First Day at Day Care*, by Gunilla Wolde (New York: Random House, 1976).

Put color paddles in the science area so that children can experiment with color in another part of the classroom.

Change the words to the familiar finger play "Open Shut Them" to describe the movement of the scissors when cutting (see *More Than Singing*, activity 7.4).

2.2 The Basic Art Area

Later in the Year

Description

As children become accustomed to using art materials in open art areas, teachers can include additional materials and more complex activities. However, many of the standard materials remain. This center includes basic materials that have been modified, such as colored glue. It also introduces new tools, such as hole punches and staplers. Colored chalk and colored pencils replace markers for variety in drawing activities.

Helpful Hints

Pasta can be colored by mixing a little food coloring in alcohol or water, dipping the pasta, and letting it dry. It dries faster if alcohol is used.

Art Experiences

- ▲ drawing
- ▲ gluing
- ▲ cutting
- ▲ stringing
- ▲ creating holes
- ▲ holding materials together

Materials

- ▲ 2 sets of colored chalk
- ▲ 2 sets of colored pencils
- ▲ multicultural crayons
- ▲ 3 jars of glue colored with food coloring (pink, blue, and yellow)
- ▲ divided tray, with pieces of colored cellophane for collage

- ▲ hole punch
- ▲ 4 pairs of children's scissors
- ▲ divided tray, with colored pasta and plastic cord for stringing
- ▲ stapler
- ▲ manila paper, 9 by 12 inches
- ▲ cellophane tape
- ▲ masking tape

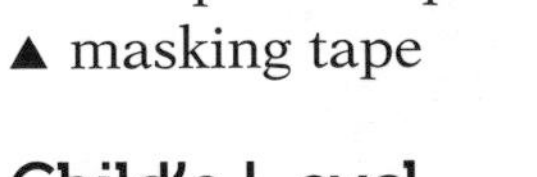

Child's Level

This art area is most appropriate for preschool and kindergarten children who have had experience using standard art materials and art areas.

What to Look For

Children will experiment with combining the colors of glue.
Children will notice that the color of the cellophane changes as it is placed on various colors of glue.
Children will experiment with materials that are new to them.
Some children will use the stapler or tape to create mixed-media products or three-dimensional art.
Children will notice that chalk and colored pencils create marks that differ from those produced by markers.

Modification

For some classes, this area might provide too many choices. If this is the case, limit the drawing choices to either chalk or colored pencils, and use only one type of tape and one color of glue.

Comments & Questions to Extend Thinking

How does the yellow cellophane look when you put it on the blue glue?
Does the pink chalk look the same as the pink pencil on your paper?
How can you hold the cutout parts of your person together?
This red cellophane looks orange here and blue on this part of the paper. I wonder why.

Integrated Curriculum Activities

Read *Little Blue and Little Yellow,* by Leo Lionni (New York: Astor-Honor, 1959). In this book, colored blobs similar to colored cellophane combine to form new colors.
Introduce colored chalk as a special activity. Children can mist their chalk drawings with water and observe how they change (see *More Than Magnets*, activity 5.23).

2.3 Art Area for Young Preschoolers

Description

Young children benefit from basic art materials that are easy to manipulate. For this area, large crayons replace markers so that young children do not have to manipulate the marker caps. Bottle caps and crepe paper pieces, which are easy to glue, are available for collage. Small pieces of paper are included for cutting, since young children have difficulty cutting large pieces of paper with scissors. There are duplicates of each type of tool or material, including collage baskets, to encourage parallel play among children.

Helpful Hints

Ask parents to collect bottle caps for the class. Milk bottle caps come in bright colors.

Art Experiences

- ▲ drawing
- ▲ cutting
- ▲ gluing

Materials

- ▲ 4 sets of large crayons
- ▲ 2 baskets of bottle caps, for collage
- ▲ 2 baskets of crepe paper pieces, for collage
- ▲ 4 small baskets, each with small squares of paper and a pair of scissors
- ▲ 4 containers of glue, with plastic glue spreaders
- ▲ manila drawing paper, 9 by 12 inches

Child's Level
This art area is most appropriate for young preschool children.

What to Look For
Children will experiment with the various tools and materials.
Children will snip the small pieces of paper as they learn to manipulate the scissors.
Children will make marks on the paper with the crayons and observe the results.
Some children will not realize that glue adheres materials after it dries. Therefore, they may put collage materials on top of the glue and then pull them off.
Some children will not realize that the glue has to go under the collage pieces. At first, they may put the glue on top.

Modification
If the children seem overwhelmed by two types of collage materials, start with just the crepe paper.

Comments & Questions to Extend Thinking
What happens when you put the bottle caps on top of the glue?
Can you cut this paper with the scissors?
Let's leave the crepe paper on top of the glue until the end of school and see what happens.
You used every color of crayon on your picture.

Integrated Curriculum Activities
Sing a simple cutting song as children learn to use the scissors (see *More Than Singing*, activity 7.4).
Document the art process by taking photographs of the children using the materials. Children can dictate or write comments to describe the photographs.

2.4 Art Area for Older Preschoolers

Description

This art area design includes a wider variety of materials for this older group. Materials that could not be used by younger children, such as hole punches and staplers, are introduced. Collage materials are presented in divided trays rather than individual baskets since older preschoolers are better able to share materials than younger children. Styrofoam modeling is also a new addition.

Art Experiences

▲ drawing
▲ gluing
▲ cutting
▲ holding materials together
▲ three-dimensional construction
▲ creating holes

Helpful Hints

Coffee stirrers also work well to stick into Styrofoam for modeling activities.

Materials

▲ 3 sets of markers
▲ 4 pencils
▲ white construction paper, 9 by 12 inches
▲ large computer paper (donated)
▲ 3 glue jars, with spreaders
▲ 4 pairs of children's scissors
▲ 2 hole punches
▲ divided collage tray, with several types of colored pasta

- ▲ divided collage tray, with colored ribbon and lace pieces
- ▲ Styrofoam plates, small Styrofoam packing pieces, and toothpicks
- ▲ 2 staplers

Child's Level

This art area is most appropriate for older preschool children who have had experience using standard art materials and art areas.

What to Look For

Children will explore the various art materials.

Children will show a variety of stages of drawing in their artwork.

Some children will draw figures or shapes and cut them out, while others will still be learning to accurately manipulate the scissors.

Children will use the toothpicks to hold the Styrofoam pieces to the Styrofoam plates.

Children may add other materials, such as pieces of lace or pasta with holes, to their Styrofoam creations.

Modification

For younger children, eliminate the toothpicks. They can glue materials onto the Styrofoam plates. Remove the hole punches and staplers if necessary.

Comments & Questions to Extend Thinking

What can you use to stick these Styrofoam pieces onto the plates?

You glued pasta wheels all around the edge of the plate to make a border.

Will the scissors cut through the Styrofoam plate?

Jenny made big holes in her plate with the hole punch and little holes with a toothpick.

Integrated Curriculum Activities

Try a group project with large pieces of Styrofoam. Children can stick a variety of materials onto the Styrofoam with pipe cleaners and toothpicks.

Put large pieces of Styrofoam packing material, golf tees, and playdough hammers in the science area. Children can hammer the golf tees into the Styrofoam and use spoons to pry them out (see *More Than Magnets*, activity 3.8).

2.5 Kindergarten Art Area

Description

Many kindergarten classrooms have art areas, but the materials are sometimes cluttered and "junky," making the area unattractive to children and difficult for them to use appropriately. This art area presents kindergarten-level materials in an aesthetically pleasing way that is easily accessible to children. The area incorporates materials, such as paint, that might not be included on open art shelves in the preschool. It illustrates a range of activities that might be planned for an art area for kindergartners.

Helpful Hints

Ask parents to save small boxes, cardboard tubes, and other containers to use for this center.

Art Experiences

- ▲ drawing
- ▲ painting
- ▲ gluing
- ▲ cutting
- ▲ stringing
- ▲ three-dimensional construction
- ▲ holding materials together
- ▲ creating holes

Materials

- ▲ 3 sets of fine-line markers
- ▲ 3 sets of colored pencils
- ▲ 3 sets of crayons
- ▲ 2 sets of tempera paint
- ▲ 4 glue containers, with spreaders
- ▲ collage tray, with squares of colored fabric or paper
- ▲ 4 pairs of children's scissors

- ▲ construction paper
- ▲ 4 pairs of children's design scissors
- ▲ stringing tray, with colored pasta, beads, and plastic cord
- ▲ container, with small cardboard boxes and tubes
- ▲ masking tape
- ▲ cellophane tape
- ▲ stapler
- ▲ 2 hole punches

Child's Level

This art area is most appropriate for kindergarten children who have had experience with a variety of types of art materials.

What to Look For

Children may combine materials to make unique creations, such as taping or gluing the cardboard boxes and tubes together and then painting them.

Some children may create patterns with the stringing activity.

Children may add cloth to their cardboard constructions.

Many children will draw representationally, but some may not yet be at this stage.

Modification

This kindergarten art area may be too complex for the beginning of the year. If so, use the design scissors for a special activity and save the paint until needed for a specific project.

Comments & Questions to Extend Thinking

What can you make with these boxes and tubes?

Would you like to design some jewelry with these beads?

Which pair of scissors made this scalloped line?

Ask Jared what he did to put shades of brown in his person's hair.

Integrated Curriculum Activities

Read the book *Galimoto*, by Karen Lynn Williams (New York: Lothrop, 1991), to the class. A boy makes unusual toys with found objects.

Add tubes to the block area. Children may incorporate them into their block creations.

2.6 Autumn Art Area

Description

Children notice many changes in the environment during autumn which may be expressed in their artwork. This art area encourages children to explore the change of season by incorporating seasonal colors and natural materials into the art area. Collage materials include nuts, seeds, pine needles, and colored leaves. Paper and marker choices are red, orange, yellow, and brown. A photograph or painting of a sunflower, displayed along with a real sunflower, may inspire some children to experiment with creating flowers.

Helpful Hints

Leaves curl up as they dry. To prevent this, press the leaves flat by placing them under a heavy book overnight. They will then stay flat indefinitely.

Art Experiences

- ▲ creating with natural materials
- ▲ gluing
- ▲ drawing
- ▲ cutting
- ▲ creating negative space with leaf hole punches

Materials

- ▲ natural materials, separated in a divided tray (includes pine needles, magnolia pods, nuts, seeds, and dried weeds)
- ▲ basket of pressed, colored leaves
- ▲ leaf template
- ▲ leaf-shape hole punches
- ▲ tape
- ▲ 3 sets of markers (red, yellow, orange, and brown)
- ▲ 3 sets of crayons (red, yellow, orange, and brown)
- ▲ construction paper (red, yellow, orange, and brown)
- ▲ 4 pairs of children's scissors
- ▲ 3 glue containers, with spreaders

Child's Level

This area is most appropriate for older preschool or kindergarten children.

What to Look For

Children will explore the natural materials.

Children will discover that varying amounts of glue are needed to hold various materials. For example, more glue is needed to hold nuts and magnolia pods than pine needles.

Some children will trace leaf shapes with the template and cut them out.

Some children will create patterns with the leaf hole punches once they are adept at using them.

Modification

Teachers may wish to start with the drawing implements and the natural collage materials. After a week or so, the hole punches and leaf template can be added to encourage other types of experimentation and art creations.

Comments & Questions to Extend Thinking

How will you arrange these materials on your picture?

How can you make this heavy buckeye stick to the paper?

I see leaf shapes on your picture and blank spaces that look like leaves.

How would you place the leaves to make them look like they're falling?

Integrated Curriculum Activities

For a movement activity, encourage children to fall like leaves and then fall like nuts.

Put a display of fall nature materials in the science area for children to explore (see *More Than Magnets*, activity 2.3).

Take a nature walk and collect more materials for the art area.

Make fall math games (see *More Than Counting*, activities 4.5, 4.6, 4.13, 5.7, 5.12, and 5.18).

Put buckeyes, buckets, and tongs on the sensory table.

Sing autumn songs (see *More Than Singing*, activities 2.5, 6.3, 6.8, and 8.4).

Put dried gourds, lotus pods, and locus pods in the music area for natural maracas (see *More Than Magnets*, activity 6.10).

2.7 Winter Art Area

Description

While winter materials, such as snow and icicles, can't be included in an art area, children enjoy creating representations of them. This art area encourages children to explore the colors and forms of winter. Collage materials are white or light blue, and black and dark blue paper provide contrast. Additional activities include a tray of materials for cutting snowflake designs and a basket of cotton balls for creating various shapes.

Helpful Hints

White fiberfill can be used instead of cotton balls for modeling activities.

Art Experiences

▲ drawing
▲ gluing
▲ cutting
▲ combining art media

Materials

▲ 3 sets of pastel markers
▲ 4 pencils
▲ 3 glue containers, with spreaders
▲ collage tray, with white and light blue tissue paper, iridescent paper confetti, white foam circles, and aluminum foil
▲ basket of white cotton balls
▲ silver and white glitter, in shakers
▲ small squares of white paper, for folding and cutting
▲ 4 pairs of children's scissors

▲ black and dark blue construction paper
▲ white drawing paper

Child's Level

This art area is appropriate for either preschool or kindergarten children.

What to Look For

Children will talk about winter as they create with the white materials.
Children who have not had experience with glitter may put glue on top of it to try to hold it.
Children will display a range of drawing stages.
Children will be fascinated with the symmetry created as they fold paper and then cut out various shapes.
Children may pull the cotton into different shapes before gluing it.

Modification

The most difficult material to control in this art area is the glitter. It can be added later or used as a special activity if it is hard to manage.

Comments & Questions to Extend Thinking

What does the foil remind you of?
How does the cotton feel?
What materials would you select to represent snow?
Fold your paper, cut out a piece, and see how it looks.
Can you tell Maria how you made that snowflake shape?
How can you change the shape of the cotton ball?

Integrated Curriculum Activities

Sing songs about snow (see *More Than Singing*, activities 2.6, 4.5, and 6.6).
Spray snow with water, colored with food coloring (activity 8.6).
Read books about snow, such as *The Snowy Day*, by Ezra Jack Keats (New York: Viking, 1962); and *In the Snow*, by Huy Voun Lee (New York: Holt, 1995).
Put snow, buckets, and scoops on the sensory table.
Use plastic snowflakes as counters for a math game (see *More Than Counting*, activity 4.16).

2.8 Spring Art Area

Description

Once again the natural materials of the season are introduced into the art area. Dried flower petals, colored eggshells, and feathers are included for collage. Pastel paper choices reflect traditional seasonal colors. Since spring falls near the end of the school year and the children are thus experienced in using the art area, some more unusual implements, such as roller bottles for painting, are included. Fresh flowers or an artist's print of flowers add a spring flavor to the art area.

Helpful Hints

Thin the paint for the roller bottles with water. Otherwise it may clog the tops. Deodorant bottles are a free source of roller bottles. The tops come off for cleaning and refilling.

Floral shops may be willing to donate dried flower petals since they often throw them out. Inexpensive potpourri is also a good source, if it is nontoxic.

Eggshells can be colored quickly with food coloring and water.

Art Experiences

- drawing
- gluing
- cutting
- painting with roller bottles

Materials

- 3 sets of pastel markers
- 2 or 3 sets of pastel chalk
- white drawing paper, 12 by 18 inches
- pastel construction paper
- 4 pairs of children's design scissors
- several pencils
- 3 glue containers, with spreaders
- collage tray, with dried flower petals, colored eggshells, and colored feathers
- collage tray, with assorted seeds
- 4 roller bottles, with pastel paint

Child's Level

This art area is most appropriate for older preschool or kindergarten children who have had experience with a variety of art materials.

What to Look For

Children will compare the types of lines made by the markers and the chalk.
Some children may create flower shapes with the design scissors.
Children will experiment with the roller bottles.

Modification

Some teachers prefer to keep the roller bottles at the easel, where they are more contained and easier to manage.

Comments & Questions to Extend Thinking

What happens to the chalk lines when you rub over them with your finger?
What kinds of lines can you make with the roller bottles?
Do any of the materials on the art shelf look like things you have seen outside?
Tell me about this chalk section of your picture.
The roller bottle has a round top but makes a straight line.

Integrated Curriculum Activities

Take photographs of the changes outside (trees, flowers, rain) to add to the classroom.
Plant some of the seeds from the art shelf with the children.
Suspend two sizes of flowerpots in the music area so children can compare the sounds of the pots when struck with a wooden mallet (see *More Than Singing*, activity 5.11).
Read books about spring from other cultures. The Native American book *Did You Hear Wind Sing Your Name?,* by Sandra De Coteau Orie (New York: Walker, 1995), combines a short, lyrical text with spectacular illustrations.
Children may want to dip chalk in water and draw with it as a special activity.

2.9 Summer Art Area

Description

Bright colors dominate the summer season, from children's colorful clothes to the bright sun, blue sky, and lush trees of nature. For this reason, bright colors are incorporated into the art area in the choices of paper, markers, and collage materials. Bright plastic, cut from beach balls that are no longer usable, provides a colorful and unusual medium for gluing. Since beach and sandbox play is popular in summer, colored sand is also included in the area.

Helpful Hints

Colored sand can be purchased, or you can color your own. Spray the sand with a mixture of food coloring and water and let it dry.

Art Experiences

- ▲ drawing
- ▲ gluing
- ▲ cutting
- ▲ creating with mixed media

Materials

- ▲ 3 sets of markers, in bright colors
- ▲ 3 sets of crayons, in bright colors
- ▲ 3 glue containers, with spreaders
- ▲ collage tray, with plastic pieces cut from beach balls
- ▲ colored sand, in salt shakers
- ▲ construction paper, in primary colors
- ▲ 4 pairs of children's scissors

Child's Level

This art area is appropriate for either preschool or kindergarten children.

What to Look For

Some children may glue pieces of plastic onto their paper and then draw around them.

Some children may experiment with putting glue on top of the sand.

Children will experiment with all of the materials.

Some children will tell stories and describe the action in their pictures as they create.

Modification

Young preschoolers may want to shake all of the sand out of the bottles. If so, save the sand shakers for a special activity which can be more closely monitored.

Comments & Questions to Extend Thinking

What can you create with this bright plastic?

Can you cut the plastic into other shapes with the scissors?

You filled in all of the shapes you drew with colored sand. How did you decide which colors to use?

Integrated Curriculum Activities

Put a tray of moist sand and tiny novelty shoes in the science area. Children can create footprints in the sand (see *More Than Magnets*, activity 2.14).

Help children create jars with layers of colored sand (activity 7.17).

Move some of the art activities outside during the summer (see chapter 8 for ideas).

Read books about summer, such as *One Hot Summer Day*, by Nina Crews (New York: Greenwillow, 1995).

2.10 Circles Art Area

Description

Children from western cultures are accustomed to using rectangular shapes, both in building and in art. This art area challenges them to explore the possibilities of the circle. Collage materials include circles that vary in size, color, and thickness. Other activities introduce printing with circular tools (cookie cutters, spools, bottle caps, etc.) and painting with bingo markers, which make circular marks. The paper is also circular rather than rectangular. An artist's print, such as "The Heartbeat of Turtle Island," by Cherokee artist James Oberle, may inspire some children to incorporate circular forms in more unique ways into their drawings.

Helpful Hints

Put a sponge in the bottom of the paint dish for the printing activity. The sponge absorbs the excess paint and makes it easier for the children to create imprints with the objects.

Art Experiences

- ▲ drawing
- ▲ cutting
- ▲ gluing
- ▲ making imprints
- ▲ exploring circular forms
- ▲ experiencing art from another culture

Materials

- ▲ 3 sets of markers
- ▲ construction paper, cut into circular shapes
- ▲ 4 pairs of children's scissors
- ▲ collage tray, with circles of various sizes and colors cut from paper, foam board, and fabric
- ▲ 4 glue containers, with spreaders

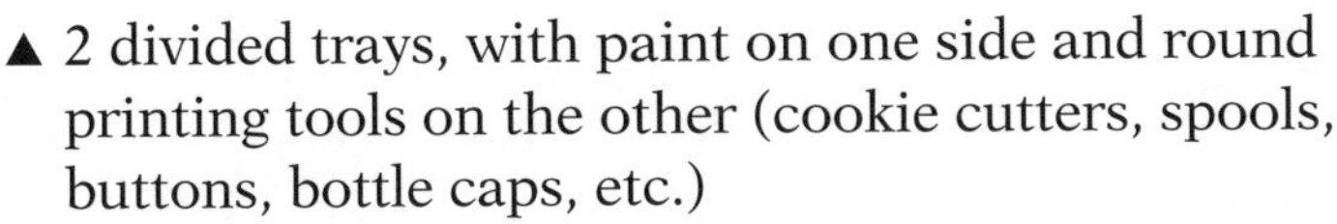

- ▲ 2 divided trays, with paint on one side and round printing tools on the other (cookie cutters, spools, buttons, bottle caps, etc.)
- ▲ 6 bingo paint markers
- ▲ several pencils
- ▲ circle hole punches
- ▲ circle template
- ▲ paper plates

Child's Level

This art area is most appropriate for older preschool or kindergarten children.

What to Look For

Children will cut the round paper to create a variety of new shapes that are different from those typically cut from rectangular paper.

Some children will initially look for rectangular paper.

Some children will create patterns with the bingo markers.

Some children will create circles with the bingo markers or printing tools and then draw or color around them.

Modification

For younger children, use the paint as a special activity rather than placing it in the art area.

Comments & Questions to Extend Thinking

What can you make with these round shapes?

Brian cut his circles to make half-circles.

How many different circles do you see in this painting?

Some of your paint circles are solid, and some have just an outline. How did you make them look different?

Integrated Curriculum Activities

Add round materials to the block area. Circular slabs cut from tree branches or purchased from craft stores are interesting.

Put a ramp in the science area, and include round and rectangular objects to roll down it. Children can compare how the various objects move (see *More Than Magnets*, activity 3.1).

Use circular tools, such as round potato mashers, spools, or bottle caps, with playdough. Children can compare the impressions made by the different materials.

2.11 Sea Art Area

Description

This art area is especially appropriate during late spring or summer, when children may be preparing to go to the beach and teachers may introduce a sea curriculum. Seashells are used for several creative purposes: making imprints, stringing, and gluing. Colored sand provides a novel art medium for children to explore. Children can also draw with colored chalk and then spray their creations with water to create a muted effect. Teachers may wish to place a copy of Leo Lionni's *Swimmy* (New York: Knopf, 1963) in the area. This Caldicott winner has lovely sea illustrations that may generate creative ideas in the children.

Helpful Hints

Look for tiny spray bottles in the cosmetic section of stores.

Many shells already have small holes. If you don't have shells with holes, drill a small hole in the shells with a narrow drill bit.

Sand can be colored by spraying it with a mixture of food coloring and water and letting it dry.

Art Experiences

- ▲ drawing
- ▲ gluing
- ▲ creating imprints
- ▲ stringing
- ▲ cutting
- ▲ creating with mixed media

Materials

- ▲ 3 sets of pastel crayons
- ▲ 3 sets of colored pencils
- ▲ 2 trays, with colored chalk and tiny spray bottles of water
- ▲ white and pastel construction paper
- ▲ 2 trays, each with a flat dish for paint and several sea shells, to create imprints

- ▲ basket of shells, for gluing
- ▲ 4 glue containers
- ▲ basket of small shells (with holes) and thin gauge wire, for stringing
- ▲ colored sand, in salt shakers
- ▲ 4 pairs of children's design scissors
- ▲ 4 pairs of children's scissors

Child's Level

This art area is most appropriate for older preschool or kindergarten children who have had experience with a variety of types of art materials.

What to Look For

Children will eagerly explore the new materials.
Children will create imprints with the shells and examine the outlines.
Some children will color inside the outlines made by the shells.
Some children will create mixed-media artwork by gluing sand and shells onto their drawings.
Children will explore how water changes their chalk creations.
Children may create jewelry with the stringing materials.

Modification

This is a very extensive art area with many types of activities. Teachers may wish to introduce the chalk and painting activities after children have already had some experience with the other materials.

Comments & Questions to Extend Thinking

Dip your shell in the paint and see what kind of mark it makes.
Do you think this shell will make the same mark as this one?
What happened to the chalk after you sprayed it?
Do you want to add some sand or shells to your beach picture?

Integrated Curriculum Activities

Kindergarten children love the book *Something Queer on Vacation*, by Elizabeth Levy (New York: Delacorte, 1980). It is a mystery set at the beach.

Make maracas by placing either sand or water in clear plastic bottles and sealing the tops. Children can compare the sounds and use them to accompany songs.

Sing songs about sea animals (see *More Than Singing*, activities 2.15 and 6.4).

Put scallops or other shells with ridges in the music area. Children can create sounds and rhythms by scraping them.

Use nets to fish for plastic fish or seashells in the water table.

2.12 Babies Art Area

Description

Since young children often have babies in their families, many teachers incorporate a baby theme into their planning. Materials commonly associated with babies can be introduced into the art area so that children can explore them creatively. This area includes collage trays of pastel cotton balls and cotton swabs (Q-tips).

Art Experiences

▲ drawing
▲ gluing
▲ painting
▲ cutting

Materials

▲ 3 sets of pastel markers
▲ 3 sets of pastel crayons
▲ pastel construction paper
▲ manila paper
▲ 4 jars of glue, colored with food coloring (pink, blue, yellow, and green)
▲ collage tray, with pastel cotton balls grouped by color
▲ collage tray, with cotton swabs in pastel colors
▲ 2 sets of pastel tempera paint, with cotton swabs instead of brushes
▲ 4 pairs of children's scissors

Helpful Hints

Cut the cotton balls in half. They will go twice as far.

Color the glue by adding a few drops of food coloring to each container.

Child's Level
This art area is appropriate for either preschool or kindergarten children.

What to Look For
Children will enjoy the soft feel of the cotton balls as they glue them.
Some children will combine the cotton swabs and cotton balls to create straight lines and circles.
Children will experiment by painting with cotton swabs.

Modification
Some teachers prefer to use the paint and cotton swabs at the easel, where it can be more easily contained.

Comments & Questions to Extend Thinking
This picture feels very soft!
Charlie used cotton to add hair to his person.
What can you create with the cotton balls and the cotton swabs?
How does it feel to paint with a Q-tip?

Integrated Curriculum Activities
Put baby rattles in the music area to use as maracas.
Sing songs about babies with the children (see *More Than Singing*, activities 2.1, 2.9, 2.12, and 2.13).
Create a baby-theme math game by making a grid board with baby stickers. Children can roll a die and use tiny novelty bottles and rattles as counters (see *More Than Counting*, activity 4.17 and *Much More Than Counting*, activities 6.9 and 8.11).
Estimate how many pacifiers are in a clear jar (see *Much More Than Counting*, activity 3.1).
Read books about babies, such as *More More More, Said the Baby*, by Vera B. Williams (New York: Greenwillow, 1990); *Sleep, Sleep, Sleep*, by Nancy Van Laan (Boston: Little Brown, 1995); and *Peter's Chair*, by Ezra Jack Keats (New York: Harper, 1967).

2.13 Valentine Art Area

Description

Children love to make valentines for their family and friends, so this art area is especially fun. It also helps eliminate pressure on families to purchase commercial valentines. Materials include heart-shaped paper, glitter, pastel cotton balls, and a collage tray of lace and ribbon. For older children, a heart-lacing activity can be added. Heart-shaped hole punches provide a unique tool for children to use.

Helpful Hints

Ask parents for donations of ribbon and lace.

For the lacing activity, use a hole punch to create holes around the edge of the hearts and attach a piece of ribbon or yarn for lacing.

Art Experiences

- ▲ drawing
- ▲ gluing
- ▲ cutting
- ▲ lacing
- ▲ combining art media
- ▲ creating negative space with heart hole punches

Materials

- ▲ 4 sets of markers
- ▲ several pencils
- ▲ construction paper (red, pink, purple, and white)
- ▲ heart-shaped template
- ▲ glitter, in shakers
- ▲ basket of pastel cotton balls
- ▲ basket of petit four cups
- ▲ collage tray, with ribbon and lace pieces
- ▲ hearts, with holes punched around the edges, for lacing

- ▲ heart-shaped hole punches
- ▲ 4 pairs of children's scissors
- ▲ 3 glue containers

Child's Level

This art area is appropriate for either preschool or kindergarten children.

What to Look For

Children will eagerly glue materials onto the hearts to create valentines.

Some children will write messages on their valentines.

Children who have not had experience with glitter may experiment by putting glue on top of the glitter.

Older children may lace around the edge of the hearts to create a border.

Modification

For young children, eliminate the lacing activity and use the glitter first as a special activity.

Comments & Questions to Extend Thinking

How can you create your own heart shape?

I notice that you made a border of cotton balls around the edge of your valentine.

What can you use to hold the glitter onto your heart?

Integrated Curriculum Activities

Read books about friendship, such as *My Best Friend*, by Pat Hutchins (New York: Greenwillow, 1993); *My Friends*, by Taro Gomi (San Francisco: Chronicle, 1990); and *A Letter to Amy*, by Ezra Jack Keats (New York: Harper, 1968).

Clap the word for *friend* in other languages as a rhythm activity (see *More Than Singing*, activity 3.3).

Use letter and envelope stickers to create grid and path games for math (see *More Than Counting*, activities 4.10, 5.6, and 5.16).

Paint with heart-shaped cookie cutters and sponges. Children can compare the impressions.

2.14 Dance Art Area

Description

Many cultures have their own dance traditions. Exploring dance, perhaps through movement activities or a multicultural dance area in dramatic play, is an excellent multicultural unit. Materials used in dance attire from various cultures make an exciting addition to the art area. Collage materials might include African print fabric, satin (used in many Asian countries), ribbon (used in many countries, including Bolivia), and tulle and lace (used in ballet). Older children can create pictures with spinning tops.

Helpful Hints

Make paper curls by cutting short lengths of curling ribbon and pulling them across a scissor blade.

Art Experiences

- ▲ gluing
- ▲ drawing
- ▲ cutting
- ▲ combining art media

Materials

- ▲ 2 sets of colored chalk
- ▲ 2 sets of colored pencils
- ▲ collage tray, containing pieces of tulle, lace, satin, ribbon, and African print fabric
- ▲ basket of colored cotton balls
- ▲ 4 glitter shakers
- ▲ 4 containers of glue, colored in pastel shades with food coloring
- ▲ 4 pairs of children's scissors
- ▲ 4 pairs of children's design scissors

▲ stapler
▲ pastel and white construction paper
▲ colored tape
▲ paper fasteners
▲ assortment of tops with marker points

Child's Level

This art area is appropriate for both preschool and kindergarten children.

What to Look For

Children will notice that the various collage materials respond differently to the glue.
Some children will initially think that the colored glue is paint.
Children will experiment with how materials look when combined with colored glue.
Some children will draw figures with chalk and use the collage materials to create costumes.
Some children will use the paper fasteners to make moving body parts on their figures.
Children will experiment with the variety of cuts made by the design scissors.

Modification

For younger or less-experienced children, remove the paper fasteners and design scissors.

Comments & Questions to Extend Thinking

What can you do to make your person move?
What happens to the glue when you put tulle on top of it?
What kind of lines does this pair of scissors make?
Raj, your person's legs move. He looks like he's dancing.

Integrated Curriculum Activities

Convert the dramatic play area into a dance studio with dance music from around the world (see *More Than Singing*, activity 6.15).
Include a variety of children's books about dance in the book area. Some possibilities are *Color Dance*, by Ann Jonas (New York: Greenwillow, 1989); *Mimi's Tutu*, by Tynia Thomassie (New York: Scholastic, 1996); *Silent Lotus*, by Jeanne M. Lee (New York: Farrar, 1991); *Lion Dancer*, by Kate Waters and Madeline Sloveny-Low (New York: Scholastic, 1990); and *Powwow*, by George Ancona (New York: Harcourt, 1993).
Use small novelty shoes, including ballet slippers, as printing tools with paint.

2.15 Quilt Art Area

Description

Many cultures have their own unique form of quilts or fabric. Thus, quilts are an excellent multicultural theme to explore with young children. This art center coordinates well with a quilt unit or class quilt project (see chapter 6). Children can organize and glue squares of a variety of types of fabrics to create small quilts. Wallpaper, cut into geometric shapes, encourages children to explore geometric combinations and arrangements. Kindergarten children can sew independently on burlap with large plastic needles. Older children can also draw on cloth with fabric markers. A small quilt displayed in the area lends aesthetic appeal and may inspire some children to create quilt designs.

Helpful Hints

Look for embroidery hoops in craft stores or fabric shops. They keep the fabric from bunching up and make sewing experiences for young children much more successful.

Art Experiences

- ▲ patterning
- ▲ gluing
- ▲ cutting
- ▲ sewing
- ▲ drawing
- ▲ working with textures

Materials

- ▲ collage tray, with a variety of types of fabric cut in squares
- ▲ collage tray, with wallpaper cut in a variety of geometric shapes
- ▲ 3 glue containers
- ▲ white construction paper (12 by 18 inches)
- ▲ colored burlap, cut in 7-inch squares

- ▲ 3 small embroidery hoops, to hold the burlap
- ▲ 3 large plastic needles
- ▲ basket of colored yarn
- ▲ white cotton fabric, cut in 7-inch squares
- ▲ fabric markers
- ▲ basket of assorted buttons
- ▲ 4 pairs of children's scissors

Child's Level

This activity is most appropriate for older preschool or kindergarten children.

What to Look For

Children will create quilts by gluing the fabric squares or wallpaper shapes onto paper.

Some children will create patterns with the materials.

Some children will cut the fabric and wallpaper to create new shapes.

Children will draw designs or pictures on the white fabric. Some children may then incorporate their fabric picture into a quilt.

Children working with the sewing materials will need to master the up and down sewing sequence. Otherwise, their yarn will wrap around the hoop.

Modification

For younger children, explore sewing and drawing on fabric as a special activity rather than as part of the art area.

Comments & Questions to Extend Thinking

How did you decide where these fabric squares should go?

What colors do you think would look good together?

Paul used the fabric squares to create a pattern.

Susan put five triangles together to make a pentagon.

What can we do with these buttons?

Integrated Curriculum Activities

Let the children work together to create class quilts (activities 6.5, 6.6, 6.7, and 6.16).

Include quilt books from many cultures in the book area. Some examples are *Luka's Quilt*, by Georgia Guback (New York: Greenwillow, 1994); *The Quilt*, by Ann Jonas (New York: Greenwillow, 1984); and *The Keeping Quilt*, by Patricia Polacco (New York: Simon & Schuster, 1988).

Cut shapes from felt to use on a flannelboard. Children can explore pattern and symmetry as they design their own quilt squares.

CHAPTER

3

Drawing

Claire used colored pencils to draw a picture of two people dressed in fancy clothes. She identified the two as Barry and Kate, who had recently gotten married. Claire had attended the wedding just two weeks before. This was the first entry into Claire's kindergarten writing journal.

▲ ▲ ▲

Stephen chose to work in the art area several times a day. One day he selected the markers and began to create an elaborate representational drawing, which he described in great detail to his teacher. He told her the house was his grandma's house, and some people broke her roof. The water around the house was a flood. Later, the teacher contacted Stephen's mother to confirm the accuracy of his descriptions. Although none of the events Stephen described in his artwork and story had actually occurred, his mother told the teacher that at home Stephen expressed concern about monsters and wanted to be near her more often than usual.

▲ ▲ ▲

Drawing implements provide opportunities for children to record their thoughts, ideas, and feelings, either in conjunction with writing or as the primary vehicle for communication. Children progress through stages in the development of drawing, just as they do in writing. Early childhood classrooms abound with opportunities for children to draw. The art area may contain one or more drawing implements, such as crayons, markers, and colored pencils. In addition, the focus of the special activity of the day may be the use of drawing implements, such as watercolor pencils or pastel chalk.

Teachers' Questions

What art activities fall under the drawing category?

Art activities that introduce children to a variety of drawing tools, used in combination with different types of paper, are considered drawing activities. Children may create scribbles, lines, designs, figures, or pictures with a pencil or other drawing implement, depending on their interest and stage of development. A wide variety of materials are available to encourage children in the exploration of drawing.

What stages do children pass through as they learn to draw?

There are two broad stages of artistic development related to drawing: scribbling and representation. Children progress through the drawing stages in a predictable manner, but at different rates depending on the individual child, just as they pass through writing stages at varying rates. Knowledge of children's stages of development in art provides important information for teachers as they plan appropriate drawing activities for the classroom. See chapter 1 for more complete information about the artistic development of young children and a chart of the drawing stages.

Why is it important to include opportunities for children to draw in early childhood classrooms?

Drawing provides a developmentally appropriate forum for young children to express themselves. Parents and educators often associate the child's first vocalizations with attempts to communicate. Drawing, in the form of scribbles, is the first permanent record that children produce as they progress towards written communication. As such, scribbles are precursors not only to representational drawings, but also to conventional writing.[1] Drawing allows children to express thoughts, ideas, and feelings through art.

Drawing activities also encourage fine-motor development. As children hold and manipulate a variety of drawing implements, they increase their muscle strength and coordination. Gradually, children develop a more mature hand grasp. The early fist grip evolves into a two-finger grasp and eventually a standard pincer grip. With increased finger strength, children are able to apply more pressure when they draw. The faint, wobbly lines of toddlers or young preschoolers develop into firm, controlled marks.

What are some goals for drawing activities?

Goals for drawing activities relate to the stages of artistic development. Drawing activities provide opportunities for children to progress through the drawing stages, from scribbling to representational. Some goals are related to drawing in general, while others are best suited to a particular activity. Examples of specific goals include the following:

- ▲ experimenting with blending colors (chalk)
- ▲ exploring the effects of water on a medium (chalk and water)

- ▲ creating illustrations to accompany literacy activities
- ▲ adding detail to drawings (colored pencils)

Do coloring books or similar activities aid in the development of children's drawing ability?

No. Most early childhood educators believe that coloring books hinder children's drawing ability and stifle creativity. Since coloring books supply children with pictures that are already drawn, there is no opportunity for children to experiment with drawing. While it might be argued that learning to color in the lines helps children develop fine motor skills, encouraging children to draw their own forms to color produces the same result while allowing them to represent objects or ideas in their own way.

What materials are needed for drawing activities?

A variety of types of drawing tools and surfaces are needed in order for children to fully explore drawing possibilities. The most common drawing tools in early childhood classrooms are crayons, pencils, and markers. However, other implements, such as watercolor crayons, chalk, oil-based chalk, and colored pencils, should also be included in the art curriculum to provide a variety of possibilities for children to record images, designs, shapes, and forms.

Teachers should also consider a variety of surfaces for drawing activities. Many early childhood programs purchase newsprint because it is the most economical paper available. Although this paper is acceptable for initial experiences with crayons, other papers may be more satisfactory and more appropriate for specific drawing activities. Markers, chalk, and oil-based chalk are easier to control and more aesthetically pleasing when used with white drawing paper. The brilliant colors of markers are highlighted against stark white paper, but are subdued on newsprint.

Paper in many colors and sizes is readily available. Teachers can cut the paper into various shapes, such as circles or triangles, to stimulate children's interest and creativity. Paper of different textures, such as corrugated paper or sandpaper, provides an interesting challenge to children and stimulates thinking as they observe the effects of the "bumps" and "ridges" on their drawing. Paper is not the only suitable drawing surface. Cloth, cardboard, and Styrofoam provide unique yet aesthetically pleasing drawing media. Children quickly notice that their drawing tool makes an indentation in Styrofoam. This allows children with visual disabilities to feel what they draw.

Where can teachers find drawing materials?

Drawing materials can be purchased through catalogs or stores that specialize in educational supplies. Some of the same materials can also be found in discount stores. Teachers should purchase the highest-quality materials they can afford. Inexpensive crayons, markers, and colored pencils do not perform satisfactorily as children attempt to draw. Children may become frustrated and lose interest in drawing. Teachers can conserve the more costly materials through careful planning of special activities.

When drawing materials are readily available, children make ample use of them. Teachers may choose to use inexpensive or donated paper for drawing activities in the art area. Parents may contribute white fabric, corrugated paper, or cardboard for classroom use.

What drawing implements are the easiest for children to use?

Thick, unwrapped crayons that are flat on one side are the easiest drawing tools for young children. Thick crayons are easy for young children to grasp and do not break as readily as thin crayons. Removal of the paper wrapping allows children to use the flat side of the crayon as well as the point. This provides opportunities for the exploration of both the width of various strokes and shading. Crayons that are flat on one side will not roll off the table. This eliminates a source of frustration for children.

How do teachers incorporate drawing activities into the classroom?

Teachers can plan drawing activities for two areas of the classroom: in the art area or as a special activity. Some standard drawing materials, such as crayons, markers, or colored pencils, may be available each day in the art area. For more complete information about the centers, see chapter 2. Teachers can also highlight drawing activities as special activities on a regular basis.

How can teachers design special activity areas to highlight drawing activities?

Teachers often designate one table near the art area, but separate from it, as the special activity area. Teachers can use this table to present drawing activities in an organized and aesthetically pleasing manner. The special activity table typically seats three to four children at one time, which allows the teacher to focus on individual children as they experiment with new materials. The teacher often displays duplicate sets of materials for each child at the table, which helps eliminate management issues. The paper for the activity can be placed in individual trays, one for each place at the special activity table, and the drawing implements can be displayed in cups, attractively covered cans, or small trays. Additional materials should be stored nearby for easy access by the teacher or the children. While older or more-experienced children may sometimes share a set of drawing materials, whenever possible each child should have access to a complete set of the drawing implements. Suggestions for how to display the materials can be found with each activity in this chapter.

What are the advantages of planning drawing activities as special activities?

Special activities allow teachers to introduce new materials, establish guidelines for their use, and monitor children's explorations of drawing materials that are too expensive or too messy to include in the art area. By introducing new activities first as a special activity, teachers can encourage children to experiment with them before they are placed in the art area. For example, the teacher of a group of young preschool children might plan a special activity using only three colors of markers and construction paper. Goals for this activity might be to introduce the markers and assist children with removing and replacing the caps. The teacher may also want to establish guidelines, such as using markers only on paper, and redirect children if they are pounding the tip, which will eventually damage the point. Later, the teacher could include markers in the art area.

How do teachers decide when to introduce specific drawing implements?

Teachers introduce drawing tools, such as markers and colored pencils, based on the ages and experiences of the group. Young children may need many opportunities to explore crayons before other drawing implements are introduced. As other drawing materials are added to the curriculum, children continue to benefit from drawing and creating with familiar drawing tools such as crayons. They experiment with new ways to use the materials and solidify newly acquired fine motor skills. Teachers can observe children as they use drawing materials to determine when to introduce new activities.

What are some of the problems or limitations children may encounter with materials such as markers or colored pencils?

Some children may experience difficulty manipulating markers and colored pencils, as well as creating desired effects as they draw. Younger, less-experienced children may not be able to remove and replace the caps on markers. Children have little control over the width of the lines markers produce and are unable to make lighter marks or contrasting shades with them. Tall, thin colored pencils may be more difficult to manage for children who have not yet developed a mature pencil grasp. The pencils produce fainter marks than crayons or markers, which may be frustrating for some children.

What can teachers do to eliminate problems associated with markers and colored pencils?

Teachers can introduce these tools in a sequential and organized manner. Teachers may wish to reduce the number of markers children initially use in a special activity. Teachers can imbed the tops of a red, yellow, and blue marker in a small amount of plaster of paris set inside a 3-inch disposable pie pan. Children can easily reseal a marker by pushing it into the stable cap. A set of three markers per child encourages each child to explore the properties of the markers rather than focusing on removing the lids. Sets of thicker, 5-inch-tall colored pencils can be purchased for use with young children.

How often should drawing activities be available for children?

Drawing implements are typically available at all times in the art area and may be planned as a special activity several times each month. Teachers can use these suggestions as guidelines, but should also observe the needs and interests of the group. Children may frequently engage in drawing activities in the art area, and therefore need fewer planned special activities that focus on drawing. On the other hand, if children spend very little time drawing with the materials in the art area, the teacher may want to plan special drawing activities more often. Special drawing materials may attract children and subsequently encourage more explorations of drawing materials at the art area.

What pitfalls should teachers avoid when commenting on children's drawings?

Teachers should avoid making judgmental comments, even when they are positive. Evaluative comments may inadvertently hinder the creative process and limit opportunities for dialogue about the artistic process. For example, adults often respond with perfunctory remarks, such as "That's nice," or "It's pretty," when children show them their artwork. While these comments are meant to be encouraging, children quickly realize that they are insincere. Not all artwork, including children's art, is meant to be pretty, and children do not view all of their endeavors as equally successful.

Teachers should also avoid questions that focus on representation. "What is it?" is a frequent response to children's artwork. This is inappropriate in several regards. First, many young children have not yet reached the stage of representational drawing, so the question is not developmentally appropriate. Second, not all art is representational, so even after children have reached the stage of representational drawing, they may choose to express themselves in a nonrepresentational style. Perhaps most importantly, when children are trying to draw a specific object, and someone asks them what it is, they may become very discouraged, avoid art, or regress in their drawing endeavors.

Sometimes teachers talk too much! Children may not want to talk about their artwork or listen to comments about it. Art is a means of expression in and of itself, and children may not always feel the need or desire to have it translated into words.

What are the best ways to respond to children's drawings?

Teachers can comment on the process of drawing, as well as the artistic elements. In many cases, teachers may act as observers and say nothing. Children benefit from the observations teachers make about artistic elements in drawings, such as color, shape, form, pattern, and symmetry. These comments supply children with the language associated with art and help draw attention to artistic elements in their drawings. Comments about the process of drawing help children focus on techniques, rather than the success of the attempt. They also help children form physical knowledge relationships related to the use of art materials. For example, the teacher might comment on whether a child used the whole arm or just the movement of the fingers to create a specific line or shape. Focusing on the process is especially helpful for children who are critical of their own drawing or who make comparisons to the drawings of other children.

How can teachers coordinate literacy experiences with drawing activities?

Teachers can plan specific drawing activities to encourage children to focus on written communication. Many teachers already record children's dictations and encourage children to write in all areas of the classroom. Some drawing activities are excellent vehicles for reading and writing experiences. For example, a group of children may demonstrate high interest in a book such as *Quick as a Cricket*, by Audrey Wood (Singapore: Child's Play, 1982). This book uses animal analogies to describe feelings. "I'm as quick as a cricket" and "I'm as quiet as a mouse," are examples from the book. Teachers might capitalize on interest in this book by creating a class book about feelings. Children are typically eager to contribute to this endeavor. The teacher can use story paper, which has a space for drawing at the top and a lined section below, for recording the children's responses. In the lined section, the teacher could preprint the pattern from the book, "I'm as ___________ as a ___________," for each child to fill in. Children at both the scribbling and representational stages can participate in the activity. Young children may describe the scribbles they make, while older children may want to write the responses themselves.

How can teachers assess children's developmental progress in drawing?

Many teachers save samples or make photocopies of children's drawings to include in a portfolio or scrapbook of each child's work. These work samples document children's progression through drawing stages as well as their creations with art media and explorations of new drawing materials. Teachers can document the art process through photographs of children creating with art materials and include comments that children make about their actions, ideas, and discoveries. Teachers may also keep anecdotal records of children's use of drawing materials.

Endnotes

1. Marjorie V. Fields, "Talking and Writing: Explaining the Whole Language Approach to Parents." *The Reading Teacher,* May 1988.

Drawing Activities

3.1 Crayons

Getting Started

Description

Crayons are perhaps the most common drawing implements associated with young children. This first drawing activity describes how teachers can introduce crayons to young preschool children. The large crayons fit easily into the immature grasp of most young preschoolers. The large newsprint provides ample drawing space for children at the stage of random scribbling, who may still use large arm movements. Later, teachers may introduce smaller sizes of paper, a larger selection of crayons, and different types of crayons.

Helpful Hints

Remove the paper from the crayons so that children can use the side of the crayon as well as the point.

Art Experiences

- ▲ exploring line, form, shape, and color
- ▲ creating scribbles
- ▲ experimenting with crayons
- ▲ expressing thoughts, ideas, and feelings
- ▲ enhancing self-concept through independent use of the medium

Materials

- ▲ newsprint or manila drawing paper, 12 by 18 inches
- ▲ 4 sets of large crayons (red, yellow, and blue)
- ▲ 4 small trays or cups, to hold the crayons

Child's Level

This first crayon activity is most appropriate for young or very inexperienced preschool children. Limiting the selection of crayons to the primary colors allows children to focus on the effects of crayons on paper and supports young children who are just beginning to recognize and name specific colors. Teachers often choose inexpensive newsprint or manila paper for early drawing experiences, when many children are at the scribbling stage. Later, teachers can vary the size and type of paper, as well as the number of crayons chosen for the activity.

What to Look For

Some children will cover the paper with scribbling marks.

Some children will make marks that extend beyond the boundaries of the paper because they do not yet have control over their large arm movements.

Some children will produce faint marks because they do not yet have sufficient muscle strength to press down on the paper.

Some children will show specific placement patterns in their scribbling.

Some children will make just one mark on the paper.

A few children may draw circles and straight lines.

Modifications

Introduce crayons in the secondary colors—orange, green, and purple.

Vary the drawing surface. Large white paper plates are easy for young children to draw on.

Put crayons at the easel. Drawing at the easel encourages large arm movements.

Comments & Questions to Extend Thinking

Let's see what kind of marks you can make with this red crayon.

Does this crayon make the same color of mark?

You have round marks all over your paper.

3.2 Crayons
More Explorations

Description

Children benefit from many drawing experiences that combine crayons with drawing surfaces of different sizes and types. Crayons, unlike markers, can be used to create more subtle lines and shadings. Children can vary the pressure applied to the crayon to change the intensity of the color. They can create lines with both the end and the flat side of the crayon. Multicolored crayons provide opportunities for children to explore the application of more than one color at the same time. To encourage further explorations of crayons, teachers can select crayons in specific colors to use with paper of various sizes, colors, and shapes.

Helpful Hints

Save broken crayons. They can be melted together to make multi-colored crayons.

Art Experiences

- ▲ developing competence with drawing implements
- ▲ creating line, form, and design
- ▲ experimenting with intensity of color, shading, and types of lines
- ▲ expressing thoughts, ideas, and feelings
- ▲ developing self-concept (children often choose to draw pictures of themselves or their families)

Materials

- ▲ white construction paper, 9 by 12 inches
- ▲ 4 sets of crayons, each with 8 colors
- ▲ 4 cups or baskets, to hold the crayons

Child's Level

Drawing activities that combine crayons with various types of paper are appropriate for preschool and kindergarten children. Some activities, such as drawing on paper with a shape cut out of the center, are more appropriate for children who have had numerous experiences exploring crayons. Teachers should assess their group of children to determine which activities to present.

What to Look For

Children will produce scribbles, named scribbles, or representational forms depending on their stage of drawing.
Some children will fill the paper with many lines and forms.
Some children will make only a few marks on the paper.
Some children will describe what they draw as they work.
Some children will use drawing as an outlet for feelings, such as experiences that may be difficult to discuss.
Some children will draw on both sides of the paper.

Modifications

Substitute paper plates for the drawing surface.
Use half-sheets of construction paper as the drawing surface to encourage children to use finger movements rather than large arm movements.
Cut the drawing paper into shapes, such as a large circle, pennant, or square.
Select interesting or unusual colors to present together:

- ▲ red, yellow, orange, and brown (when children show interest in autumn colors)
- ▲ purple and red
- ▲ red, blue, and purple
- ▲ red, yellow, and black
- ▲ fluorescent red, yellow, and blue

Introduce negative space by cutting geometric or irregular shapes in the center of the drawing paper.
Assemble various shades of the same color of crayon, such as blue, blue-green, turquoise, cyan, navy, and blue-violet, for children who are able to manage thinner crayons.

Comments & Questions to Extend Thinking

I see dark red on this part of your paper and light red over here.
You used all of the colors in your basket on this picture.
What do you have to do to make a thick line?

3.3 Chalk

Description

This activity introduces chalk as a drawing medium. As children experiment with chalk and compare it to the more familiar crayons, they quickly notice both similarities and differences. As with crayons, children can use both the end and the side of chalk. They can create lines, shapes, and representational forms with chalk, and any negative spaces left in their designs can be filled in with more chalk. On the other hand, chalk blends and smudges more easily than crayon, and its color and texture can be changed by spraying it with water. Children quickly observe that chalk leaves a dust residue on their paper.

Chalk is available in several types. The most appropriate chalk for young children is thick sidewalk chalk or thin sticks of white or colored chalk sold in sets. Other types of chalk are more suitable for older children because they can stain both hands and clothing. Teachers can display colored chalk in a small tray so that children can quickly observe the selection of colors available.

Helpful Hints

Break each stick of chalk into two pieces to conserve the supply.

Pieces of chalk about 1-inch long may encourage children to explore the effects of drawing with the flat side.

Art Experiences

▲ exploring the physical properties of chalk
▲ creating line, form, and design
▲ experimenting with blending colors
▲ using fingers or sponges to alter chalk creations

Materials

- ▲ white construction paper, 9 by 12 inches
- ▲ 4 sets of chalk, each with 3 or 4 colors
- ▲ 4 small trays or cups, to hold the chalk
- ▲ smocks (optional)

Child's Level

Chalk is easily manipulated by both preschool and kindergarten children. Some of the variations are best suited to children who have had previous experience with chalk. Younger or more-inexperienced children may not be able to follow multiple steps in the activities using water and chalk.

What to Look For

Some children will cover the paper with chalk lines and forms.

Some children will create representational drawings.

Some children will discover how to use their fingers to soften the chalk lines.

Some children will experiment with both the end and the side of chalk in their drawings.

Modifications

Focus on contrast by combining several colors of chalk with a black base, or white chalk with a dark base.

Vary the color of chalk in response to children's interest in seasonal changes, such as orange and yellow chalk with a dark brown base (autumn).

Apply chalk to a wet base by first spraying the paper with water.

Allow children to spray their chalk drawings with water after they draw.

Change the size of the paper to 12- by 18-inch white construction paper.

Comments & Questions to Extend Thinking

What happens when you rub the chalk with your finger?

The pink and blue seem to blend together on this part of your picture.

3.4 Colored Pencils

Description

Colored pencils offer children opportunities to elaborate on the familiar forms that they often draw. Since colored pencils produce fine lines, unlike the relatively thick lines created by crayons or chalk, they may encourage children to add greater detail to their drawings. For example, when a child draws a face with crayons, the eyes, nose, and mouth often fill up the entire head because the lines are so wide. On the other hand, the thin lines produced by colored pencils leave plenty of room for detail, such as eyelashes, hair, and teeth. In addition, since children can vary the intensity of the color produced by colored pencils, they are a useful tool for shading.

Helpful Hints

Keep the points of the pencils sharpened for best results.

Art Experiences

- ▲ drawing with fine lines
- ▲ adding greater detail to drawings
- ▲ adding shading to drawings

Materials

- ▲ white construction paper, 9 by 12 inches
- ▲ 4 sets of fine-point colored pencils, each with 8 colors
- ▲ 4 baskets or trays, to hold the pencils

Child's Level

Although many preschool and kindergarten children can manipulate colored pencils, some children cannot yet hold them in a pincer grasp. A more mature pencil grasp is helpful in producing marks with colored pencils, which often have hard points that require considerable effort to make a dark mark on the paper. Faint marks are difficult for children to see, which may frustrate some children. Teachers of very young children may want to purchase colored pencils made especially for beginners. The thicker point allows children to be more successful when exploring drawing activities with colored pencils.

What to Look For

Children will produce scribbles, named scribbles, or representational forms, depending on their stage of drawing.
Some children will fill the paper with many lines and forms.
Some children will make only a few marks on the paper.
Some children will add more detail to the pictures they draw, such as putting eyelashes on faces.
Some children will describe what they draw as they work.
Some children will use drawing as an outlet for feelings.

Modifications

Use sets of colored pencils with a variety of drawing surfaces, such as pastel duplicating paper or paper plates.
Select colors of pencils to coordinate with children's interests, such as pastel colored pencils when children show interest in spring flowers.
Focus on contrast by providing white colored pencils with dark blue or black paper.
Cut the drawing paper into shapes, such as circles, pennants, or squares.

Comments & Questions to Extend Thinking

I see lots of flowers in your picture. It reminds me of spring.
What did you do to make this part of the tree darker?

3.5 Felt-Tipped Markers

Description

Brilliantly colored felt-tipped markers immediately attract children to drawing activities. The selection of available markers keeps growing as companies invent new shades of colors. Markers are relatively expensive, and children can easily damage the tips, even with normal use. For these reasons, many teachers plan drawing activities with markers as special activities before including them in the art area. The teacher or another adult can monitor the special activity, remind children to replace the lids, and redirect children who may misuse the markers.

Helpful Hints

Storing the markers upside down when not in use may help prevent them from drying out.

Some teachers imbed the marker lids in plaster of paris so they do not get misplaced. This also encourages children to replace the markers in the holder.

Art Experiences

- ▲ exploring a fluid drawing tool
- ▲ experimenting with broader lines
- ▲ creating designs with brilliant colors
- ▲ expressing thoughts, ideas, and feelings

Materials

- ▲ white construction paper, 9 by 12 inches
- ▲ 4 sets of markers, each with 3 or more colors
- ▲ 4 trays or marker holders

Child's Level

Virtually all preschool and kindergarten children are interested in drawing activities with markers. However, teachers may want to delay the introduction of markers to very young or inexperienced children until they have adjusted to school routines and have had some experience with crayons. When teachers introduce markers to very young children, they can limit the selection to three or four colors at a time.

What to Look For

Children will experiment with the marks they can make.
Some children will write letters, letterlike forms, or their names.
Some children will make one or two marks with each of the colors available.
Some children will create representational figures.
Some children will learn the names of colors while using markers.
Some children will not be able to remove the marker lids.
Some very young children will chew on the marker lids as they try to remove them.

Modifications

Vary the color selections:

- primary colors (red, blue, yellow)
- red, yellow, and orange (perhaps for a pizza unit)
- pastel colors (after an extended exploration of primary colors)

Focus on contrast by providing two colors of markers with high contrast, such as red and black or green and yellow.
Vary the drawing surface to include white and pastel construction or duplicating paper, paper plates, paper towels, coffee filters, doilies, or white paper bags.
Introduce markers with thin tips.

Comments & Questions to Extend Thinking

I see one person drawn with each color in your tray.
What kinds of lines can you make with these markers?

3.6 Specialty Crayons

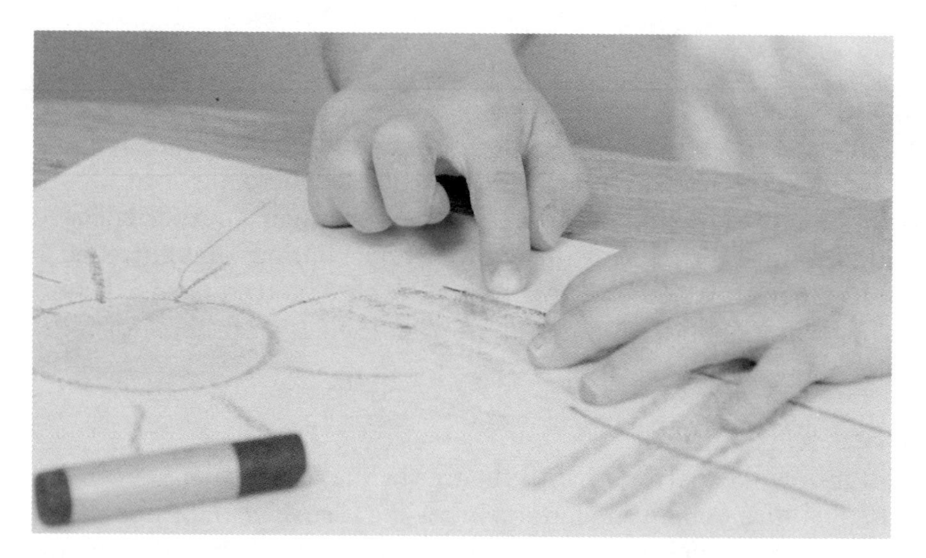

Description

The explorations in this activity are similar to those in chalk and crayon drawing experiences. These special drawing tools combine elements of both chalk and crayons. While the colors are brilliant, like crayons, the marks on the paper can be smudged or blended with water, like chalk. Specialty drawing crayons, which combine an oil-based substance and chalk, are available from several art supply catalogs.

Helpful Hints

Store the specialty crayons in the original container to keep them from easily breaking.

Art Experiences

- ▲ experimenting with a unique drawing tool
- ▲ exploring line, form, and design
- ▲ comparing chalk and crayons to specialty crayons
- ▲ blending colors with fingers or water

Materials

- ▲ white construction paper, 9 by 12 inches
- ▲ 4 sets of specialty crayons, each with 3 or more colors
- ▲ smocks

Child's Level

Explorations with specialty crayons are most appropriate for older preschool and kindergarten children. Since children apply color to paper in the same way as with crayons and chalk, teachers can introduce specialty crayons after children have had some experience with chalk and crayons. Some of the variations listed below, such as those using water, are most appropriate for older or more experienced children.

What to Look For

Children will produce scribbles, named scribbles, or representational forms, depending on their stage of drawing.

Some children will fill the paper with many lines and forms.

Some children will make only a few marks on the paper.

Some children will draw faces, people, or people with many body parts, clothes, and details, such as eyelashes.

Some children will blend the colors on the paper.

Some children will smudge the colors with their fingers or a sponge.

Modifications

Introduce a variety of drawing surfaces, such as paper plates, paper towels, or white or pastel duplicating paper.

Use half-sheets of construction paper as the drawing surface to encourage children to use finger movements rather than large arm movements.

Cut the drawing paper into various shapes, such as a large circle, pennant, or square.

Select interesting or unusual colors to present together:

- ▲ greens, blues, and purples (to coordinate with children's interest in water or the sea
- ▲ purple and red
- ▲ red, yellow, and black
- ▲ pastel colors (to stimulate renewed interest in drawing or to coordinate with children's interest in ballet, for example)

Introduce negative space by cutting geometric or irregular shapes in the center of the drawing paper.

Include small sponges or spray bottles to encourage children to explore blending the specialty crayons with water.

Comments & Questions to Extend Thinking

Does this special crayon look any different from our other crayons?

Rub the lines with your finger and see what happens.

3.7 Watercolor Crayons

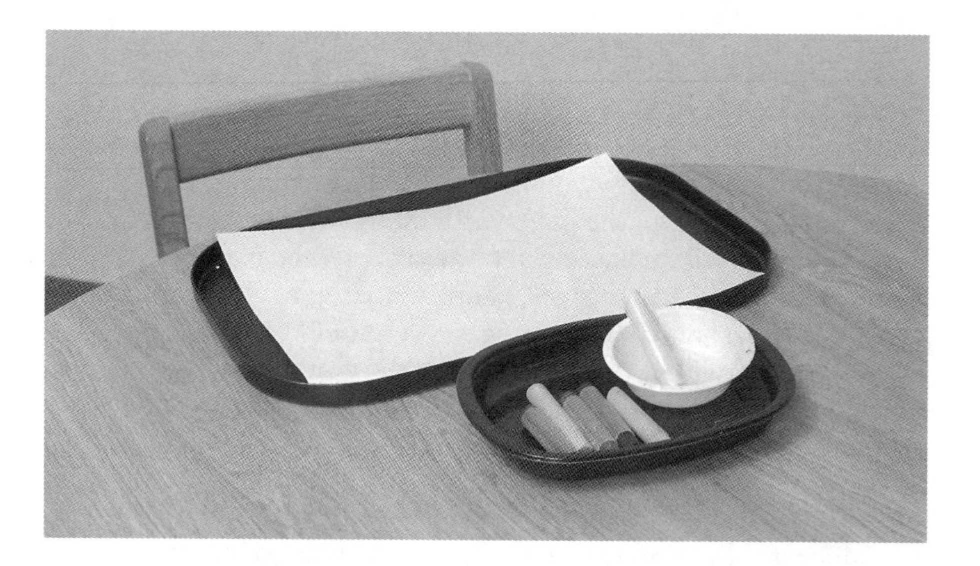

Description

Watercolor crayons are crayons that are dipped into water before applying the color to paper. The effect is similar to painting with watercolor paints; however, the colors are more brilliant. In some instances, the watercolor crayon is encased inside a cardboard tube to provide a dry surface for holding the crayon. Children can experiment with adding more or less water to the watercolor crayon and observe the results.

Helpful Hints

A small moist sponge can also be used to wet the watercolor crayons.

Art Experiences

- ▲ exploring a familiar drawing activity with an unusual tool
- ▲ comparing the lines made in this activity to those made with watercolor paints
- ▲ creating lines and forms with blurred edges

Materials

- ▲ white construction paper, 9 by 12 inches
- ▲ 4 sets of watercolor crayons, each with 3 or more colors
- ▲ 4 small trays, to hold the watercolor crayons
- ▲ 4 cups, each with a small amount of water
- ▲ smocks (optional)

Child's Level

This drawing activity is most appropriate for preschool and kindergarten children who have had experience drawing with crayons or chalk and painting with watercolor paints. Children can compare this activity to their previous experiences. Younger or inexperienced children may not be able to follow the sequence of steps necessary in this activity. Teachers can plan watercolor crayon activities to stimulate renewed interest in drawing as well as to build on the knowledge of materials constructed in other drawing and painting activities.

What to Look For

Children will dip the watercolor crayon into the water and experiment with making marks on the paper.

Some children will quickly become adept at the process of wetting the watercolor crayon and create designs and representational figures, such as people, flowers, and hearts.

Some children will use the watercolor crayon without first wetting the tip.

A few children will view the watercolor crayon as "broken" when it does not respond as they expect.

Modifications

Change the drawing surface to one of the following:

- white tagboard
- white or pastel duplicating paper
- white paper plates
- white paper towels
- white doilies
- coffee filters

Use watercolor crayons at the easel.

Comments & Questions to Extend Thinking

What kind of marks do these crayons make when you dip them in water and draw with them?

You made three lines with each color in your tray.

3.8 Crayon Melting

Description

This activity combines art with science exploration as children use crayons to draw on aluminum foil placed on top of a warming tray. As the crayons melt, they slide across the surface and produce brilliant colors. Although the warming tray does not get extremely hot on the surface, teachers must carefully supervise this activity. Teachers may want to use a variety of surfaces over a period of a few days to allow children to compare the results.

Helpful Hints

Create crayons on a stick to elevate children's hands high above the warming tray. Heat an oven to 250 degrees and turn it off. Place crayon shavings, about ½-inch deep, in muffin tins and melt in the oven. Insert a craft stick into the blob before it completely solidifies.

Art Experiences

- ▲ exploring the physical properties of crayons when heat is applied
- ▲ observing crayons as they change from a solid to a liquid state
- ▲ creating lines with a more fluid medium
- ▲ comparing the effects of drawing with crayons on a heated surface to drawing on paper at room temperature
- ▲ expressing creativity with an unusual medium

Materials

- ▲ one or more warming trays (depending on the number of adults to supervise)
- ▲ aluminum foil, cut to the size of the warming tray
- ▲ selection of large crayons, with the paper removed
- ▲ pot holder or child's glove, for protection from the heat (optional)

Child's Level

This unusual activity is appropriate for older preschool and kindergarten children. Younger preschool children may not be able to withhold the impulse to lean on the warming tray. Children need many drawing experiences with crayons before teachers introduce this activity.

What to Look For

Children will experiment with the crayons on the warming tray and observe the results.
Some children may comment on the changes in the crayons as they melt and later return to a solid state.
Some children will create lines, shapes, and designs with the crayons.
Some children will hold the crayon in one place to observe the melting process.
Some children will lay the crayons on the foil and watch them turn into puddles.

Modifications

Substitute waxed paper, colored cellophane, or clear cellophane for the aluminum foil.
Substitute colored foil for the aluminum foil.
Vary the colors of crayons in the activity.
Sprinkle glitter onto the melted crayon drawings.

Comments & Questions to Extend Thinking

What is happening to the crayon?
How does it feel when you move the crayon across the tray?
Look where that red line crosses the yellow line. It turned to orange.
Look how quickly the crayon got hard again after we took it off the tray.

3.9 Multiple Lines

Crayons, Markers, & Colored Pencils

Description

This activity introduces the possibility of creating more than one line with a single movement of the hand. It is an outgrowth of observations made of children who sometimes grasp several markers or crayons in one hand and draw with them. Teachers can provide this experience for all children. Several crayons, markers, or colored pencils are bundled together with a thick rubber band. This activity often encourages children to verbalize descriptions of their multiline drawings. They may be so curious that they repeat this activity many times!

Helpful Hints

If too many implements are bundled together, children may remove some from the center.

Masking tape cannot be used to bundle more than two or three implements together.

Art Experiences

- ▲ experimenting with creating more than one line at a time
- ▲ encouraging verbal communication about art
- ▲ creating relationships about the position of the markers or crayons in the bundle and the location of the lines on the paper
- ▲ stimulating renewed interest in drawing activities

Materials

- ▲ white construction paper, 9 by 12 inches
- ▲ 4 "bundles," each with 2 or more crayons, markers, or colored pencils
- ▲ thick rubber bands or masking tape, to bundle together the crayons, markers, or colored pencils

Child's Level

This activity is most appropriate for older preschool and kindergarten children. Younger children have not yet fully explored drawing with a single implement and don't understand where the extra lines come from. Older children are fascinated by the creation of duplicate lines, shapes, and designs with a single stroke of their hand and arm.

What to Look For

Some children will explore the unusual drawing tool at the scribbling stage, even if they have progressed to the representation stage when using a single crayon or marker.

Some children will create repeated lines and loops on the paper.

A few children may be unhappy with the results of the drawing and ask for a single crayon, marker, or colored pencil.

Modifications

Change the paper to 12- by 18-inch white construction paper.

Vary the color selection in the bundle of crayons, markers, or colored pencils.

Change the quantity of drawing implements in the bundle.

Plan this activity for the easel, and use 18- by 24-inch paper.

Comments & Questions to Extend Thinking

How did you make three lines at once?

How can you make the blue line come out on top?

I see three outlines of this person. It looks like the person is moving.

3.10 Fabric Markers

Description

The fabric markers used in this activity are similar to the familiar felt-tipped markers in activity 3.5. They create permanent marks on fabric but do not blur, as permanent markers do, when used on cloth. Children are excited about the possibilities of drawing on fabric, since this is usually a "no-no." Children may incorporate their fabric drawings into other projects, such as quilts (activity 6.6). Teachers may wish to place paper under the fabric to absorb the color as it "bleeds" through the lightweight fabric.

Helpful Hints

Use masking tape to secure the fabric to the tray if children are unable to hold it as they draw.

Fabric markers can be found in many fabric, art supply, and craft stores.

Art Experiences

- ▲ exploring a unique drawing surface
- ▲ creating lines, shapes, and forms
- ▲ observing the duplications of the drawing as the lines "bleed" through the fabric onto the paper

Materials

- ▲ white cotton, such as muslin, cut into 8-inch squares
- ▲ 4 trays, to provide a work surface and protect the table
- ▲ paper, to place under the fabric
- ▲ assortment of fabric markers

Child's Level

Drawing with fabric markers is most appropriate for older preschool and kindergarten children. This activity should be introduced after children have had some experiences using regular felt-tipped markers on paper. The fabric is more flexible than paper and may be difficult for younger children to support while drawing.

What to Look For

Children will eagerly experiment with the fabric markers and the fabric.

Some children will create scribbles on the fabric.

Some children will create representational figures, such as faces, on the fabric.

Some children may have difficulty holding the fabric as they draw.

Some children will observe the image that bleeds onto the paper under the fabric and compare it to the original drawing on the fabric.

Some children will tell stories about the pictures they draw.

Modification

Substitute other fabric for the muslin. Some possibilities include quilted fabric, gingham checks, white tone-on-tone designs, and pastel colors.

Comments & Questions to Extend Thinking

Beth made a pattern of lines with the fabric markers—red-green-purple, red-green-purple.

Can you see your drawing on the reverse side of your fabric?

3.11 Embossing on Foil

Description

Children can use a soft-point pencil as a drawing tool on aluminum or other foil. The lead pencil marks do not show on the foil, but slight depressions are left behind. This is similar to the art of embossing paper, which uses a blunt metal tool.

Art Experiences

▲ drawing by creating an indentation rather than by leaving a color impression
▲ using a common writing tool with a new medium
▲ comparing drawing to embossing

Materials

▲ 4 trays
▲ aluminum foil, cut to approximately 9 by 12 inches
▲ soft lead pencils without a sharp point

Child's Level

This activity is most appropriate for older preschool and kindergarten children. While it uses a familiar pencil as a tool for drawing, it is not well-suited to very young children who may have difficulty exerting sufficient pressure on the pencil to create an indentation.

Helpful Hints

Large beginner pencils work well for this activity.

Place a paper towel under the foil. It allows the pencil to create a deeper indentation.

What to Look For

Children will experiment with moving the pencil over the foil and observe the results.

Some children may comment on the depressions the pencil makes in the foil.

Some children will create lines, shapes, and designs with the pencil.

Some children will not be able to manipulate the pencil successfully. They may press too hard, and make holes in the foil, or not press hard enough, and therefore not create an impression.

Modifications

Provide other types of foil for children to draw on, such as foil wrapping paper.

Use Styrofoam plates as a drawing surface for embossing.

Comments & Questions to Extend Thinking

Can you feel the lines you drew?

What does it look like on the other side of your foil?

I can see your drawing, even though there's no color.

3.12 Class Book

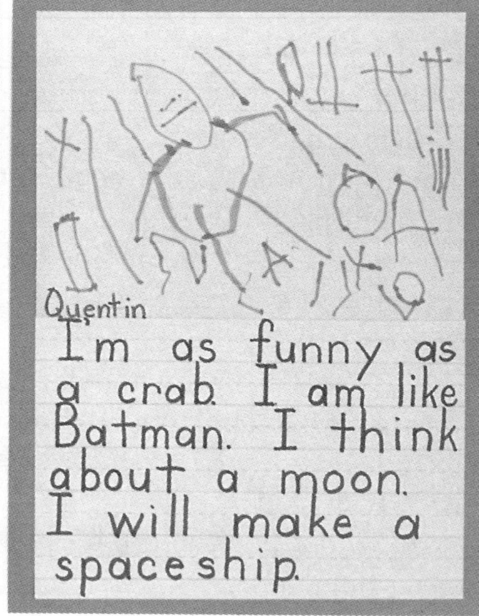

Helpful Hints

Children may wish to decorate the cover of the book. Staple the pages together, or use a binder, if available.

Description

Teachers may use drawing as the impetus for creating a class book. Once a popular topic is selected, children can each create a page. Examples might include remembrances of a field trip, such as a visit to a fire station; a class book based on a popular curriculum topic, such as families; or a class project inspired by a popular book or song, such as "Hush Little Baby." Once children have completed their drawings, they can write or dictate their stories or comments, which can be included on their page of the book. This allows each child to create individually while contributing to a group project. Story paper, which is plain on the top and lined on the bottom, is ideal for this project.

Art Experiences

- ▲ using artwork to support literacy
- ▲ drawing
- ▲ contributing to a group project

Materials

- ▲ 4 sets of markers
- ▲ 4 sets of multicultural markers
- ▲ story paper, 12 by 18 inches, cut in half
- ▲ 2 pieces of construction paper, to use for the front and back covers of the book

Child's Level

This activity is most appropriate for older preschool and kindergarten children, who are more likely to be interested in contributing to a group project.

What to Look For

Children will talk about their drawings.
Children will explore a variety of lines and shapes in their drawings.
Some children will create representational drawings.
Children will eagerly look at each other's pages and read and reread the book.

Modification

Write stories or comments on a separate piece of paper, which can be stapled to the bottom of the picture. The drawings and stories can be displayed in the classroom.

Comments & Questions to Extend Thinking

Liz used lots of orange to draw pictures of pumpkins from our trip to the pumpkin farm.
What should I write about your picture?
Tell Will what your page of the book says.
The people look happy in this picture. They must like being together.

3.13 Ice Cube Drawings

Description

For this activity, children use colored ice cubes as drawing tools. The activity is an outgrowth of discoveries that children made while exploring an ice project in their class. In order to understand how to create ice, which was the children's goal, they experimented with both clear and colored ice cubes. Children quickly began using the ice cubes as drawing tools. They were fascinated with the way the ice melted as they moved the ice cubes across the paper and eagerly described the lovely pastel lines left behind.

Helpful Hints

Store the ice cubes in a cooler so that they don't all melt while children are waiting for a turn.

Art Experiences

- ▲ drawing with a fluid medium
- ▲ combining colors to create new colors
- ▲ creating with an unusual material
- ▲ observing changes in materials

Materials

- ▲ colored ice cubes, made in plastic freezer pop molds by adding a drop of red, yellow, or blue food coloring to the water before freezing it
- ▲ white construction paper, 9 by 12 inches
- ▲ 4 trays, to hold the paper
- ▲ smocks

Child's Level

This activity is most appropriate for older preschool and kindergarten children, who may use the materials to create a specific result and are less bothered by the coldness of the ice cubes.

What to Look For

Children will move the ice across the paper and observe the results.

Some children will draw specific lines or shapes with the ice cubes.

Children will experiment with mixing colors as the ice cubes melt.

Some children will attempt to suck on the ice and may need redirection.

Modifications

Emphasize narrow lines by switching to smaller ice cubes.

Use colored ice cubes to create a group mural.

Make colored ice in freezer pop molds for use at the easel.

Comments & Questions to Extend Thinking

What is happening to the ice?

Are these colored lines on your paper made of ice?

Sjaya says she drew her name with ice.

I see purple on your paper, but I don't see a purple ice cube. Where did the purple come from?

3.14 Misting Over Crayons

Description

Children who are accustomed to working with crayons are intrigued by the changes that occur when they spray their crayon creations with colored water. They are particularly surprised to discover that the colored water does not obscure the crayon. For this activity, children draw with crayons at the easel. When they have completed their drawing, they spray the picture with colored water and observe the results.

Helpful Hints

Look for tiny spray bottles in the cosmetic section of drugstores.

Art Experiences

▲ drawing
▲ combining art materials
▲ observing the effects of colored water on crayon marks
▲ observing changes in materials

Materials

▲ easel (the activity can also be done at a table or on the floor)
▲ manila easel paper
▲ assorted crayons
▲ small spray bottle containing water colored with blue food coloring
▲ smock

Child's Level

This activity is most appropriate for older preschool or kindergarten children who are able to follow a two-step process.

What to Look For

Children will draw with the crayons, spray their pictures with colored water, and carefully observe the results.
Children will create scribbles, named scribbles, or more representational drawings, depending on their level of development.
Some children will try to draw over wet paper with the crayons.
Some children may only be interested in spraying water on the paper.
Children will talk about their drawings and discuss the results of spraying water on them.

Modifications

Explore different colors of water to spray on the drawings.
Use two primary colors (red, yellow, or blue) of water to spray on the drawings. Children will observe that the two colors of water combine to produce a new color, but the colored water does not combine with the crayon marks to create a new color.
Substitute watercolor paint for the colored water.

Comments & Questions to Extend Thinking

What do you think will happen if you spray water over the crayon drawing?
Do you think this blue water will cover up the crayon?
The blue water changed the color of the paper but not the color of the crayon.

CHAPTER 4

Collage

Megan used glue to attach colorful, curly ribbon and sequins onto a black paper plate. She brushed a small dab of glue onto her plate and placed a piece of ribbon on top. When she wanted to attach the sequins to the paper, however, she placed a dab of glue directly onto each sequin. When she completed her collage activity, she showed it to her teacher. Megan explained that she needed more glue to attach the ribbon than she did for the sequins.

▲ ▲ ▲

Wesley joined Ahmer and Sierra at the special activity table. The children each had a piece of white construction paper and three colors of rug yarn, which had been donated by one of the parents. Wesley glued three pieces of yarn to make a triangle. The other two children were very interested in how he did this and immediately tried to create shapes of their own. They discussed how to make other shapes, and were especially interested in solving the problem of making circles out of the short, straight pieces of yarn.

▲ ▲ ▲

Young children consider the use of space and the arrangement of objects and materials from very early ages. They line up stuffed animals on a pillow, place toy cars in the parking spaces of a garage, and try to fit pieces into a shape sorter. Collage activities allow children to continue the exploration of space and arrangement as well as express their creativity. As children combine glue with paper or other materials, they must think about size, shape, and form. How many pieces of paper fit around the edge of a paper plate? What is the relationship between the rectangular pieces of paper and the circular shape of the plate? Can the paper shapes be arranged to create a pleasing design? These are a few of the artistic aspects that children explore with collage materials.

Teachers' Questions

What are collage activities?

Collage activities are combinations of two or more materials secured to a base surface, usually with glue. A wide variety of materials can be incorporated in collage activities. Construction paper is a common base for collages, but many other materials, such as cardboard, paper plates, and wood, also make excellent surfaces for the activities. The materials available to use in combination with glue and base surfaces are almost unlimited: buttons, pasta, torn or cut paper, shells, fabric, wallpaper, leaves, nuts, ribbon, and bottle caps, to name a few. Many collage materials are free, collected by teachers, parents, or children, perhaps during explorations of the natural environment.

Why are collage activities an important component of the art curriculum?

Collage activities allow children to explore many artistic elements as they interact with a wide variety of materials. As they combine materials in collage activities, children must consider the artistic use of space, texture, shape, color, and design. They also construct information about pattern, symmetry, and balance. Collage activities are open-ended, without a predetermined outcome. Artistic elements emerge gradually after children have had many opportunities to experiment with glue and various collage materials.

Collage activities foster the construction of physical knowledge and logical-mathematical relationships. As children participate in collage activities, they explore the physical properties of materials, such as color, weight, texture, and size (***physical knowledge***) and form relationships based on these observations (***logical-mathematical knowledge***). They discover whether or not materials can be cut or torn, are fluid or nonfluid, or have any properties that change over time. For example, glue is white, sticky, and fluid. When it dries, it is clear, hard, and can adhere one material to another. Paper, on the other hand, has color, weight, and shape. It can be folded, torn, and cut, and is not fluid. Paper cannot be used to secure one material to another.

The creation of relationships flourishes in situations such as collage activities, where children can explore the physical properties of materials. For example, a child who constructs physical knowledge about the weight of objects and adhesion properties of glue may accurately decide that more glue is needed to secure acorns than leaves to paper. The child constructs a relationship between the weight of various objects and the amount of glue needed to make them stick to the surface. Similarly, a child who constructs physical knowledge about tissue paper learns that it has color that "bleeds" when wet with glue. This child may choose to place a yellow piece of tissue on top of a red piece in order to produce a new color. The child's understanding of the relationship between the wetness of the glue and the properties of the paper results in blending colors. Information such as this allows children to use collage materials in the most effective and creative ways.

What are some of the goals for collage activities?

Goals for collage activities include those specifically related to collage materials as well as general goals for art. Goals specific to collage activities include the following:

- ▲ exploring the placement of shapes within a confined space
- ▲ experimenting with pattern and symmetry
- ▲ creating unique forms and shapes
- ▲ exploring the use of textures
- ▲ elaborating on the use of common materials
- ▲ encouraging flexible thinking
- ▲ extending previous knowledge
- ▲ fostering the construction of physical knowledge and logical-mathematical relationships

Some general goals for art, such as fostering creativity, expressing thoughts, and encouraging art appreciation, apply to experiences with collage materials as well as to most artistic explorations. Additional information about goals for the art curriculum can be found in chapter 1. Specific goals for individual collage activities are included with each activity.

What materials are needed for collage activities?

Collage activities require a base surface, a selection of materials to mount to the base, and a substance to secure the materials to the base. Although paper is the most common material used for a collage base, many other materials can be substituted. Cardboard, poster board, mat board scraps, paper plates, wood, and fabric are possibilities. Teachers should select the base surface depending on the weight of the collage materials, aesthetic appeal, and coordination with other activities in the curriculum. For example, a shell collage might be mounted on heavy cardboard to support the weight of the shells, while lightweight and more delicate tissue paper could be combined with white construction paper. Wood scraps might be selected as the base for gluing craft sticks, spools, and toothpicks when the dramatic play area is designed as a construction site.

Many materials make excellent collage components. Paper, fabric, ribbon, cotton balls, and natural materials, such as dried weeds, leaves, and shells, are perhaps the most common types of collage materials.

Glue is the most common substance used to mount collage materials to the base. It is much more effective than paste, which can be difficult to spread and may not hold heavy items to the base surface.

What kind of glue is most suitable for collage activities?

White liquid glue, sometimes called school glue, is the most common type of glue used for collage activities. White glue spreads easily, has good adhesion properties, dries clear, and is a readily available resource for early childhood programs. This type of glue can be thinned with water to make it easier to spread or to conserve the available supply. Teachers should add small amounts of water and experiment with the results to discover the best ratio of water to glue. If the glue is too thin, children will experience difficulty controlling it and become frustrated when it will not adequately hold materials together. Teachers should avoid using squeeze bottles of glue for collage activities. Even older children enjoy squeezing out all of the glue at once! Instead, teachers can store glue in paint containers that have a hole in the lid, or smaller containers with flip-top lids. These are available in many art supply catalogues.

An inexpensive, flexible spreader is commercially available for use with glue. This is more satisfactory than metal glue brushes, which are difficult for children to manipulate and begin to rust after only a few washings. The bristles of the brushes are stiff and frustrating for children to use, especially on small collage objects. The glue spreaders, which hold a small amount of glue, are easy to use as applicators on various collage materials.

When should color be added to glue?

Glue with added color should be used after children have had many experiences exploring white glue and collage materials. Very often young children initially expect white glue to respond in the same way as paint. They are surprised when the picture they "painted" with the glue disappears as it dries. After many experiences with white glue, children develop an understanding of the properties of glue. At this point, the introduction of glue with added color may stimulate new interest in collage activities as well as add a new dimension to the activities. While colored glue is commercially available, teachers may wish to color glue themselves by adding small amounts of paint or food coloring to white glue.

Should teachers cut the base paper into shapes?

Teachers can occasionally vary the shape of the base paper to encourage children to focus on the use of space. Changes in the shape of the base paper stimulate additional interest in a familiar activity, force children to consider the use of space in a new way, and encourage creative thinking. Teachers should take care, however, not to select shapes just to make the collage more attractive to adults or to "fit" a theme. A collage made by gluing acorns to a rectangular piece of poster board is as valuable as using a leaf-shaped base. In fact, it may be more valuable because it does not suggest a specific outcome to the children.

What should teachers consider when selecting materials for collage activities?

Collage materials should be developmentally appropriate for individual children as well as the group; aesthetically pleasing; suitable for the gluing surfaces selected; and meet budget constraints. Younger, less-experienced children need lightweight materials to glue onto a stable, flat surface, while more-experienced children may be able to solve problems such as how to adhere a heavy material to a flimsy surface. Aesthetically pleasing materials, such as colorful paper, ribbon, and fabric, introduce children to beautiful media for collage activities. These should be neatly cut or trimmed and selected to coordinate with the color of the base surface and with each other. Suggestions for color combinations are included with specific activities in this chapter. Finally, teachers must consider the budget when selecting collage materials. Many of the materials can be found in discount stores or may be donated by parents. Although teachers often seek and appreciate free resources, the materials should always be evaluated for their aesthetic qualities before being included in the art curriculum.

What is the best way to display collage activities for children?

Collage activities should be displayed in an organized and aesthetic manner. A selection of collage materials, organized in divided trays and attractively presented on an art shelf or special activity table, immediately attracts children to the activity. The systematic presentation of the materials helps children organize their thoughts and consider multiple ways to combine the materials. For example, when three colors of cellophane are placed in one basket in the center of the table, children do not know what colors are available. Young children may be concerned about whether there will be enough materials for each of them. Such concerns often lead to management issues. Children may grab cellophane by the handful in order to assure that they have enough. They may not be aware of the three colors available and therefore be unable to explore all the possibilities. On the other hand, the cellophane can be sorted by color and placed into divided trays, one for each child at the table. The teacher may need to periodically replenish the supplies. Children can quickly observe the materials available and feel secure that there is a sufficient amount. They can then concentrate on more artistic pursuits.

Collage activities can be designed for placement in an art area or as special activities. Collage materials are often placed in the art area where they are available for children to use over an extended period of time. More information about collage activities planned for the art area can be found in chapter 2. Many teachers also plan special activities that are typically available for one or two days at a time. As a collage special activity, the teacher might provide each child at the special activity table with a white paper plate, glue, two colors of netting fabric, and two colors of curly ribbon. Each child can glue the ribbon and netting onto the paper plate in a variety of designs. Similar collage activities may be introduced at various times during the year.

Why do teachers plan specific collage activities?

Teachers plan specific collage activities to introduce varieties of collage materials to children. Specific collage activities provide opportunities for children to construct knowledge about the physical properties of materials and create relationships among them. Explorations of individual collage materials, such as a variety of fabrics, enhance a child's understanding of how these materials respond to the glue and to each other. At a later time, the same child might combine silk, corduroy, and felt in a different activity. Previous experiences with glue and fabric provide a foundation for the new activity and allow the child to elaborate on the ideas gleaned from the earlier experience. Elaboration is a component of creativity.

Teachers may also plan collage activities to allow children to explore new materials before they are placed in the art area. Some teachers may wish to introduce glue as a special activity several times before placing it on the art area shelves. This allows the teacher to monitor the abilities of the group and individual children. The teacher may adjust the amount of glue provided or perhaps decide to delay introducing glue at the art area until children have more experience in the more controlled situation of a special activity. During special activities teachers can restate guidelines, such as using the glue only on the paper, and assist children when problems arise. Teachers typically monitor the special activity table more closely than the art area.

Why is the sequencing of collage activities an important consideration?

Sequencing collage activities contributes to children's understanding of the materials and provides opportunities for children to explore such artistic elements as color, pattern, and form. Careful sequencing of the collage activities furthers the development of the skills necessary to continue creative explorations of collage materials. Collage activities that include too many choices may hinder children's ability to be creative as they struggle to figure out how to make items stick to the paper.

How should teachers sequence collage activities?

Teachers should begin with the simplest form of the collage activity and introduce more complex variations one at a time. For example, an activity that includes construction paper, glue, and small squares of blue paper is a good beginning collage activity. Subsequently, the teacher might plan the same activity, changing only the color of the paper squares. This minor change provides new interest and stimulates children to repeat the experience, thus developing the skills necessary to become more competent and creative using collage materials. Teachers may plan paper collage activities many times throughout the year. Competence with a particular art medium allows children to be more creative in their artistic endeavors.

Should teachers plan collage activities related to other curriculum areas?

Teachers can plan collage activities to coordinate with other experiences in the curriculum; however, they must be careful ***not*** *to contrive activities merely to correlate with an existing curriculum topic.* Art experiences should be designed for their inherent creative possibilities rather than to fit a topic. A collage activity that includes animal-print paper is an example of an art activity contrived to fit a zoo theme. An alternative selection of collage materials might include materials of various textures, such as corrugated paper, velvet fabric, sandpaper, and shiny paper. Children interested in creating zoo animals may choose from these materials to represent the animals. Children who are not interested in creating zoo animals may explore the materials and combine them in unique ways. The possibilities for flexible thinking are more limited with animal-print paper.

What curriculum areas provide the best opportunities for coordination with collage activities?

The literacy area provides some of the best opportunities for teachers to plan related collage activities. Teachers may be able to build on children's interest in books as they plan collage activities. For example, many children are interested in the books *Color Dance*, by Ann Jonas (New York: Greenwillow, 1989), and *Mouse Paint*, by Ellen Stoll Walsh (New York: Harcourt, 1989). Both books focus on mixing colors. Teachers may plan a collage activity that combines white paper with red, yellow, and blue cellophane. This combination of colors may provide opportunities for children to make connections to the book. Some children may think about overlapping the cellophane to create new colors. Other children may not think about the book, but explore the placement of the cellophane in a pleasing design. Teachers may also structure the activity in a way that encourages children to think about the story line of the book. For example, children may be encouraged to contribute collage pictures and dictations about them to create a class book about colors.

How can teachers assess children's use of collage materials?

As with other art experiences, teachers can save examples of children's collages to include in a portfolio. Teachers can also photograph children working with collage materials to document the process and write anecdotal notes to describe children's experiences with collage activities.

Collage Activities

4.1 Paper Collage

Description

Young children delight in dabbing glue onto paper and placing other colorful pieces of paper on top of the glue. Many children continue the process until they have several layers of paper and glue. Still other children may cover the paper with glue, but may or may not place any collage pieces on top of the glue. This activity suggests ways teachers can introduce paper collage to young children, as well as variations that encourage children to further explore this first collage activity. Repeated experiences with simple materials build a foundation for later, more complex collage activities.

Helpful Hints

For very young children, begin with a half-sheet of paper for the base. They often glue only a few collage pieces to their paper.

Art Experiences

- ▲ exploring the physical properties of glue
- ▲ exploring glue with a flexible material
- ▲ creating pattern relationships
- ▲ considering form and contrast
- ▲ planning within boundaries

Materials

- ▲ 4 trays (one for each child)
- ▲ white construction paper, 9 by 12 inches
- ▲ small squares of construction paper, all the same color (8 to 10 per child, replenished by the teacher as needed)
- ▲ 4 small trays, to hold the collage pieces
- ▲ 4 jar lids, each with a small amount of glue and a glue spreader
- ▲ smocks (optional)

Child's Level

This simple collage activity is appropriate for preschool children. The minimal amounts of glue and collage pieces and the structured presentation of the materials allow children to explore the necessary skills for later, more complex paper collage activities. Similar activities can be planned many times throughout the year.

What to Look For

Some children will place a small amount of glue on the base paper and put the collage squares on top of the glue. They will repeat the process until they are satisfied with the result.

Some children will cover the base paper with glue and then place some of the collage squares on top of the glue.

Some children may arrange the collage squares on the base paper without using the glue. They are often surprised when they lift the paper and the collage pieces fall off.

Some children may focus only on the glue and not use any of the collage pieces. They are usually surprised when the glue dries clear and their picture appears to be gone.

A few children may create a design using the collage squares.

Modifications

Use other shapes of paper for collage pieces, such as triangles and rectangles.

Vary the color combinations:

- red, yellow, or blue collage pieces with a white or black base
- red, yellow, and orange collage pieces with a brown base (when children show interest in autumn colors)
- white collage pieces with a black base (when children notice snow on the ground, for example)
- black collage pieces with a white base (to focus on contrast, or when children show interest in shadows)
- pastel collage pieces with a white base (when children notice spring colors in the environment)
- several shades of the same color, such as blue or red, with a white base

Substitute paper plates for the base material.

Cut the base paper into other shapes, such as pennants or squares.

Comments & Questions to Extend Thinking

Let's leave the paper squares on top of the glue until after class and see what happens.

What happens when you put the paper squares on top of the glue?

4.2 Ribbon Creations

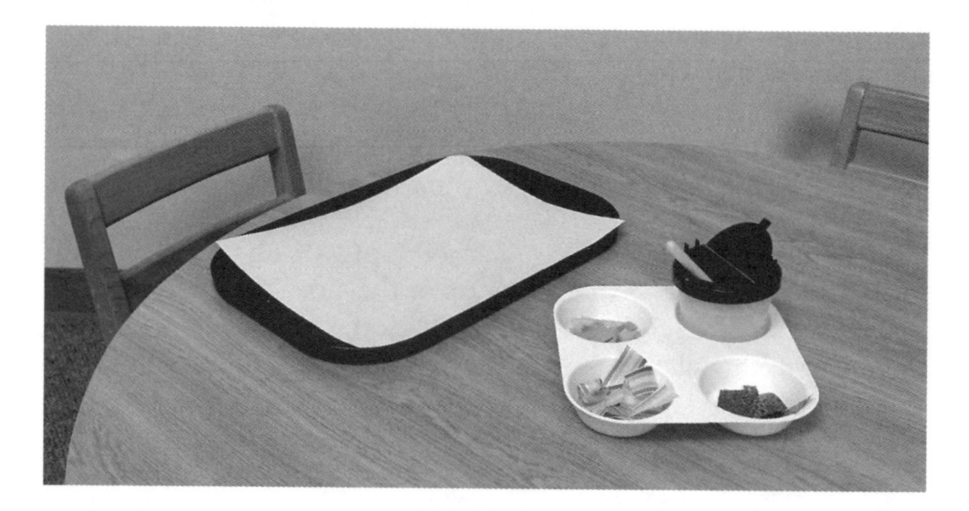

Description

In this activity, children create collages with ribbon of various colors and textures. Ribbon provides an inexpensive source of collage material. The pieces of ribbon are arranged in a divided container so children can easily observe their color, width, and design. Teachers can also plan collage activities that combine ribbon with other materials, such as tissue paper, sequins, glitter, or fabric. However, children require many experiences using a single type of collage material, such as ribbons, before combining several collage materials.

Helpful Hints

Shop after any holiday or change of season for an inexpensive source of ribbon.

Ask parents for donations of unusual ribbon.

Floral shops, department stores, and gift shops may donate end rolls of ribbon or scraps left from gift wrapping.

Art Experiences

- ▲ exploring glue with flexible materials
- ▲ observing and creating patterns and symmetry
- ▲ planning within boundaries
- ▲ experimenting with color and texture

Materials

- ▲ 4 trays (1 for each child)
- ▲ white construction paper, 9 by 12 inches
- ▲ divided tray, with pieces of colored ribbon
- ▲ 4 glue containers, each with a small amount of glue and a glue spreader
- ▲ smocks (optional)

Child's Level

This activity is most appropriate for preschool or kindergarten children who have had some experience using paper collage pieces. Children can manipulate the flat pieces of ribbon in a similar way.

What to Look For

Children will glue pieces of ribbon onto the base paper in random designs.
Some children will create patterns with the ribbon.
Some children will create representational designs, such as faces or houses, with the ribbon.
Some children will glue several layers of ribbon on top of each other.

Modifications

Start with one color of ribbon and a white base for children who need a very simple collage activity.
Encourage patterning by providing two colors of ribbon. This often leads to alternating patterns.
Use three to five colors of ribbon with a white base.
Combine metallic ribbon with a black or white base.
Introduce various types of base surfaces, such as paper plates, scraps of poster board, or white fabric.
Combine ribbon with pieces of fabric, tissue, sequins, and glitter.
Cut the base paper into a variety of shapes, such as pennants or squares.

Comments & Questions to Extend Thinking

Where do you think this gold ribbon should go?
I see a row of red ribbon across the top of your paper.
How does this grosgrain ribbon feel?

4.3 Fabric Collage

Description

Interesting fabric provides opportunities for children to explore color, pattern, and texture as they create designs with collage materials. The fabrics may range from plain cotton and calico prints to more unusual tulle, netting, and velvet. Fabric from many cultures, such as African prints or silk from India, may be introduced. Many children are unfamiliar with fabric other than the material used in their own clothing and homes. Working with various fabrics encourages children to more carefully consider the physical properties of the materials, such as weight and thickness. Heavier pieces of fabric require more glue to secure them to a base surface than materials such as ribbon.

Helpful Hints

Store fabric pieces in separate plastic bags for easy access.

Look for fabric remnants in fabric stores. They are usually inexpensive.

Art Experiences

- ▲ creating form and design with various colors and shapes
- ▲ exploring textures
- ▲ discovering how much glue is needed to secure various materials

Materials

- ▲ 4 trays (1 for each child)
- ▲ white construction paper, 9 by 12 inches
- ▲ divided tray, with small squares of fabric for collage pieces
- ▲ 4 jars, each with a small amount of glue and a glue spreader
- ▲ smocks (optional)

Child's Level

Although this activity is slightly more difficult than gluing lighter-weight collage materials, it is appropriate for both preschool and kindergarten children. Fabric collages can be introduced after children have had experience with gluing paper or ribbon. A divided tray to hold the fabric pieces provides children with easy access to the various materials.

What to Look For

Some children will create an overall design with the fabric.
Some children will create representational designs with the fabric.
Some children will combine two pieces of fabric to create a new shape.
Some children may glue fabric on top of fabric in some places on the base.
A few children may glue pieces of fabric onto other fabric without regard for the base.

Modifications

Draw attention to color by combining two or three colors of lightweight cotton fabric with white paper or a paper plate for the base.
Change the thickness of the fabric by supplying two or more colors of felt, cut into 2-inch squares, with cardboard or a paper plate for the base.
Explore a loose-weave, coarse material, such as burlap, cut into small squares, with a neutral base, such as tan burlap or dark brown construction paper.
Assemble several types of fancy fabric, such as tulle, netting, velvet, and lamé, to glue to a white or black base.
Emphasize texture by combining fabrics such as velvet, burlap, and "fuzzy" material with a base of black paper or poster board.
Use white "fuzzy" fabric with dark paper to focus on contrast.

Comments & Questions to Extend Thinking

What happens to the glue when you put the netting on top of it?
Julie put a piece of velvet in the middle of her netting.
Which fabric is the thickest?
How much glue will you need to hold the quilted fabric?

4.4 Wonderful Wallpaper

Description

Wallpaper, which is available in many colors, patterns, designs, and textures, is ideal for creating collages. Teachers have easy access to sample books that parents or decorating shops willingly donate. The books contain a wealth of interesting selections. In many instances, the same design or pattern is shown in several colors. Through careful selection of the specific types of wallpaper, teachers can enhance the possibility for the creation of patterns. For example, children may create alternating stripes if two colors of wallpaper strips are available. Since wallpaper often has colors with high contrast, children may more easily perceive repetition of designs in wallpaper samples than in other materials. In addition, the designs in the wallpaper samples may stimulate children to consider unique ways to use the pieces in their artwork. For example, striped paper might become the dress on a person, while textured paper might become the hair.

Helpful Hints

Include a tray of wallpaper collage pieces in the art area to encourage further explorations.

Art Experiences

- ▲ observing and creating patterns
- ▲ exploring and comparing textures
- ▲ experimenting with the arrangement of shapes
- ▲ creating unique designs with familiar materials

Materials

▲ 4 trays (1 for each child)
▲ cardboard or poster board, for the base
▲ divided tray, with a selection of wallpaper pieces for collage
▲ 4 jars, each with a small amount of glue and a glue spreader
▲ smocks (optional)

Child's Level

Both preschool and kindergarten children can experiment with wallpaper collage pieces to create unique outcomes. Since wallpaper samples are heavier than most paper, this activity is better suited to children who have already had experience gluing paper, ribbon, or other lightweight collage materials. It would not be an appropriate first collage experience.

What to Look For

Some children will arrange the wallpaper pieces in a random design.
Some children will use the wallpaper pieces to create a representational design, such as a house.
Some children will create patterns using the wallpaper.
Some children will comment about the various textures of the wallpaper.
Some children may combine the wallpaper pieces to form new shapes.

Modifications

Highlight use of color by selecting one color of wallpaper in several designs, such as a solid texture, stripes, and a floral print.
Focus on design by choosing one wallpaper design, such as flowers, printed in several colors.
Draw attention to texture by providing several colors of wallpaper with the same texture.
Emphasize contrast through several white tone-on-tone designs, used with a dark blue base.
Encourage patterning by limiting choices to two colors or textures of wallpaper.
Encourage children to combine shapes to create new ones by cutting wallpaper into geometric shapes, such as triangles.

Comments & Questions to Extend Thinking

Tommy says he put two triangles together to make a kite.
What color of stripe comes next in your pattern?

4.5 Yarn Collage

Description

In this activity, children experiment with short pieces of yarn to create designs and shapes. This flexible collage material easily conforms to children's explorations as they bend, twist, and curl it. Later, teachers can cut the yarn into pieces of various lengths or display the yarn in balls so that children can cut yarn for themselves. Teachers can purchase yarn at discount stores or ask for donations from parents or local artisans.

Helpful Hints

Display small amounts of yarn to encourage children to select individual pieces of yarn rather than grabbing a handful.

Art Experiences

- ▲ experimenting with a flexible material
- ▲ exploring curves and straight lines
- ▲ creating designs, shapes, and representational figures
- ▲ creating part-whole relationships by combining individual pieces to make shapes
- ▲ exploring the negative space created by curving pieces of yarn to form a perimeter

Materials

- ▲ 4 trays (1 for each child)
- ▲ white construction paper, 9 by 12 inches
- ▲ divided tray, with 2-inch-long pieces of yarn in several colors
- ▲ 4 jar lids, each with a small amount of glue and a glue spreader
- ▲ smocks (optional)

Child's Level

This activity is most appropriate for preschool and kindergarten children who have had many experiences with less-flexible collage materials. Yarn is more difficult to manage than collage materials such as paper and ribbon, and therefore can be frustrating for some children. Longer pieces of yarn are more difficult for young children to manipulate than shorter pieces. Previous experiences with collage materials help lay a foundation for children to effectively manipulate yarn.

What to Look For

Children will place small amounts of glue on the base paper and lay the yarn on the glue.
Some children will apply the glue directly to the yarn before pressing the yarn onto the paper.
Children will create an overall design on the paper.
Some children will create representational pictures, such as people.
Children may create shapes by combining separate pieces of yarn.
A few children may dip the yarn into the glue without using the glue spreader.

Modifications

Vary the color choices:

- ▲ primary colors of yarn with white or black paper plates
- ▲ red, yellow, orange, and brown yarn with dark brown construction paper (to coordinate with activity 2.5, the Autumn Art Area)
- ▲ white yarn with dark blue or black construction paper (when children notice clouds in the sky, or snow, for example)
- ▲ black yarn with white construction paper (to focus on contrast)
- ▲ pastel yarn with white construction paper (perhaps in spring or summer when children notice the colors of flowers)

Encourage the formation of shapes by cutting the yarn into longer lengths.
Combine a collage material that has length and width, such as pieces of fabric, with yarn, which emphasizes line.
Experiment with other base materials, such as white fabric squares, paper plates, or scraps of poster board.

Comments & Questions to Extend Thinking

Nikhil used yarn to make the wheels on his car.
Can you create a shape with the yarn?
Which colors do you like together?

4.6 Transparent Collage
Cellophane

Description

The transparent quality of cellophane adds a new dimension to collage activities. The glue is visible through the cellophane, and primary colors of cellophane can be combined to produce new colors. This collage activity provides ample opportunities for children to explore color combinations as well as the smooth texture of the cellophane. Combining the cellophane with a variety of base materials stimulates additional explorations and encourages children to form relationships, such as the effect of the color of the base on the color of the cellophane.

Helpful Hints

To reduce static electricity, teachers may use hand lotion before handling the cellophane.

Art Experiences

- ▲ exploring transparent materials
- ▲ combining colors
- ▲ experimenting with folding cellophane

Materials

- ▲ 4 trays (1 for each child)
- ▲ white construction paper, 9 by 12 inches
- ▲ divided tray, with small squares of red, yellow, and blue cellophane
- ▲ 4 glue containers, each with a small amount of glue and a glue spreader
- ▲ smocks (optional)

Child's Level

This activity is most appropriate for older preschool and kindergarten children. Static electricity often causes the cellophane pieces to stick together, which can be frustrating for young children. When teachers display small amounts of cellophane in divided trays or containers, children can more easily view the selection of colors.

What to Look For

Children will apply glue to the base surface and add individual pieces of cellophane.

Some children will place one color of cellophane on top of another and observe the change in color.

Some children will create patterns or designs with the pieces of cellophane.

A few children may spread glue on the individual pieces of cellophane before applying them to the paper.

Some children will create representational pictures with the cellophane.

Some children will fold the cellophane before gluing it, to create new shapes.

Modifications

Explore a variety of base surfaces, such white paper plates, clear cellophane, aluminum foil, cardboard tubes, wax paper, or small plastic tumblers.

Highlight color change by incorporating a colored base:

- ▲ red cellophane collage pieces with a yellow or blue base
- ▲ blue cellophane collage pieces with a yellow or red base
- ▲ yellow cellophane collage pieces with a blue or red base

Experiment with an unusual base surface, such as clear contact paper or clear self-adhesive lamination sheets. The cellophane pieces adhere to the sticky surface. A separate piece of contact paper or lamination can be placed on top of the collage.

Focus on color change by using a primary color of glue, such as red or blue, with yellow cellophane.

Comments & Questions to Extend Thinking

How did you get a green shape on your paper? There's no green cellophane.

What happens when you put yellow cellophane on top of red?

I can see your name through the cellophane.

4.7 Glitter Collage

Description

The sparkling colors of glitter appeal to both children and adults. In this activity, children experiment with the effects of glue and glitter. They discover that glue is necessary before the glitter will adhere to the paper. The pieces of glitter are very tiny compared to other collage pieces, and more of them are needed to create a design. Children cannot glue individual pieces of glitter to create the end result. Instead, they must first create the desired design with glue. A tray or box to hold the activity encourages children to shake off the excess glitter so that they can observe the design they have made.

Helpful Hints

Some glitter is made from metal and may injure children's eyes. Safer types are available through art catalogs.

Tape the tops of the shakers closed or children may open them and empty the jars.

To conserve the glitter, tape over some of the holes in the lids of the shakers.

Art Experiences

- ▲ exploring an unusual art medium
- ▲ experimenting with adhering glitter to paper
- ▲ creating designs with glue before covering them with glitter
- ▲ observing changes in glue as it dries
- ▲ participating in a multistep activity

Materials

- ▲ 4 trays or cardboard shirt boxes (1 for each child)
- ▲ white construction paper, 9 by 12 inches
- ▲ 1 or more colors of glitter, in small shakers, per child
- ▲ 4 jar lids, each with a small amount of glue and a glue spreader
- ▲ smocks (optional)

Child's Level

This activity is most appropriate for older preschool and kindergarten children. Younger children have more difficulty following the steps involved in the process: applying the glue, shaking the glitter, and removing the excess glitter. They may not yet understand the adhesion properties of glue, especially when used with a material such as glitter.

What to Look For

Some children will follow the steps in the process and apply glue to the paper first, then sprinkle glitter on top, and finally shake off the excess glitter.

Some children will create several layers by putting glitter on top of glue and glue on top of glitter.

Some children will create shapes and forms with the glue and cover them with the glitter.

Some children will sprinkle glitter on the paper without using any glue.

Modifications

Begin with one color of glitter and a half-sheet of construction paper for very young children.

Vary the colors of glitter, such as two colors of glitter or multi-colored glitter with a white base.

Introduce a variety of types of bases, such as paper plates, foil, cellophane, clear plastic yogurt lids, or metal lids from juice containers.

Comments & Questions to Extend Thinking

How can you make the glitter stay on the paper?

Look. When Nancy shook the glitter off her paper, it left the outline of a house.

4.8 Colored Salt or Sand

Description

Colored salt and sand collages are similar to glitter collages in several ways. First, the process of applying glue, adding the salt or sand, and shaking off the excess is the same as the process for glitter activities. The colored salt or sand is contained in shakers like those used for glitter. In addition, children who want to create a representational picture must first use the glue to create the desired forms and then apply the salt or sand. However, since salt and sand are heavier than glitter, they require a sturdier base. With repeated art experiences that involve either glitter, salt, or sand, children construct relationships involving the similarities and differences among them.

Helpful Hints

Colored sand is commercially available.

Teachers can easily color salt or white sand by placing some on a paper plate and rubbing it with colored chalk.

Art Experiences

- ▲ exploring an unusual art medium
- ▲ experimenting with how to make salt or sand stick to paper
- ▲ creating designs with glue and either salt or sand
- ▲ participating in a multistep activity
- ▲ creating relationships between salt or sand and glitter activities

Materials

- ▲ 4 trays or cardboard shirt boxes (1 for each child)
- ▲ white poster board, approximately 9 by 12 inches
- ▲ 1 or more colors of colored salt or sand, in small shakers, per child
- ▲ 4 jar lids, each with a small amount of glue and a glue spreader
- ▲ smocks (optional)

Child's Level

Like glitter activities, this activity is most appropriate for older preschool and kindergarten children. Younger children have more difficulty following the steps involved in the process. They may not yet understand the adhesion properties of glue when used with a substance such as salt or sand.

What to Look For

Some children will follow the steps in the process: first apply glue to the paper, then sprinkle salt or sand on top, and finally shake off the excess.

Some children will create several layers by putting salt or sand on top of glue and glue on top of salt or sand.

Some children will create shapes and forms with the glue and then cover them with salt or sand.

A few children will apply glue to the paper without adding any salt or sand.

Modifications

Begin with one color of salt or sand with a white poster board base.

Vary the color possibilities:

- ▲ two colors of salt or sand with a white base
- ▲ orange and yellow salt or sand with a brown base
- ▲ pastel colors of salt or sand with a white base

Focus on contrast by introducing white salt or sand with a black base.

Use other materials for the base, such as paper plates.

Comments & Questions to Extend Thinking

I see sand all over your paper. What happens when you hold it up?

I see a strip of red at the bottom and a strip of blue on top of it. What color will come next?

4.9 Tissue Paper Collage

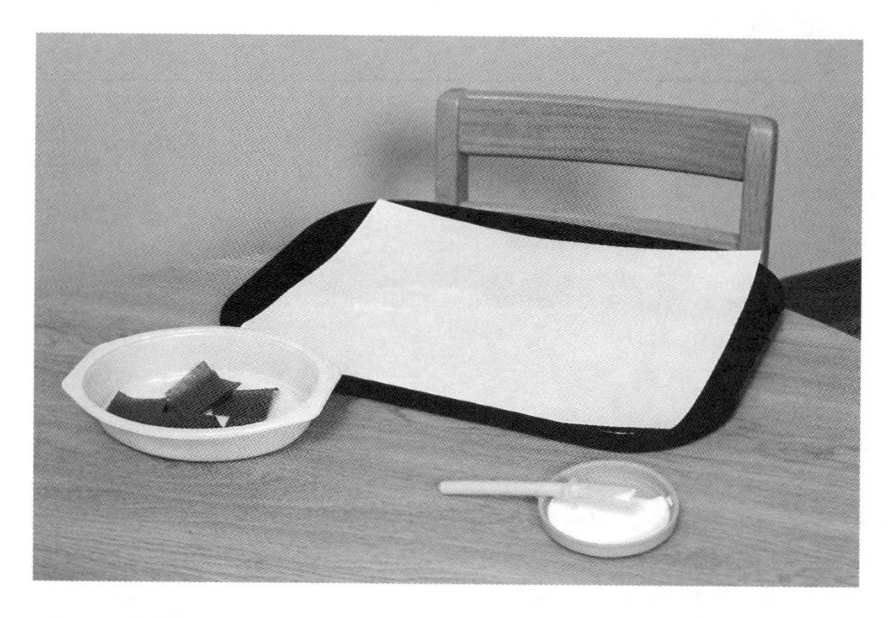

Description

The physical properties of tissue paper both fascinate and frustrate young children. For example, the colors "bleed" when wet with glue, and some colors are translucent. However, while the tissue paper is flexible and can easily be cut or torn, it often sticks to children's fingers. Tissue paper can be shaped to conform to three-dimensional surfaces, such as paper towel tubes and clear plastic tumblers. Since children are more familiar with working on a flat surface, this provides an added challenge. Tissue paper collage activities further children's thinking and problem-solving skills as they explore this new medium.

Helpful Hints

Ask parents to save tissue paper left over from wrapping gifts. Local gift shops may donate small amounts of leftover tissue paper.

Art Experiences

- ▲ experimenting with translucent paper
- ▲ exploring the effects of glue on tissue paper
- ▲ creating relationships between glue and tissue paper
- ▲ blending colors

Materials

- ▲ 4 trays (1 for each child)
- ▲ white construction paper, 9 by 12 inches
- ▲ 1½-inch squares of tissue paper for collage pieces
- ▲ 4 small trays, to hold the collage pieces
- ▲ 4 jar lids, each with a small amount of glue (thinned with water) and a glue spreader
- ▲ smocks

Child's Level

This activity, as well as the variations, is most appropriate for older preschool and kindergarten children. The tissue paper is more difficult to manipulate than construction paper. Children often get glue on their hands, and the tissue then sticks to their fingers. Tissue paper tears easily and often becomes bunched in a ball. This can be frustrating to inexperienced children. For this reason, teachers may wish to begin with a small amount of one color of tissue paper. This enables children to be more successful with the medium. They can focus on gluing rather than manipulating all the color choices. Later, they will be able to blend colors and create designs.

What to Look For

Some children will place tissue paper on top of glue in random designs.

Some children will create patterns with the tissue paper.

Some children will experiment with creating layers by placing tissue paper on top of glue, glue on top of tissue paper, and then more tissue paper on top of the glue.

Some children will explore the ability of glue to make the colors of the tissue "bleed."

Some children will experiment with blending two colors of tissue to create a new color.

Modifications

Start with one color of tissue and a white base.

Combine two colors of tissue to create a third color, such as red and yellow, blue and yellow, or red and blue, all with a white base.

Explore the color change created by a primary color of tissue paper applied to a different primary color of base:

- ▲ red tissue with a yellow or blue base
- ▲ yellow tissue with a red or blue base
- ▲ blue tissue with a red or yellow base

Experiment with various bases, such as paper plates, clear cellophane, cardboard tubes, or clear plastic tumblers.

Encourage children to tear tissue to create uneven edges.

Comments & Questions to Extend Thinking

What do you see when you overlap the blue and yellow tissue?

Is there any way to make purple?

Taizo's squares go around in a circle.

4.10 Cotton Ball Collage

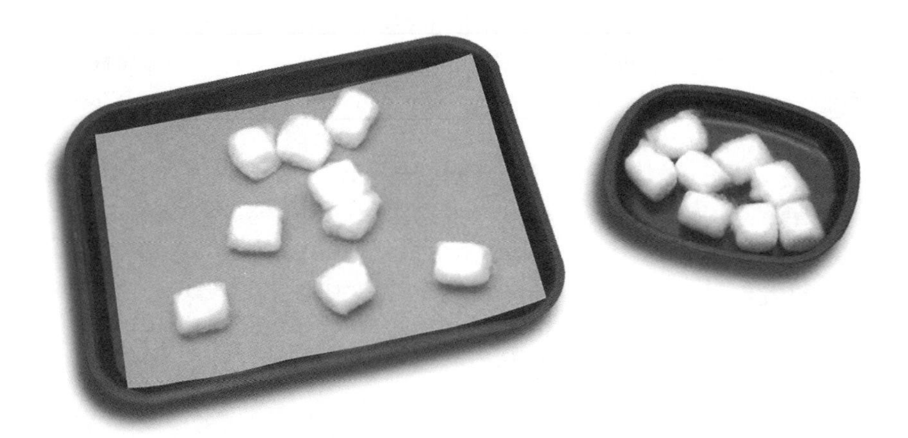

Description

Cotton balls, which are inexpensive and come in a variety of pastel shades, make an excellent material for collages. Young children can easily manipulate the lightweight cotton balls, and the soft texture is very appealing. Since cotton balls are not flat like paper, the result of this activity is a three-dimensional formation that is different from many of the collage activities that children explore.

Art Experiences

▲ creating three-dimensional forms
▲ exploring the soft texture of cotton balls
▲ arranging cotton balls within set boundaries
▲ exploring contrast
▲ creating patterns (see *Modifications*)

Helpful Hints

Cotton balls can be cut into halves or thirds to conserve the supply.

Materials

▲ 4 trays (1 for each child)
▲ colorful construction paper, 9 by 12 inches
▲ 8 to 10 white cotton balls for each child (replenished as needed)
▲ 4 small trays, to hold the cotton balls
▲ 4 jars, each with a small amount of glue and a glue spreader
▲ smocks (optional)

Child's Level

This collage activity is appropriate for both preschool and kindergarten children. Some of the variations are more complex and should be introduced after children have had experiences with cotton balls. For the initial experience, teachers can provide small numbers of cotton balls on a tray for each child. This encourages children to pick up individual cotton balls and glue them one at a time rather than grabbing a handful.

What to Look For

Some children will glue one cotton ball at a time onto the base.
Some children will create patterns with two or more colors of cotton balls (see *Modifications*).
Some children will arrange the cotton balls to create shapes, such as a large circle or square.
A few children will glue cotton balls on top of other cotton balls.
A few children will attempt to arrange cotton balls on the paper without using glue.

Modifications

Focus on contrast by providing white cotton balls to use with dark construction paper.
Explore a variety of color combinations, such as pastel cotton balls with a white base.
Encourage patterning by selecting two colors of cotton balls to use with a white base.
Vary the base materials by introducing paper plates or cardboard tubes.

Comments & Questions to Extend Thinking

How do cotton balls feel?
Does it take very much glue to hold a cotton ball?
These cotton balls make a face.
Andy made a border with cotton balls.

4.11 Sparkling Collages

Spangles & Sequins

Description

Sequins and spangles are available in many colors and shapes. Children enjoy gluing them onto clear lids from yogurt containers. The colors, which are striking, are visible from both sides of the clear lid. The tiny sequins and spangles provide an interesting challenge for children who are accustomed to larger collage pieces and base surfaces.

Art Experiences

- ▲ creating designs within small spaces
- ▲ experimenting with the amount of glue needed to secure sequins and spangles
- ▲ exploring materials glued to a clear background
- ▲ observing the change in glue as it dries on a clear surface
- ▲ planning on a base with a circular perimeter

Materials

- ▲ 4 trays (1 for each child)
- ▲ clear lids from yogurt containers, to use as the base
- ▲ sequins or spangles, in various colors and shapes
- ▲ 4 small dishes, to hold the sequins or spangles
- ▲ 4 jar lids, each with a small amount of glue and a glue spreader
- ▲ smocks (optional)

Helpful Hints

Inexpensive sequins and spangles can be found in odd lot stores.

Ask parents to save the clear lids from yogurt containers.

Portion cups can be used to hold a small selection of sequins or spangles.

Child's Level

Since sequins and spangles are very small, this activity is most appropriate for older preschool and kindergarten children. They are more likely to have the fine motor control needed to manipulate the tiny pieces and the small gluing surface.

What to Look For

Some children will carefully apply a small amount of glue to individual sequins or spangles and place them on the clear lids.

Some children will cover the lids with glue and then place the sequins or spangles on top.

A few children may have difficulty manipulating the small sequins or spangles.

Children will be fascinated with the clear appearance of the glue after it dries. This is readily apparent on the clear surface of the lids.

Modifications

Start with one color of sequin or spangle to glue to the lids.

Combine several colors of sequins or spangles to glue to the lids.

Explore unusual shapes of sequins or spangles to glue to the lids.

Comments & Questions to Extend Thinking

Let's see if a tiny dab of glue will hold this sequin.

How will you decide where to place the sequins?

4.12 Wood Collage

Description

Many materials made from wood are available to use for collages. Craft sticks are a common component of the early childhood curriculum; however, toothpicks, wooden spools, and wooden shapes are also available. Wooden objects are more closely related to natural materials, such as sticks, than many typical art materials. The wooden materials allow children to create three-dimensional collages. Children must consider not only form and design but also the weight of the wood as they secure together individual pieces. How much glue is needed? Which pieces can be attached to each other using glue? What is the drying time necessary for the amount of glue needed for the activity? These questions further children's thinking and pose interesting problems to solve.

Helpful Hints

Some carpet cleaning companies may use circular pieces of wood to place under furniture legs. Parents can save these for you.

Local contractors, lumberyards, and parents may donate leftover scraps of pine 2 x 4s.

Art Experiences

▲ creating three-dimensional structures
▲ exploring the physical properties of wood
▲ creating relationships between the glue and the wood
▲ exploring balance and symmetry
▲ creating representational sculptures

Materials

▲ scraps of poster board, to use as the base
▲ varieties of small wooden materials, such as craft sticks, toothpicks, and wooden shapes, sorted into separate containers
▲ 4 glue containers, with spreaders
▲ smocks (optional)

Child's Level

Three-dimensional collage activities are intriguing to both preschool and kindergarten children. They are most appropriate for older preschool and kindergarten children who have had many experiences using glue with a variety of collage materials. Wood collage activities may be frustrating to very young children. The pieces can be difficult to secure, and the thicker applications of glue needed to hold the wood take much longer to dry. Pieces that have not been sufficiently secured will fall apart.

What to Look For

Some children will glue small pieces of wood to the base to create a three-dimensional sculpture.

Some children will glue the pieces of wood together to create representational objects, such as cars and buildings.

Some children will glue pieces of wood together without regard for the base.

At first, some children will have difficulty determining the amount of glue needed to secure the heavier pieces of wood to the base.

A few children may ask for additional supplies to complete the wood collage, such as wheels, pasta, or buttons.

Modifications

Use a variety of materials for the base:

- ▲ 4- to 6-inch lengths of wood cut from 2 x 4s
- ▲ corrugated paper
- ▲ pieces of Styrofoam
- ▲ small gift boxes
- ▲ scraps of mat board

Allow children to paint their creations after they dry.

Combine the wood scraps with other collage materials, such as buttons, fabric, sandpaper, and pasta.

Comments & Questions to Extend Thinking

What can you do with all of these different wood pieces?

This wood shape is a triangle. Can you make a triangle with toothpicks?

4.13 Rough & Smooth Collage

Description

This activity can be included in the art curriculum to coordinate with a construction unit or to build on children's experiences sanding wood. Children use several grades of sandpaper for this collage. The texture of sandpaper is unusual and interesting to young children. The roughness of the sandpaper contrasts with the smooth surface of the base used in this collage activity. Most sandpaper selections are various shades of brown. This is different from other collage activities that often focus on color and color combinations.

Helpful Hints

Odd lot stores are sources of inexpensive sandpaper.

Sandpaper can be purchased in packages of assorted grades.

Art Experiences

- ▲ exploring texture
- ▲ experimenting with unusual collage materials
- ▲ creating with rigid materials
- ▲ creating monochromatic (single color) designs

Materials

- ▲ 4 trays (1 for each child)
- ▲ manila tagboard, 9 by 12 inches, to use as the base
- ▲ divided tray, with 1-inch squares of several grades of sandpaper to use as the collage pieces
- ▲ 4 jar lids, each with a small amount of glue and a glue spreader
- ▲ smocks (optional)

Child's Level

This is an appropriate collage activity for both preschool and kindergarten children. Sandpaper pieces are similar in size and weight to familiar construction paper collage pieces. Some children may initially avoid the monochromatic display if they are more accustomed to brightly colored collage materials. Teachers may wish to substitute colored construction paper for the manila tagboard in subsequent activities using sandpaper.

What to Look For

Some children will place a small amount of glue onto the base surface and put the sandpaper squares on top of the glue.

Some children will place a small amount of glue on each piece of sandpaper and arrange the pieces on the base surface.

Some children may arrange the sandpaper squares on the base surface without using the glue. They are usually surprised when they lift the collage and all of the squares fall off.

Some children will cover the base surface with glue and then place sandpaper squares on top of the glue.

Some children may create a design using the sandpaper squares.

Some children may create patterns with the varying textures of sandpaper.

Modifications

Combine the sandpaper squares with other base materials:

- mat board
- 4- to 6-inch lengths of wood cut from 2 x 4s
- large pieces of sandpaper
- construction paper

Cut the base paper into shapes, such as circles, triangles, or squares.

Cut the sandpaper collage pieces into shapes, such as triangles or rectangles.

Comments & Questions to Extend Thinking

Does all the sandpaper feel the same?

Is there a way to create a pattern with the sandpaper?

I see a row of coarse sandpaper on your paper.

4.14 Nature Collage

Description

Natural materials provide an inexpensive medium for collage activities with young children. The possibilities vary according to the resources available in a particular geographic area as well as the ingenuity of the teacher. Children can collect many of the natural materials on a nature walk. Teachers may introduce collage materials related to seasonal changes; for example, seed pods and seed carriers would be most appropriate for an autumn collage activity. Collages of natural materials may also correlate with other curriculum plans. For example, teachers might plan a shell collage to coordinate with a science display of shells. Similar collage materials can be displayed for extended periods of time in art areas, such as an autumn art area (activity 2.6) and a spring art area (activity 2.8). Teachers of younger children may want to introduce natural materials one at a time before combining several in one activity.

Helpful Hints

Gather dried materials, such as weeds or leaves, no earlier than a day or two before implementation of the activity. They often wither after a few days.

Art Experiences

- ▲ exploring and combining natural materials
- ▲ observing differences in materials
- ▲ comparing textures of natural materials

Materials

- ▲ 4 trays (1 for each child)
- ▲ white construction paper or tagboard, 9 by 12 inches, to use as the base, depending on the weight of the collage materials

- ▲ one of the following collections of natural materials:
  - ▲ seeds, seed pods, and seed carriers
  - ▲ pine needles, magnolia seed pods, and colored leaves
  - ▲ various types of flower petals
  - ▲ various types of dried weeds
  - ▲ tiny shells
  - ▲ acorns or other local nuts
- ▲ individual baskets or divided trays, to display the collage materials
- ▲ 4 jars, each with a small amount of glue and a glue spreader
- ▲ smocks (optional)

Child's Level

This activity is most appropriate for older preschool and kindergarten children. Some of the materials break easily or are more difficult to secure with glue, which may frustrate young preschool children.

What to Look For

Some children will apply the glue to the collage materials and then secure them to the base.

Some children will apply the glue to the base and then secure the collage materials to it.

Some children will arrange the collage materials in a random design.

Some children will plan the arrangement of the collage materials.

Some children will create representational figures with the collage materials.

Modifications

Use any of the following as a base for the collage materials: colored construction paper, poster board, mat board, or small gift boxes.

Cut the base paper or cardboard into shapes, such as circles, pennants, and rectangles.

Comments & Questions to Extend Thinking

This picture reminds me of our trip to the park.

Lela arranged her shells to look like flowers.

How can you make these heavy nuts stick to your paper?

4.15 Button Collage

Description

Children enjoy rummaging through collections of buttons of many sizes, colors, and designs. Teachers can capitalize on this interest by including a button collage in the art curriculum. This activity can be planned to coordinate with high interest in a book such as *Corduroy*, by Don Freeman (New York: Viking, 1968). In the story, Corduroy, a toy bear, searches for his missing button.

Helpful Hints

Do not plan this activity if you also plan a button collection for the math area. Children may use buttons from your collection as part of the gluing activity!

Ask parents for donations rather than purchasing buttons at retail stores. Garage sales may also be a good resource.

Art Experiences

- ▲ exploring spatial arrangement with buttons
- ▲ creating patterns
- ▲ observing similarities and differences
- ▲ creating representational forms

Materials

- ▲ 4 trays (1 for each child)
- ▲ small pieces of poster board, to use as the base
- ▲ 1 basket, with a selection of buttons to use as the collage pieces
- ▲ 4 glue containers, each with a small amount of glue and a glue spreader
- ▲ smocks (optional)

Child's Level

This activity is most appropriate for preschool and kindergarten children who have had some experience with lightweight collage materials, such as paper and ribbon. Buttons require more glue to adhere them to a surface. Children construct this relationship as they experiment with the materials and compare the results to previous experiences involving other materials.

What to Look For

Some children will glue one button at a time onto the base.
Some children will create patterns with two or more colors of buttons.
Some children will arrange the buttons into shapes, such as a large circle or square, on the base surface.
Some children will create representational figures, especially faces, with the buttons.
A few children will glue buttons on top of other buttons.
A few children will attempt to arrange the buttons on the paper without using glue.

Modifications

Encourage patterning by selecting two colors or sizes of buttons.
Introduce other base surfaces, such as paper plates or mat board.
Cut the base material into shapes, such as pennants and squares.

Comments & Questions to Extend Thinking

Which buttons would you like to use on your collage?
It took a lot of glue to hold that big button. How much glue do you need for this little one?

4.16 Sea Collage

Group Project

Helpful Hints

Children can help generate a list of necessary supplies. Parents can help assemble the materials.

Description

Group art projects allow children to work together toward a common goal while expressing their individual ideas. This activity coordinates with a sea project or curriculum design in the classroom. Children start by drawing or painting underwater colors, forms, and representations on a large mural. Then they add a variety of collage materials to create a three-dimensional sea representation. Plastic grass, shells, pipe cleaners bent into formations, and sponges cut into various shapes are some of the possibilities.

Art Experiences

- ▲ contributing to a group project
- ▲ creating with multi-media
- ▲ gluing with a variety of materials
- ▲ drawing
- ▲ painting with watercolors

Materials

▲ large sheet of blue mural paper
▲ crayons or markers
▲ watercolor paint
▲ variety of collage materials, such as plastic grass, shells, pipe cleaners, sponges, colored cellophane, and pastel doilies
▲ 4 glue jars, with spreaders
▲ smocks

Child's Level

This activity is most appropriate for kindergarten children. They are typically interested in cooperating with peers on a group project and can follow a multistep process.

What to Look For

Children will draw their ideas about sea representations, from abstract to more realistic.

Children will add paint to the mural to represent water and sea life.

Children will collaborate with one another about what to include in the mural.

Children will glue a variety of materials to the mural.

Children will discuss the process of creating forms for the mural, such as bending pipe cleaners or cutting sponges to achieve a desired effect.

Children will tell stories about their sea mural.

Modifications

This project emerges in large part from the ideas of the children. Variations are incorporated as children suggest them. The teacher can facilitate by asking leading questions and contributing observations.

Comments & Questions to Extend Thinking

What would you like to include in your sea scene?

What could we use to represent seaweed?

What colors of paint do we need?

It looks like that striped fish is swimming through the seaweed.

Paul wants to add a shark. Who has some ideas about how he could create a shark?

Painting & Printing

Ping completed an easel painting by using pastel shades of pink, green, and yellow. At first glance, the teacher thought Ping had covered the entire paper with the paint and had created a free-form design rather than a recognizable picture. Ping exclaimed that she had created a pattern. She had made strokes of pink-yellow-green, pink-yellow-green for several repetitions and in several places on the large sheet of paper. The pattern had not been apparent to the teacher at first.

▲ ▲ ▲

Annie initially made random marks with teddy bear cookie cutters dipped in paint. When she finished her painting, she stayed at the easel and began a second picture. This time she was more deliberate in her placement of the cookie cutter impressions. When Annie finished, she had created a heart shape composed of the teddy bear prints.

▲ ▲ ▲

Many adults have fond memories of early experiences with thick, brilliant paints, large brushes, and the huge expanse of paper at the easel. Perhaps they also remember the routines associated with the experience: the smock made from an old shirt, the ritual rinsing of each brush, and the special place to hang the painting to dry. Painting is a traditional component of many programs for young children, such as nursery schools, child care settings, kindergartens, day camps, and art classes. Current early childhood programs go beyond the traditional easel painting to include opportunities to paint and print with a variety of tools at both the easel and a special activity table.

Teachers' Questions

What are painting and printing activities?

Painting activities are art experiences in which children use a variety of brushes or brush-like tools and a stroking motion to apply paint to paper. Children dip the brush into the paint and often use the whole shoulder and arm to sweep the brush across the paper. At other times, children use smaller hand movements to apply the paint to the paper.

Fingerpainting activities are specific art experiences in which children use their hands to explore the paint. Children can experiment with the paint directly on special paper. Sometimes children explore finger paint inside the confines of a tray or on top of a table. They may later want to record the lines, squiggles, and designs made in the paint by placing paper on top of the paint.

Printing activities are art experiences in which children dip a variety of sponges or rigid tools, such as cookie cutters or spools, into paint and use a pressing motion to apply the paint to the paper. The process of printing differs from painting in several ways. For example, children can create several repetitions of the same print with a printing tool. There is a direct relationship between the shape of the printing tool and the resulting print. Children sometimes have less control over the results of printing than the results of painting.

Why is it important to include painting and printing activities in the art curriculum?

Painting activities allow children to explore the creative process through a fluid medium. The paint flows across the paper in response to the child's shoulder and arm movements. Children blend colors, create shades of color, and change the intensity of colors. When painting with watercolors, they may also experiment with translucent colors as they add more water to the paint.

Printing activities provide opportunities for children to explore repetitions of design and placement of prints on paper. The initial explorations of printing tools are usually random but become more purposeful with additional experiences. Children eventually consider the shape of the printing tool before determining the arrangement of the prints on the paper. Children also create relationships related to their actions and the resulting print. They may consider the amount of paint on the tool and the intensity of the color of the print; the shape of the tool and the print that it makes; and pattern and symmetry relationships.

What are some of the goals for painting and printing activities?

Painting and printing activities allow children to express themselves creatively; explore the process of creating a design; and experiment with shape, color, and form. Children are drawn to the medium of paint. Their goals usually include exploration of the vibrant colors they apply to large sheets of paper. While they sometimes express ideas and emotions, at other times they apply paint merely for the pleasure they gain from the experience. Teachers may plan with some of the following goals in mind:

- ▲ exploring pattern, symmetry, and design
- ▲ creating symbolic representations of thoughts, ideas, and feelings
- ▲ communicating information using paint as an art medium
- ▲ exploring the blending of colors to form a different color
- ▲ experimenting with shape and form
- ▲ exploring the physical properties of paint

What equipment is needed for painting and printing activities?

An easel is an important component of the art curriculum for painting and printing activities. The traditional easel is a standard part of many early childhood classrooms. If budget constraints prohibit the purchase of a traditional easel, other types of easels can be created from inexpensive materials. Teachers can even make a temporary easel with a cardboard box.

In addition to the easel, a separate table or other flat surface is needed for explorations of painting and printing on a horizontal surface. Children do not need to consider the effects of gravity when they explore paints on the horizontal plane of a table. Teachers often designate one table, separate from the art area, as a special activity table. Many children eagerly anticipate the daily display of the new special activity.

What types of paint are needed for painting and printing activities?

Tempera paints and watercolor paints are needed for painting activities. Many teachers are familiar with the dry and liquid forms of tempera paint. Although the liquid form is more expensive, it is highly recommended for use with young children.

Watercolor paints are typically available in sets of eight or more colors in one container. Individual refill pans, packaged with one color per box, are also readily available. Teachers should invest in several boxes of refills in the primary colors (red, yellow, and blue), plus black and white, so that they can regulate the number of colors that they present to children. Young children may be overwhelmed by sets of eight or more colors. While they often enjoy the process of adding water to the watercolor cakes, it is difficult for them to remember to rinse the brush each time. Very often they simply mix all the colors in the set, thus producing muddy-colored cakes of paint. The refill pans allow teachers to determine how many and which colors of watercolor paint to display for each activity. When the display includes only a few colors, such as red, yellow, and blue, children are less likely to mix the colors in the pans.

Finger paint is available in both dry and liquid forms. The dry form can be mixed with water or sprinkled on top of liquid starch to form a fingerpainting solution. The liquid form is actually a thick substance that is used directly on paper. The same substance can also be used inside a tray or on top of a table. Children can create a mono-print by placing paper on top of the finger paint.

Tempera paint is used for printing activities. The implements used for printing, such as potato mashers and cookie cutters, are fairly large and need a thick paint to adhere to them.

What types of paper are most appropriate for painting and printing activities?

The most suitable paper for painting and printing activities planned for the easel is newsprint or manila paper that measures 18 by 24 inches. Painting and printing activities at the easel encourage children to use large shoulder and arm movements. The large paper provides an appropriate amount of space for both sweeping motions with a paintbrush and for extensive explorations with printing tools that make large impressions on paper. The size of the paper may affect how children plan the painting and printing activities. The large blank space may encourage children to continue to paint or print until most of the space is filled. Relatively few children have access to easel painting in the home environment.

The most suitable paper for special painting and printing activities is construction paper (9 by 12 inches); inexpensive white paper (8½ by 11 inches); and recycled computer paper. Teachers may also choose other painting surfaces, such as paper plates, shelf paper, corrugated paper, cardboard, brown craft paper, and other donated paper. Watercolor painting activities are best suited to absorbent paper, such as white or pastel construction paper. Other possibilities include white and pastel duplicating paper, paper plates, coffee filters, and doilies. The translucent quality of the paint is compromised when children apply watercolor paints to other colors of paper.

When should teachers cut paper into different shapes for painting and printing activities?

Teachers may occasionally cut easel paper or special activity paper into different shapes, such as circles, triangles, and irregular forms. Children are intrigued by a change in the shape of the paper. Sometimes teachers may create negative space by cutting holes in the paper, which challenges children to think about the available space in new ways. However, teachers must be careful not to cut the paper into shapes merely to fit a theme. Cutting the paper into representational shapes, such as turtles or trees, is similar to providing models for children to copy or predrawn pictures for children to paint. These shapes may limit creativity, as well as inadvertently communicate a lack of acceptance of the children's ability to create something worthwhile. Children may come to believe that teachers expect paintings to look like something specific.

What types of tools are needed for painting activities?

The basic brush used for easel painting activities has stiff, flat bristles about ¾-inch wide. The stiff bristles of easel brushes are designed to successfully apply thick tempera paint. Sometimes very young children have difficulty managing the long handles of easel brushes. If this is a problem, teachers can saw off the handles of existing brushes to make them a more manageable length (about 5 inches). Teachers should avoid brushes wider than ¾-inch if the paint containers have a hole in the lid. The bristles of a wider brush will not fit through the opening, and the brush will eventually be damaged as the bristles are forced through the hole.

The most appropriate brush for use with watercolor paints is a high-quality brush with soft bristles and a fine point. The paint must be moistened with a small amount of water before it can be used. Inexpensive brushes will not hold enough water to sufficiently wet the dry cake of paint. Brushes with stiff bristles cannot be formed into a point, thus limiting the designs children can create.

What types of tools are needed for printing activities?

The most common printing tools are sponges, cookie cutters, and recycled materials, such as spools and jar lids. Other unique materials, including potato mashers, back scrubbers, and disposable toothbrushes, are also used in printing activities. Many of these materials can be found in discount stores or may be donated by parents or businesses.

How often should painting and printing activities be planned for the classroom?

Painting at the easel is an activity that should be available for children almost every day of the year. Children require extensive periods of time to fully explore the materials and express themselves through this medium. Occasionally, teachers should vary the types of brushes and paint at the easel to further artistic development, stimulate new interest, and provide opportunities to experiment with a variety of painting tools on a vertical surface. For example, watercolor paints and brushes may be placed at the easel for a week at a time. The teacher might also include small pots of tempera paint, with cotton swabs instead of brushes.

Painting should be planned as a special activity on a regular basis—as often as once a week. Painting is one of the special activities, such as creating collages, printing, drawing, modeling with clay or dough, and stringing, that teachers plan frequently. Painting on a flat surface is a valuable experience for young children. They may be able to exert more control over their painting efforts on a table than at the easel. Teachers typically use a wider variety of painting tools and smaller sizes of paper for special activities than for painting at the easel. The special painting activities may repeat many times throughout the year, with different colors of paint and paper, as well as a variety of painting implements. For example, the teacher may combine cotton swabs and watercolor paints as a special activity numerous times during the year, while watercolors may be planned for the easel only once or twice each year.

Teachers may plan printing activities for the easel on a regular basis—perhaps once a month. The easel is primarily a venue for painting activities; however, printing is an interesting variation for children to explore on the vertical plane. Children must determine the best ways to grip printing tools in order to press them onto the paper. Very often this involves a great deal of experimentation. They can also compare the results of using a specific printing tool at the easel as opposed to on a flat surface.

Printing activities, like painting activities, should be planned as a special activity on a regular basis. Teachers may decide to plan either a painting or a printing activity each week. Occasionally, teachers may plan painting and printing in the same week.

Why is sequencing an important consideration when planning painting and printing activities?

Careful sequencing helps prevent management issues that might otherwise arise, provides opportunities for children to build on previous knowledge of the materials, and helps children elaborate on ideas they have tried in past experiences. Early childhood professionals understand the value of implementing the curriculum in an organized and sequential manner. Teachers begin with simple versions of art activities, make small changes in the activities, and repeat the experiences on a regular basis. Suggestions for how to sequence painting and printing activities can be found with the activities in this chapter.

How do teachers select the combinations of colors for painting and printing activities?

Teachers often select colors to coordinate with seasonal changes in the environment, to stimulate interest in the activity, to encourage patterning, to enhance artistic appreciation, and to provide opportunities for children to blend colors. The aesthetic presentation of painting and printing activities significantly contributes to the process as well as the outcome of the artistic explorations. The teacher might select red, yellow, and blue paint for the easel as an initial experience. This assures that children are not overwhelmed by too many choices. They can experiment with combinations of the primary colors and observe the results. Teachers might plan an autumn printing activity that uses two leaf-shaped cookie cutters with red and yellow paint. While this may encourage children to think about the changing colors of the leaves in the environment, they are free to arrange the prints in any form they choose. Similarly, pastel colors are sometimes chosen for spring activities. At times teachers may provide a selection of shades of one color, such as blue. This often generates conversation about how to create light blue and dark blue.

How do painting and printing activities encourage creativity?

Painting and printing activities encourage children to be divergent thinkers, a common attribute of creativity. Since painting and printing activities are open-ended, children may use them in a variety of ways. For example, the teacher might set up a combination painting-printing activity at the easel. The materials could include a leaf cookie cutter, displayed in a tray with a small amount of gold paint, and a thin watercolor brush, in a cup of red paint. While some children might use the cookie cutter to create random prints, others might use the watercolor brush to produce many thin strokes. Some children might create many leaf prints and use the red paint to fill in the empty spaces inside the leaf outlines. Still other children might make several red dots and then use the cookie cutter to make a leaf print around the dots. The same materials thus lead to many individual outcomes.

What is the role of the teacher?

Teachers plan activities, organize the materials, set up the activities in an aesthetically pleasing manner, replenish supplies, and ask questions or make comments sparingly. They also observe the needs and interests of children in order to plan future painting and printing activities. Teachers are most involved before children explore the activities. Effective planning by the teacher and careful organization of the materials helps assure that children use them independently. This allows the teacher to interact with children in many areas of the classroom, instead of remaining only in the art area. Some painting and printing activities that are implemented as special activities may require more teacher interaction. For example, fingerpainting is messy and necessitates one adult to supervise the area most of the time. Other activities, such as printing with circular cookie cutters or tools, require very little supervision. The teacher can go to the area occasionally to converse with children, replenish supplies, or help children solve problems they encounter. Teachers can ask questions related to the process of painting, such as "What did you do to make all the small lines? I only see large brushes." They can comment on symmetry and pattern, colors selected, and use of the space.

What pitfalls should teachers avoid when commenting on children's paintings and prints?

Teachers should avoid making judgmental comments, even when they are positive. Evaluative comments about painting and printing activities are often stereotypic and overused. Comments such as "Good job" and "Beautiful painting" do not apply to all creative endeavors by children. Even young children are capable of evaluating their own efforts. Children may not be satisfied with a particular painting and choose to throw it away. Evaluative comments may lead some children to become dependent on the teacher's judgment of what is pretty or acceptable. This often leads to more stereotypic painting by children who want to please the teacher.

Teachers should avoid asking too many questions about the paintings and prints children create. Children are intrinsically motivated to use painting and printing materials. They do not necessarily produce an end product that can be described. When teachers ask questions such as, "What did you paint?" children may feel compelled to make up an answer. Some children may avoid painting and printing activities simply to avoid the teacher's questions.

Sometimes teachers should not talk at all. Children may want to explore the painting and printing supplies without interruption. Teachers may inadvertently interrupt the child's thinking and problem-solving processes.

What are the best ways to respond to children's paintings and prints?

Teachers should make comments and ask questions that focus on the process of painting and printing or emphasize artistic elements. Even these types of comments and questions should be used sparingly. As teachers observe children, they can occasionally comment about color, pattern, symmetry, and other artistic elements. Sometimes teachers can ask questions that focus on relationships, such as the movement of the child's arm and the resulting line of color, or the creation of a different color as the child blends the paint together. Examples of these types of questions and comments might include the following:

> *What would you do to make a thinner line of paint?*
> *How did you make the lighter prints with the sponge?*
> *I notice orange paint in your picture, but I don't see any orange paint at the easel.*
> *How can you make a broader line with the thin brush?*

How can teachers coordinate literacy experiences with painting and printing activities?

Teachers can plan specific painting and printing activities to encourage children to focus on written communication. Many teachers already record children's dictations and encourage children to write in all areas of the classroom. Some painting and printing activities are excellent vehicles for reading and writing experiences. For example, if children demonstrate high interest in the book *It Looked Like Spilt Milk*, by Charles G. Shaw (New York: Harper, 1947), the teacher can plan a painting activity using blue paper and white paint like the illustrations in the book. Later, children might dictate descriptions of the paintings using the pattern from the book. The teacher can record the children's responses to complete the sentence, "Sometimes it looked like ________." Older children may be able to write the responses themselves.

How can teachers incorporate math concepts into painting and printing activities?

Teachers can plan specific painting and printing activities that encourage children to consider the math concepts of one-to-one correspondence, pattern, and symmetry. Easel paper marked into 2-inch squares encourages children to think about painting one mark, design, or picture inside each square. Likewise, children often make one impression with a printing tool inside each square of the paper. Careful planning may stimulate children to consider pattern as they engage in painting and printing experiences. For example, in an activity that includes three colors of paint, many children alternate one stripe or dot of each color for several repetitions, thus creating a pattern. A printing activity using two sizes of sponge also encourages children to consider patterning. Sometimes the patterns are accidentally created, but later the child continues the pattern or intentionally reproduces it. Fold-over paper activities highlight symmetry in painting and printing activities. Children observe the outcome of painting on one side of the paper and creating a mirror image of the painting on the other side by folding the paper.

How can teachers assess developmental progress in painting and printing?

Teachers can save samples of painting and printing, take photographs, and keep anecdotal records to document children's progress. Young children are often more interested in the process of painting or printing than in the final outcome. They may repeat the same experience numerous times. Teachers can ask children if they want to display their paintings or prints at school. Sometimes children abandon art they have created, and teachers may collect these to document progress.

Painting & Printing Activities

5.1 Painting with Brushes

Easel

Description

Painting with tempera paint at the easel is typically associated with the art curriculum in early childhood classrooms. However, the suggested variations in the colors of paint and the types of brushes in this activity assure continued interest in painting at the easel. These variations also help children create relationships between the type of brush and the stroke it makes, the blending of colors, and the use of color to express mood.

Art Experiences

- ▲ exploring a fluid medium
- ▲ blending colors
- ▲ creating line, form, shape, and design
- ▲ exploring the effects of gravity
- ▲ comparing painting on a vertical surface to painting on a horizontal surface

Materials

- ▲ newsprint paper, 18 by 24 inches
- ▲ 3 paint containers for each easel station
- ▲ 3 easel brushes for each easel station
- ▲ red, yellow, and blue paint for each easel station
- ▲ smocks

Child's Level

This activity is appropriate as a beginning of the year painting experience for preschool and kindergarten children. The selection of colors is limited to allow children to explore the medium in a simple form; however, more-experienced children can blend the primary colors to create additional colors. Teachers of very young children may want to begin with only one primary color of paint. This allows children to focus on the painting process. Teachers can assist children with routines, such as hanging up the paper, and redirect them to wear smocks and paint only on the paper. Within a week, teachers can increase the selection to two colors and eventually all three primary colors.

What to Look For

Some children will create designs that cover the entire paper.
Some children will combine colors to create new colors.
Some children will make only one or two strokes of color.
Some children will cover the entire paper and mix all three colors.
A few children will paint with a brush in each hand.
A few children will mix the colors in the paint jars by switching the brushes in the paint containers.

Modifications

Vary the color combinations:

- red, yellow, orange, and brown (when children show interest in autumn colors, fire, or a pizza unit)
- pastel colors (when children notice spring colors in the environment)
- various forms of blue, such as turquoise, light blue, and blue-violet
- paints that contain red, such as pink, red-orange, and maroon

Use other sizes and types of brushes:

- watercolor brushes
- "chubby" brushes
- regular household paintbrushes, 1 to 2 inches wide
- pastry and barbecue brushes
- several different brushes, 1 of each type

Vary the type, size, and shape of the paper:

- white or colored construction paper, 12 by 18 inches
- paper cut in large shapes, such as circles, squares, or pennants
- paper with a hole cut in the middle (geometric or irregular shapes)

Helpful Hints

The paint in the containers should be lower than the top of the bristles on the brush. This not only conserves paint, but also reduces dripping.

Comments & Questions to Extend Thinking

I see straight marks and curved lines on your paper.
What happened when you put blue paint on top of yellow?

5.2 Painting with Brushes
Special Activity

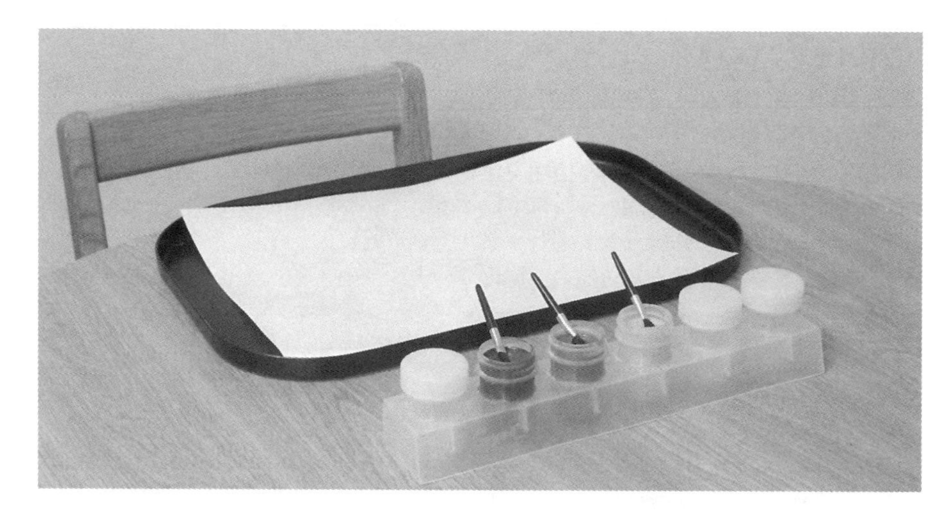

Description
This activity and its variations focus on painting on a horizontal surface with tempera paint and a variety of brushes. Children explore many of the same artistic elements as they do at the easel, but they do not have to consider the effects of gravity. Since special activities use smaller-sized paper than easel activities, teachers rarely incorporate large easel brushes for these experiences.

Helpful Hints
Make your own paint containers. Clear film canisters can be secured to a piece of wood by drilling a hole through the bottom and placing a screw through the hole into the wood.

Art Experiences
- ▲ exploring a fluid medium
- ▲ blending colors
- ▲ creating line, form, shape, and design
- ▲ comparing painting on vertical and horizontal surfaces

Materials
- ▲ 4 trays, to hold the paper
- ▲ white construction or drawing paper, 9 by 12 inches
- ▲ red, yellow, and blue paint
- ▲ 4 sets of small paint containers (fill 3 jars per set)
- ▲ 4 sets of makeup brushes (3 per child)
- ▲ smocks

Child's Level

This special activity is appropriate for both preschool and kindergarten children. The selection of primary colors allows younger children to experiment with the paints and small brushes, while older or more-experienced children can build on their previous experiences with paint and brushes.

What to Look For

Some children will use each of the paints to create designs and figures.
Some children will blend the primary colors to create new colors.
Some children will mix the colors in the small cups.
Some children will use only one or two of the colors.
Some children may create patterns of color.

Modifications

Vary the color combinations:

- various shades of blue, such as turquoise, light blue, blue-violet, and fluorescent blue
- paints that contain red, such as pink, red-orange, and maroon
- red, gold, and black (high contrast)
- green, orange, and purple (secondary colors)
- purple and red (two colors encourages patterning)
- fluorescent red, blue, and yellow
- red, yellow, blue, green, orange, and purple (primary and secondary colors)
- red, yellow, and blue, used with black or white paper

Use other painting tools:

- cotton swabs
- brushes used to butter corn on the cob

Comments & Questions to Extend Thinking

How did you get purple paint on your paper? I don't see any purple paint in your jar.
Some of your lines are thin, and some are thick. Which brush makes the thin lines?
I see a blue, a red, and a yellow person. They look like they're holding hands. Are they friends?

5.3 Double-Brushes

Easel or Special Activity

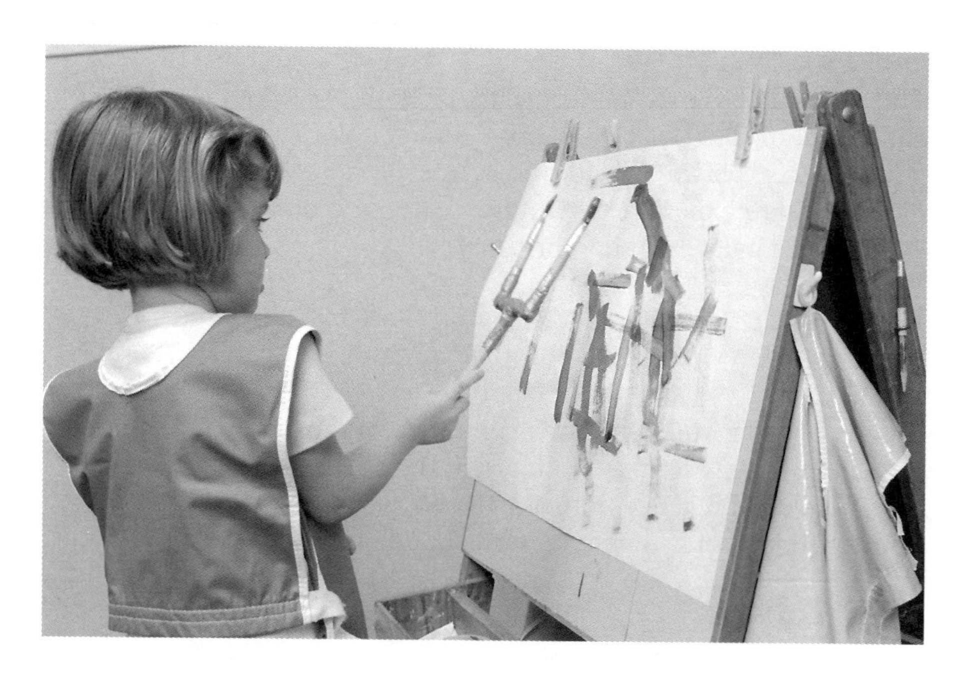

Helpful Hints

Packages containing several brushes in a variety of sizes can be found in many craft stores.

Description

Children are often surprised by the reaction of double-brushes to a single arm movement. They are accustomed to the paintbrush responding as an extension of their arm, thus producing a single stroke of paint each time they move their arm. However, double-brushes produce more than one mark with each arm movement. Children must consider this new information in order to produce the desired effect with the paint. Double-brushes are available through several art supply catalogs, or teachers can make their own. To make double-brushes, select inexpensive brushes with plastic handles. Drill two holes (the diameter of the brush handle) into a block of wood. Use a quick-bonding glue to secure the handle of the brush in each hole.

Art Experiences

- ▲ experimenting with an unusual type of painting tool
- ▲ comparing double-brushes to other brushes
- ▲ creating relationships between arm movements and the placement of the paint on the paper
- ▲ producing duplicate designs with a single motion
- ▲ solving the problem of how to load paint onto the brushes

Materials

Easel

- ▲ newsprint paper, 18 by 24 inches
- ▲ 2 primary colors of paint for each easel station
- ▲ 2 paint containers
- ▲ smocks

Special Activity Table

- ▲ white construction or drawing paper, 9 by 12 inches
- ▲ 4 trays, to hold the paper
- ▲ 2 primary colors of paint per child
- ▲ 2 paint containers per child
- ▲ smocks

Child's Level

This unique activity is most appropriate for older preschool and kindergarten children who have had numerous experiences with single brushes.

What to Look For

Children will solve the problem of how to get paint onto each brush and experiment with creating strokes and designs.

Some children may load paint onto only one brush, hold the handle of a single brush, and paint as usual.

Some children will notice that a single arm movement produces more than one line of paint.

Modifications

Vary the size of the brushes made into the double-brush.

Use two different diameters of brush in the same handle.

Vary the colors of paint:

- ▲ red and yellow, blue and yellow, or red and blue
- ▲ black and gold (for contrast)
- ▲ green and purple (secondary colors)
- ▲ black and white

Plan double-brushes for the special activity table during the same week that double-brushes are planned for the easel.

Make a different style of double-brush by banding two brushes together with a large rubber band. Combine this type of brush with only one color of paint.

Comments & Questions to Extend Thinking

How do you think these brushes work?

How did you get a double-circle on your paper?

I see a blue line next to every red line on your paper.

5.4 Silly Brushes

Easel or Special Activity

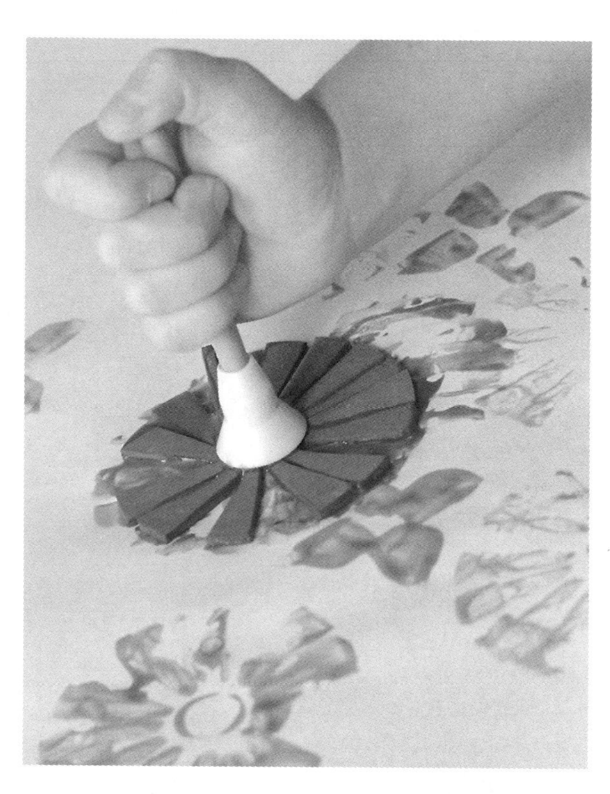

Description

The brushes in this activity are not brushes in the traditional sense. They are made with a rubber band-like material and are often available through discount school supply catalogs. Children use the same motions to apply paint with these tools as they do with brushes, but the results are very different. The implements hold a different amount of paint than brushes and create a different type of mark.

Art Experiences

- ▲ experimenting with paint and unusual implements
- ▲ creating relationships between these implements and traditional brushes
- ▲ exploring line, form, and design
- ▲ comparing the design of the implement to the design made with paint

Materials

Easel

- ▲ newsprint paper, 18 by 24 inches
- ▲ 2 different brushes, for each easel station
- ▲ small tray, to hold the paint, for each easel station
- ▲ 1 color of paint
- ▲ smocks

Special Activity Table

- ▲ white construction or drawing paper, 9 by 12 inches
- ▲ 4 trays, to hold the paper
- ▲ 2 different brushes per child
- ▲ 4 small trays (1 per child), to hold the paint
- ▲ 1 color of paint
- ▲ smocks

Child's Level

Painting with silly brushes is appropriate for both preschool and kindergarten children. Younger children may use the unusual brushes in the same way as regular brushes, while older children may use them in more unique ways.

What to Look For

Children will compare the silly brushes to regular brushes.

Some children will use a stroking motion to apply the paint to the paper, while others will use a dabbing motion.

Some children may notice the different designs the silly brushes make.

Children may observe the lighter prints made with repeated strokes of the silly brushes.

Modifications

Vary the colors of paint:

- red and yellow, blue and yellow, or red and blue (for color mixing)
- black and gold (for contrast)
- green and purple (secondary colors)
- black and white

Coordinate the colors of construction paper used in special activities with the colors of paint:

- primary colors with black paper
- red, yellow, and orange with brown paper
- green with yellow paper
- black with white paper
- white with dark blue or black paper

Comments & Questions to Extend Thinking

What kind of marks can you make with these silly brushes?

How did you make that flower design?

You made lots of **X**s on your paper. They all look alike. How did you do that?

Helpful Hints

Do not use paint cups or jars to hold the paint in this activity. Children are able to load too much paint onto the brushes, thus altering the desired effects of painting with silly brushes.

5.5 Nature's Brushes

Easel or Special Activity

Description

Natural materials used as painting tools, such as evergreen branches or weeds, provide opportunities for the development of flexible thinking as children explore items not typically associated with art. Most of the materials suggested in the variations of this activity respond similarly to paintbrushes as children apply paint. This allows children to quickly comprehend how to create the desired results.

Helpful Hints

Disposable microwave trays can be used to hold the paint.

Be sure to use fresh materials each day. Natural materials quickly wear out.

Art Experiences

- ▲ creating large, sweeping arm and shoulder movements
- ▲ exploring the pattern and symmetry in natural materials
- ▲ generating alternative methods for moving natural brushes
- ▲ expanding flexible thinking

Materials

Easel

- ▲ newsprint paper, 18 by 24 inches
- ▲ small tray, to hold the paint, for each easel station
- ▲ evergreen branch, about 6 inches long, for each easel station
- ▲ 1 color of paint
- ▲ smocks

Special Activity Table

- ▲ white construction or drawing paper, 9 by 12 inches
- ▲ 4 trays, to hold the paper
- ▲ 4 small trays (1 per child), to hold the paint
- ▲ 4 evergreen branches (1 per child), about 6 inches long
- ▲ 1 color of paint
- ▲ smocks

Child's Level

This activity is most appropriate for older preschool and kindergarten children. The atypical painting tool may confuse very young children.

What to Look For

Some children will use a large, sweeping motion to apply the paint to the paper.

Some children will apply the paint with a dabbing motion.

Some children may compare the natural brushes to regular brushes.

Some children may notice the different designs the natural brushes make.

Children may observe the lighter prints made with repeated strokes of the natural brushes.

Modifications

Substitute other natural materials for the evergreen branch, such as weeds, small branches, cattails, or feathers.

Combine two natural materials in one activity.

Comments & Questions to Extend Thinking

I wonder what kind of marks this pine branch will make.

What does the spruce branch feel like when you paint with it?

Is there a way to make a single line with the branch?

5.6 Feather Dusters

Easel

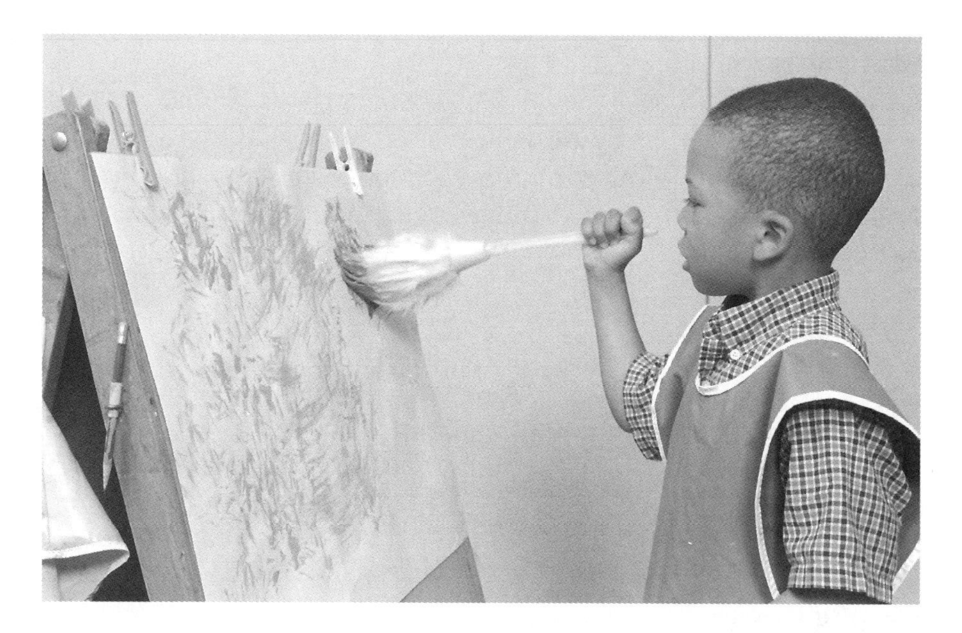

Description

Painting with feather dusters is best suited to the large pieces of paper typically used at the easel. Children may want to explore large sweeping motions with the feather duster, and this is not possible with smaller pieces of paper. The feather dusters create unusual and aesthetically pleasing marks when used with paint.

Helpful Hints

Feather dusters will dry to their original shape after a gentle washing with a mild soap.

Art Experiences

- ▲ experimenting with the amount of paint needed to create a feather design
- ▲ exploring large arm and shoulder movements
- ▲ comparing feather dusters to other painting tools
- ▲ observing the specific designs made with feathers
- ▲ creating different intensities of color with feather dusters (depending on how much paint is on the feather duster and how recently it was applied)

Materials

- ▲ newsprint, 18 by 24 inches
- ▲ 1 feather duster for each easel station
- ▲ 1 small tray for each easel station, to hold the paint
- ▲ 1 color of paint
- ▲ smocks

Child's Level

Painting with feather dusters is most appropriate for older preschool and kindergarten children. Very young children may experience difficulty manipulating the feather duster and applying just enough paint to create the design of the feathers. They often want to reapply paint after each stroke.

What to Look For

Some children will cover the entire paper with paint.
Some children will create designs with the feather duster.
Some children will create varying intensities of color—from light to dark.
A few children may reapply paint after each stroke of the feather duster.

Modifications

Plan painting with feathers as a special activity at the same time that feather dusters are at the easel. This gives children opportunities to make comparisons between the related activities.
Vary the color of paint in the activity.

Comments & Questions to Extend Thinking

What kind of marks does the feather duster make?
You covered your whole paper with paint, but I can still see the marks of the feathers.

5.7 Painting on a Revolving Surface

Special Activity

Description

In this activity, children paint on paper taped to a spinning lazy Susan. This poses many challenges! Many children require a great deal of experimentation before they are successful. Children can explore making concentric circles of color by holding the paint-brush over the revolving paper. Some children discover how to create specific designs by moving their paintbrush in a particular way as the surface rotates.

Helpful Hints

Ask a volunteer to assist you in this activity. Children may need assistance to keep the tray revolving.

Art Experiences

- ▲ applying paint to paper without moving the arm
- ▲ creating circles
- ▲ observing the effects of painting on a moving surface
- ▲ creating relationships between the placement of the paintbrush and the location of the resulting line

Materials

- ▲ 2 lazy Susans
- ▲ paper cut to fit the top of the tray
- ▲ 2 watercolor or other fine-point brushes (1 per child)
- ▲ 2 small paint cups, with the same color of paint
- ▲ smocks

Child's Level

This complex activity is most appropriate for older preschool and kindergarten children who can more easily manipulate the lazy Susan as they paint.

What to Look For

Many children will initially move the brush in a back and forth motion as the tray spins in a circular motion.

Some children will hold the brush steady as the paper spins on the tray.

Children will become aware of the circles of paint they are able to produce.

Some children will create patterns of alternating colors of paint when two or more colors are available.

Children will experiment with varying the speed of the rotating tray.

Some children will initially move the brush along with the rotating surface, and thus not make any marks.

Modifications

Vary the colors of paint in the activity.

Substitute cotton swabs for the watercolor brush.

Use two colors of paint and two brushes to encourage patterning and color mixing.

Use paper plates taped to the revolving tray as the painting surface.

Comments & Questions to Extend Thinking

Can you paint without moving the brush?

How can you make a little circle?

I see concentric circles on your paper. Look. They're getting bigger.

5.8 Brayers

Easel or Special Activity

Description

In this activity, children roll paint with a brayer. These tools, used for linoleum printing, have a hard rubber cylinder mounted on a handle. Although the cylinder does not have a texture, the rolling motion creates interesting designs on paper. Brayers are available in several sizes.

Helpful Hints

Brayers are sold in many craft stores.

Art Experiences

▲ applying paint with a different movement of the arm
▲ observing the results of a continuous flow of paint
▲ comparing the results of painting with brayers to painting with sponge rollers, traditional brushes, and other implements
▲ encouraging flexible thinking

Materials

Easel

▲ newsprint paper, 18 by 24 inches
▲ small tray, to hold the paint, for each easel station
▲ brayer, 4 inches wide, for each easel station
▲ smocks

Special Activity Table

▲ white construction or drawing paper, 9 by 12 inches
▲ 4 trays, to hold the paper
▲ 4 small trays (1 per child), to hold the paint
▲ 4 brayers (4 inches wide)
▲ smocks

Child's Level

This painting activity is appropriate for both preschool and kindergarten children. Although the painting tool is unusual, most children can create the movement needed to apply the paint. Loading the brayer with paint is also easy for most children.

What to Look For

Children will roll paint across the entire paper.

Some children will experiment with up-and-down and side-to-side motions with the brayer.

A few children will notice a mark made as the handle removes some of the paint. The mark is similar to creating lines in finger paint. Children may continue to intentionally explore these phenomena.

Modifications

Repeat this activity several times using a single 4-inch-wide brayer per child, changing only the color of paint.

Plan this activity several times using a single 2-inch-wide brayer per child, changing only the color of paint.

Combine two brayers, each 4 inches wide, and vary the combinations of colors:

- red and yellow, blue and yellow, or red and blue (to produce new colors)
- black and white (to produce shades of gray)
- black and gold (for contrast)
- purple and yellow

Combine two different sizes of brayers, and vary the combinations of colors.

Combine three brayers.

Combine brayers and sponge rollers. This encourages children to make comparisons between the two painting implements.

Combine brayers and regular brushes. This also encourages children to make comparisons.

Comments & Questions to Extend Thinking

What kind of mark does this brayer make?

I see marks going in two directions on your paper, up and down and sideways.

5.9 Sponge Rollers
Easel or Special Activity

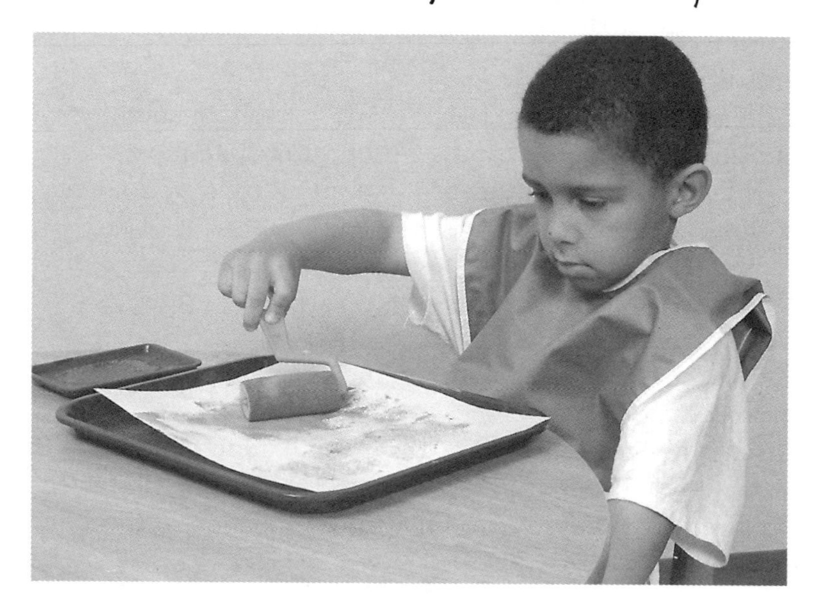

Description
The sponge paint rollers used in this activity are similar to the brayers in the previous activity; however, they have a soft, spongy cylinder attached to a handle instead of a hard cylinder. The sponge surface holds more paint and creates a different texture than the brayer. Children use the same arm movements to apply paint with both the sponge roller and brayer.

Helpful Hints
Replacement sponges are available for these painting tools.

Art Experiences
- ▲ applying paint with a different movement of the arm
- ▲ observing the results of a continuous flow of paint
- ▲ comparing the results of painting with sponge rollers to painting with brayers, traditional brushes, and other implements
- ▲ encouraging flexible thinking

Materials
Easel
- ▲ newsprint paper, 18 by 24 inches
- ▲ small tray, to hold the paint, for each easel station
- ▲ sponge roller, 4 inches wide, for each easel station
- ▲ 1 color of paint
- ▲ smocks

Special Activity Table
- ▲ white construction or drawing paper, 9 by 12 inches
- ▲ 4 trays, to hold the paper

- ▲ 4 small trays, to hold the paint (one per child)
- ▲ 4 sponge rollers (4 inches wide)
- ▲ 1 color of paint
- ▲ smocks

Child's Level

This painting activity is appropriate for both preschool and kindergarten children. Although the painting tool is unusual, most children can create the movement needed to apply the paint. Loading the sponge roller with paint is also easy for most children.

What to Look For

Children will roll paint across the entire paper.

Some children will notice the texture of the paint impression made by the tiny holes in the sponge.

Some children will use the sponge roller to make stripes of color.

Some children will compare the marks made by the roller to previous experiences with brayers.

Modifications

Repeat this activity several times using a single 4-inch-wide sponge roller per child, changing only the color of paint.

Plan this activity using a single 2-inch-wide sponge roller per child, changing only the color of paint.

Combine two sponge rollers, each 4 inches wide, and vary the combinations of colors:

- ▲ red and yellow, blue and yellow, or red and blue (for color mixing)
- ▲ black and white (to create shades of gray)
- ▲ black and gold (for contrast)
- ▲ purple and yellow

Combine two different sizes of sponge rollers, and vary the combinations of colors, such as those listed above.

Combine three sponge rollers.

Combine sponge rollers and brayers in the same activity. This encourages children to make comparisons between the two implements.

Combine sponge rollers and regular brushes. This also encourages children to make comparisons.

Comments & Questions to Extend Thinking

What kind of mark does the sponge roller make?

Kenny made wide stripes on his paper.

What happens when you move the roller in a different direction?

5.10 Spray Painting
Easel

Helpful Hints

Prepare a supply of colored water ahead of time so you can quickly refill empty spray bottles. This activity is very popular!

Description

Young children enjoy the process of spraying colored water and observing the colors dripping and mixing on the paper. In this activity, which combines science and art, young children use tiny spray bottles to create muted color combinations. Children can also explore this activity outside.

Art Experiences

- ▲ observing the mixing of colors
- ▲ planning color arrangements
- ▲ observing the effects of gravity

Materials

- ▲ newsprint, 18 by 24 inches
- ▲ small spray bottles (3 for each easel station), filled with colored water
- ▲ red, blue, and yellow water, made by adding food coloring
- ▲ smocks
- ▲ protective covering under the easel and drying rack (these paintings drip a lot)

Child's Level

This activity is most appropriate for older preschool and kindergarten children. The tiny spray bottles may be difficult for young preschoolers to manipulate.

What to Look For

Children will soak the paper with colored water.
Children will notice the blending of colors.
Some children will experiment to find out how to mix the colors.
Some children will know how to produce specific colors and will plan their picture accordingly.
Some children will verbalize the process of blending colors.
A few children may have difficulty manipulating the spray bottles.

Modifications

Begin with only two colors for an easier version of this activity.
Add complexity for experienced children by letting them first draw with crayon and then spray their creations with colored water (activity 3.14).
Create a group mural in the outside area with larger spray bottles of colored water (activity 8.1).

Comments & Questions to Extend Thinking

I see green on your paper where you sprayed yellow over the blue.
Is there any way to make orange?
Joseph says he made the sunrise.
What colors would look like rain?

5.11 Painting with Wheels

Easel or Special Activity

Description

Children use small cars to create paint tracks in this activity. They can experiment on both the vertical surface of the easel and the horizontal surface of the special activity table. Children observe the paint tracks they make with the cars and begin to construct relationships between their arm movements and the locations of the tracks.

Helpful Hints

Use a small amount of paint in the trays. Less paint on the wheels makes the tracks easier to observe.

Be sure to use a dark shade of paint. Yellow or white tracks are difficult to see.

Art Experiences

▲ painting with an unusual implement
▲ comparing different painting implements
▲ creating relationships between arm movements and paint tracks
▲ planning the arrangement of the tracks on paper
▲ creating two lines of paint with one motion
▲ observing the pattern of the tire tracks

Materials

Easel

▲ newsprint paper, 18 by 24 inches
▲ 1 small plastic vehicle for each easel station
▲ 1 color of paint, in a dark shade
▲ small trays (1 for each easel station), to hold the paint
▲ smocks

Special Activity Table

- ▲ white construction paper, 12 by 18 inches
- ▲ 1 small plastic vehicle per child
- ▲ 1 color of paint, in a dark shade
- ▲ small trays (1 per child), to hold the paint
- ▲ smocks

Child's Level

Painting with wheels is appropriate for both preschool and kindergarten children. Older children may be able to use more than one vehicle for painting.

What to Look For

Children will dip the cars in the paint and observe the tracks they make on the paper.

Some children will explore side-to-side movements and up-and-down movements to make paint tracks.

Some children will create relationships between their movements and the tracks they make. These children may create a track around the perimeter of the paper or make the tracks cross in specific places.

Children may enjoy moving the vehicle around the paper and not notice the paint tracks.

Modifications

Repeat this activity several times using a single vehicle with wheels, but varying the color of paint.

Plan this activity several times using a different type or size of wheel. Some possibilities include casters, pastry wheels, and pizza wheels.

Combine two different wheels and vary the combinations of colors:

- ▲ 2 primary colors (red and yellow, red and blue, or blue and yellow)
- ▲ black and white (to create contrast, as well as shades of gray)
- ▲ black and gold (for high contrast)

Combine wheels and regular brushes in the same activity. This encourages children to closely observe and compare the designs made by each implement.

Comments & Questions to Extend Thinking

How did you make two tracks at the same time?

I see four wheels. Why aren't there four tracks?

All of the lines are straight on your paper. Is there a way to make a curved line?

5.12 Painting with Objects

Easel or Special Activity

Description

Children use familiar objects, such as combs, toothbrushes, and plastic hairbrushes, as painting implements in this activity. Painting with many of these of materials provides opportunities for children to pay special attention to pattern and symmetry in their paintings. Combs, for example, create a seriated design (wide to narrow lines) that children can repeat on the paper.

Helpful Hints

Ask parents for donations of household items to use in this activity. Be sure combs and brushes are sterilized.

Art Experiences

- ▲ exploring an unusual painting implement
- ▲ creating repeated designs
- ▲ focusing on pattern and symmetry
- ▲ planning a specific design based on the implement
- ▲ experimenting with the designs made by different sides or edges of the implements

Materials

Easel

- ▲ newsprint paper, 18 by 24 inches
- ▲ 1 or more unusual painting tools (comb, toothbrush, etc.)
- ▲ small tray to hold the paint (1 for each easel station)
- ▲ 1 color of paint
- ▲ smocks

Special Activity Table

- ▲ white construction or drawing paper, 9 by 12 inches
- ▲ 1 or more unusual painting tools for each child
- ▲ small tray to hold the paint (1 per child)
- ▲ 1 color of paint
- ▲ smocks

Child's Level

This activity is most appropriate for older preschool and kindergarten children. Younger or less experienced children may not be ready to explore unusual implements until they have had extensive experiences with more traditional paintbrushes.

What to Look For

Some children will apply the paint to the paper using a stroking motion.

Some children will apply the paint with a dabbing motion.

Some children may notice the different designs made by the different implements.

Children may observe changes in the intensity of color from the start to the finish of a stroke of paint.

Some children may initially be confused by the idea of using familiar objects for painting.

Modifications

Begin with one or two different implements and one color of paint. This provides sufficient opportunities for children to fully explore the designs made by the individual tools. Later, one color of paint can be used for each implement in the activity.

Vary the color combinations:

- ▲ several shades of the same color (navy, medium blue, light blue)
- ▲ gold and silver, used with black paper
- ▲ white paint on black paper

Comments & Questions to Extend Thinking

How did you make these parallel lines?

What part of the comb made the thick lines?

Look at the way these lines crisscross each other.

5.13 Straw-Blown Paintings

Special Activity

Description

In this activity, children explore artistic concepts, such as blending colors, as well as scientific information about the movement of air and the properties of paint. Children blow air through a straw to move paint across the paper. At first, children's explorations create random designs, but later they plan which colors of paint to move and in what directions.

Helpful Hints

Cut a small hole in the straws to prevent children from sucking up paint.

Art Experiences

- ▲ observing the properties of paint
- ▲ creating relationships between their actions and the reactions of the paint
- ▲ blending colors (see *Modifications*)
- ▲ encouraging communication about the reactions of the paint

Materials

- ▲ white construction or drawing paper, 9 by 12 inches
- ▲ 4 trays, to hold the paper
- ▲ 6-inch pieces of plastic straws (1 for each child)
- ▲ small cups, to hold the paint (1 for each child)
- ▲ 1 primary color of tempera or watercolor paint, thinned with water
- ▲ small spoons, for applying the paint to the paper
- ▲ smocks

Child's Level

This activity is most appropriate for older preschool or kindergarten children since it requires that they be able to blow air through a straw. This may be difficult for very young preschool children. Older preschool and kindergarten children usually have little or no difficulty blowing air through a straw.

What to Look For

Children will experiment with blowing air to move the paint.

Some children will become aware of how they moved the paint, gain more control over the process, and then create intentional results.

Some children will be unable to accurately aim the stream of air to move the paint.

Some children will use the straw like a brush to move the paint.

Children may need assistance using the tasting spoons to place small amounts of paint on the paper.

Modifications

Add a second primary color of paint to encourage children to focus on blending colors, such as red and blue, yellow and blue, or yellow and red.

Include all three primary colors (red, yellow, and blue) to encourage additional blending of colors.

Substitute bulb syringes for the straws in this activity. The bulb syringe may be too difficult for some children to squeeze. You can observe the abilities of children in the group and determine whether or not to use this variation.

Plan the activity using 12- by 18-inch white construction or drawing paper.

Comments & Questions to Extend Thinking

Can you make the paint move without touching it with the straw?

What do you have to do to make this red paint reach the blue paint?

The paint made a fan shape when you blew on it through the straw.

5.14 Rolling Marble Paintings

Special Activity

Description

This painting activity combines science and art. Children create a permanent record of tracks made by a marble, dipped in paint, that they roll across paper in the bottom of a shoe box. As they tilt the box to vary the angle and slope, they can observe the track made by the rolling marble. Teachers can begin with one marble for each child and a single color of paint. This allows children to experiment with how to move the marble before they explore concepts related to blending colors.

Helpful Hints

Do not use marbles in this activity if children still put objects into their mouths. Use balls instead.

Art Experiences

- ▲ moving paint in an unusual manner
- ▲ exploring the relationship between the action of the marble and the reaction of the paint
- ▲ comparing the movement of the box and the resulting paint track
- ▲ blending colors (when using more than one color of paint)

Materials

- ▲ 4 clear plastic shoe boxes (1 for each child)
- ▲ white construction or drawing paper, cut to fit inside the box
- ▲ 4 marbles (1 for each child)
- ▲ 4 tasting spoons (1 for each child), for lifting the marbles out of the paint

▲ 1 color of paint in a dark shade (yellow is difficult to see)
▲ smocks

Child's Level

This activity is most appropriate for older preschool and kindergarten children. Younger children may have more difficulty keeping the marbles inside the box.

What to Look For

Some children will carefully tip the box and observe the track made by the marble.
Some children will initially shake the box up and down to watch the marbles jump.
Some children will tip the box back and forth without attending to the reactions of the marble.
A few children may attempt to control the movement of the marble. This control increases with experience.

Modifications

Plan this activity several times, but vary the color of paint each time.
Try the activity with various types of balls, such as whiffle, golf, Ping-Pong, and Koosh balls.
Use a marble and one type of ball with a single color of paint. Children can focus on the different tracks made by each of the balls.
Use a marble with one color of paint and a ball with another color of paint. Children can focus on creating lines that cross. The different colors highlight the tracks made by each ball.
Substitute a larger box for the activity. Children can make longer tracks.
Create a ramp from a hollow block or a piece of wood elevated at one end by a small box. Cut paper to fit the length and width of the ramp. Children can roll marbles or balls dipped in paint down the ramp.

Comments & Questions to Extend Thinking

The marble is round, but it made a straight track.
How can you get marble tracks on this side of your paper?
Your marble keeps going around the edge of the box. What can you do to make it roll across the center?

5.15 Watercolor Painting

Easel or Special Activity

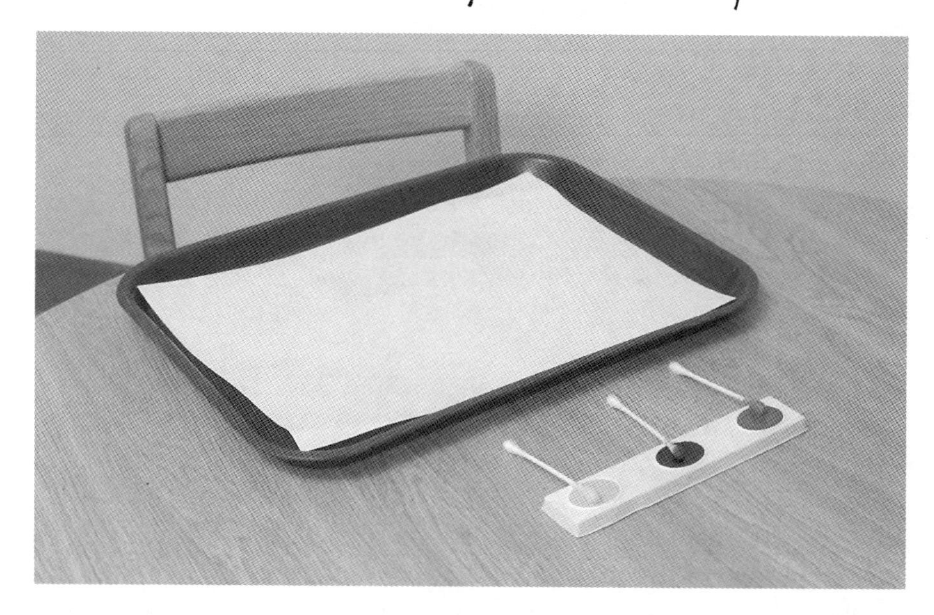

Description

Children explore watercolor paints in this activity. They can experiment with how to load the brush with color and how to affect the intensity of the color as they add more or less water. Watercolor paints are more translucent than tempera paints. The soft bristle brushes used with watercolors may encourage children to add greater detail to their paintings. The organization of materials and limited selection of paint colors (red, blue, and yellow) help children focus on blending colors.

Art Experiences

- ▲ painting with watercolors
- ▲ exploring translucent colors
- ▲ blending colors
- ▲ observing absorption
- ▲ comparing watercolor paints to tempera paints

Materials

Easel

- ▲ white construction paper, 12 by 18 inches
- ▲ sets of red, yellow, and blue watercolor pans, slightly moistened with water (1 set for each easel station)
- ▲ wet cotton swabs (1 for each watercolor pan)
- ▲ smocks

Helpful Hints

Watercolor refills are packaged by color in sets of three per plastic holder. The individual pans can be removed from the holder. Replace them with one red, one yellow, and one blue refill pan.

Place thin sponge pieces, such as those found in gift boxes of fruit, under the paper towels and coffee filters to absorb the excess paint. This makes cleanup easier.

Special Activity Table

- ▲ white construction paper, 9 by 12 inches
- ▲ sets of red, yellow, and blue watercolor pans, slightly moistened with water (1 set per child)
- ▲ wet cotton swabs (1 for each watercolor pan)
- ▲ smocks

Child's Level

Watercolor painting activities are appropriate for both preschool and kindergarten children. The description of this activity shows one of the simplest ways to present watercolor painting. Children do not have to rinse a brush after using each color, and they are less likely to mix all the colors together.

What to Look For

Children may experiment with applying one dot or stroke of each color of paint.

Some children will create lines and designs with each of the three colors of paint.

Some children will blend the primary colors to create new colors.

Some children will use only one or two of the colors.

Some children may create patterns of color.

Modifications

For very young children, begin with just one or two colors of paint. Children can explore the process of adding paint to the cotton swabs.

Use just two colors of watercolor paints to encourage children to explore the creation of patterns.

Vary the surface for painting by including such materials as white paper plates, white paper towels, and coffee filters.

Use a watercolor brush and a small amount of water for rinsing the brush.

Comments & Questions to Extend Thinking

Is there a way to make green paint?

What kind of lines can you make with these swabs?

You made a pattern of lines: red-blue-yellow, red-blue-yellow.

5.16 Fingerpainting
Special Activity

Description

Fingerpainting is a special category of painting. In this activity, children use their hands to create designs in the paint. Teachers may want to sequence a series of fingerpainting activities to prepare children for exploring paint on paper. For example, children can use finger paint inside the confined space of a tray and then on a tabletop. Pressing a piece of paper on top of the designs, thus creating a monoprint, permanently records the designs, if desired. Later, children can use finger paint directly on paper. Many children are so fascinated by the process that they never want a permanent record. Some children, who are less willing to take risks painting, drawing, and writing, are willing to experiment with fingerpainting. The images in the paint are easily changed or completely wiped away with a few strokes of the child's hand.

Helpful Hints

Liquid starch, with a small amount of tempera paint added, is an inexpensive substitute for commercial finger paint.

Keep a bucket of water and towels near the special activity table. Children can wash off most of the paint before going to the sink.

Commercial finger paint paper often cracks as it dries. This can be very frustrating to children.

Art Experiences

- ▲ exploring texture
- ▲ creating nonpermanent lines, shapes, and designs (when exploring finger paint inside a tray or on a tabletop)
- ▲ using fingers and hands to experiment with a fluid medium
- ▲ tactilely exploring an art medium

Materials

- ▲ white construction or drawing paper, 9 by 12 inches
- ▲ 2 or 3 trays, for the paper
- ▲ finger paint (1 color)
- ▲ small cups, to hold the paint (1 for each child)
- ▲ plastic spoons, for applying the paint to the paper
- ▲ sponges, for cleaning the table in between children
- ▲ smocks

Child's Level

This activity is appropriate for both preschool and kindergarten children. It is a very messy experience! For younger, less-experienced groups of children, teachers may want children to paint inside a tray before experimenting on paper.

What to Look For

Some children may initially be apprehensive about putting their hands into the finger paint. Teachers can model touching the paint themselves, allow children to place their hands on top of the teacher's hands, or offer craft sticks as a tool to explore the paint.

Children will discover that they can create lines, swirls, and pictures by moving their fingers through the paint.

Some children will explore the finger paint with hands, fingers, and elbows.

Some children will paint themselves rather than on the paper!

Modifications

After initial explorations with a single color of finger paint, add a second color.

Select two primary colors (red, yellow, or blue) that blend to form a secondary color. Other color combinations will always produce a muddy brown color. Even combining all three primary colors together makes a muddy brown.

Comments & Questions to Extend Thinking

You can move this paint around with your hands.

How does the paint feel?

I see round, swirling lines in the paint. I wonder if we'll be able to see them after you press the paper over the paint.

5.17 Cookie Cutter Prints

Easel or Special Activity

Description

Printing with cookie cutters provides opportunities for children to explore the placement of one or more shapes within the boundaries of the paper. They can also focus on the repetition of the same shape on the paper. Very few young children can accurately recreate a particular shape or figure over and over again in the exact size and form as the first in the series. Printing activities allow them to explore this possibility.

Art Experiences

- ▲ exploring the technique of printing with a rigid tool
- ▲ experimenting with paint by pressing rather than stroking
- ▲ creating relationships between the shape of the cookie cutter and the shape of the print it makes
- ▲ creating different intensities of color with the cookie cutter
- ▲ exploring the placement and arrangement of forms
- ▲ exploring negative space created by the outline of the cookie cutter
- ▲ observing and creating patterns and symmetrical designs

Materials

Easel

- ▲ newsprint paper, 18 by 24 inches
- ▲ red paint
- ▲ small tray, to hold the paint (1 for each easel station)
- ▲ cookie cutter in an interesting shape, such as a leaf or heart (1 for each easel station)
- ▲ smocks

Special Activity Table

- ▲ white construction or drawing paper, 9 by 12 inches
- ▲ 4 trays, to hold the paper
- ▲ red paint
- ▲ small tray, to hold the paint (1 per child)
- ▲ cookie cutter in an interesting shape (1 per child)
- ▲ smocks

Child's Level

This activity is appropriate for both preschool and kindergarten children.

What to Look For

Some children will fill the paper with prints and partial prints.

Some children will experiment by printing with both sides of the cookie cutter as well as the edges.

Children may create patterns in activities with two cookie cutters.

Some children may verbalize observations about the printing activity.

Children often use the cookie cutter like a brush, a familiar art tool. They move the cookie cutter across and down the paper with the arm and shoulder. This is similar to how they apply paint with a brush.

Modifications

Vary the color of paint used with a single cookie cutter. This allows children to thoroughly explore the printing process.

Use two different but related cookie cutters (such as one oak and one maple leaf or a big and little circle) and two colors of paint. This helps children consider patterning possibilities.

Use two different but related cookie cutters and a single color of paint. This also encourages children to think about patterns.

Use very small cookie cutters, available in cake decorating shops, and a half-sheet of construction paper (6 by 4½ inches).

Draw lines to divide the easel paper into a grid. This encourages children to print one cookie cutter impression in each square and think about one-to-one correspondence relationships. Make the squares slightly larger than the cookie cutter.

Helpful Hints

Collect cookie cutters in multiple sets so each child at the special activity table has duplicate materials for printing activities.

Do not use metal cookie cutters that easily bend.

Comments & Questions to Extend Thinking

You've created a pattern—up-down, up-down. Which cookie cutter will you use next?

You made a leaf shape in each corner of your paper.

5.18 Rolling Cookie Cutter Prints

Easel or Special Activity

Description

The unique tool in this activity combines many cookie cutters on a wheel attached to a single handle. Children can create multiple prints with one motion. They observe the repetition of pattern, compare the shapes on the wheel, and sometimes use their whole body in creating the design. Children need large pieces of paper to fully explore this printing tool. Teachers may need to limit the number of children who participate in this activity at the same time. Children at the table need sufficient space for a large piece of paper and the paint container. They also need room to move their body as they roll the wheel.

Helpful Hints

Look for this unusual tool in odd lot stores and specialty kitchen supply shops.

Art Experiences

- ▲ experimenting with a unique printing tool
- ▲ comparing the multiple prints made with one motion to the single prints made in other printing activities
- ▲ exploring patterns

Materials

Easel

- ▲ newsprint paper, 18 by 24 inches
- ▲ long tray or pan, to hold the paint (1 for each easel station)
- ▲ 1 dark shade of paint

- ▲ printing wheel, as pictured
- ▲ smocks

Special Activity Table

- ▲ white construction or drawing paper, 12 by 18 inches
- ▲ long tray or pan, to hold the paint (1 per child)
- ▲ 1 dark shade of paint
- ▲ printing wheel, 1 per child
- ▲ smocks

Child's Level

This activity is most appropriate for older preschool and kindergarten children. Younger children may have difficulty manipulating the unusual implement. They need more experience with single printing tools before exploring the rolling cookie cutter.

What to Look For

Children will dip the printing wheel in paint and observe the shapes it creates as they roll it over the paper.

Some children will notice that patterns are created.

Some children will move the roller back and forth in the same place on the paper, obscuring the individual prints.

Some children will move the roller only a short distance, lift it from the paper, and move it to a different part of the paper. This does not provide opportunities to fully explore the prints the tool makes.

Some children will move the roller as far as they can reach. Some may even walk forward or around the table to continue moving the roller.

Modifications

Vary the color of paint.

Plan a group mural that children create with several rolling cookie cutters. Select paint in several coordinating colors, such as red, yellow, and blue, or magenta, purple, and pink. Place the containers of paint on a small table to prevent children from stepping on them.

Comments & Questions to Extend Thinking

Do you see this print in any other place on your paper? (Point to a specific shape.)

How can you get paint on all of the shapes at the same time?

The shapes always follow each other in the same order. Why is that?

5.19 Potato Masher Prints

Easel or Special Activity

Description

The potato mashers in this activity are similar to the cookie cutters used for making prints in activity 5.17. Potato mashers have rigid shapes, like cookie cutters, but also have a long handle. Children grasp this handle as they use the potato masher to press the paint onto paper. Potato mashers vary widely in design. This makes them a perfect printing tool.

Helpful Hints

To provide enough space for the large size paper, have fewer children at the special activity table.

Art Experiences

- ▲ exploring the technique of printing
- ▲ experimenting with paint by pressing rather than stroking
- ▲ creating relationships between the shape of the potato masher and the shape of the print it makes
- ▲ creating different intensities of color with the potato masher
- ▲ exploring the placement and arrangement of forms
- ▲ observing and creating patterns and symmetrical designs

Materials

Easel

- ▲ newsprint paper, 18 by 24 inches
- ▲ small tray, to hold the paint (1 for each easel station)
- ▲ dark shade of paint
- ▲ potato masher, for printing (1 for each easel station)
- ▲ smocks

Special Activity Table

- ▲ white construction or drawing paper, 12 by 18 inches
- ▲ small tray, to hold the paint (1 per child)
- ▲ dark shade of paint
- ▲ potato masher, for printing (1 per child)
- ▲ smocks

Child's Level

Printing with potato mashers is appropriate for both preschool and kindergarten children.

What to Look For

Children will observe the specific prints created by the potato mashers as they apply the paint.

Some children will cover the paper with many potato masher prints.

Some children will reapply paint to the potato masher before making each print.

Some children may not be able to figure out how to hold the potato masher to make a print. This is especially true for younger children exploring this activity at the easel.

Some children will create patterns with a single color of paint and two different types of potato mashers (see *Modifications*).

Some children will create patterns with two different colors of paint and a single type of potato masher (see *Modifications*).

Some children will notice the symmetrical design of potato mashers.

Modifications

Vary the color of paint used with a single potato masher. This allows children to thoroughly explore the printing process.

Use two different potato mashers and two colors of paint. This helps children consider patterning possibilities.

Use two different potato mashers and a single color of paint. This also encourages children to think about patterns.

Plan a group mural that children create with several different potato mashers. Select coordinating colors of paint, such as red, yellow, orange, and brown, or red, pink, and lavender. Place the containers of paint on a small table to prevent children from stepping in the paint.

Comments & Questions to Extend Thinking

What will happen if you make more prints without adding paint?

Is there a way you can make a lighter print?

You started a pattern—upside-down–sideways, upside-down–sideways. What will you print next?

5.20 Sponge Prints

Easel or Special Activity

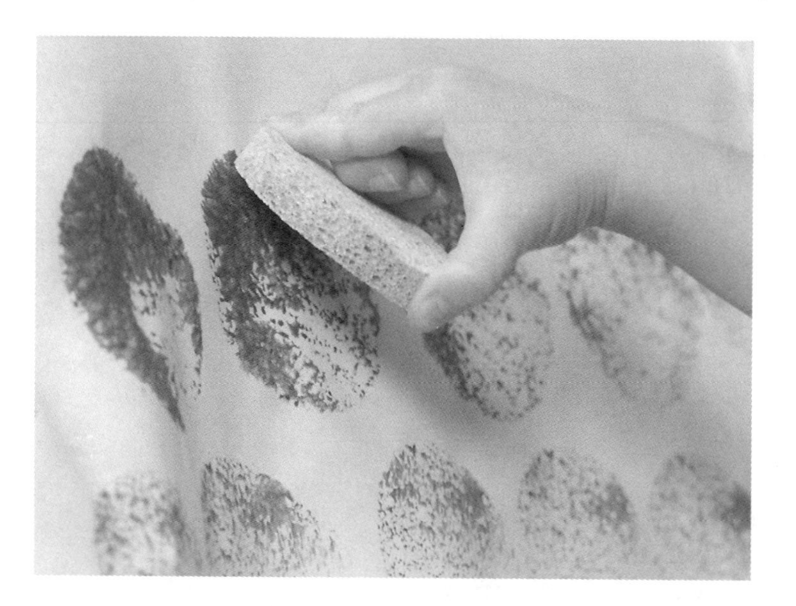

Description

In this printing activity, children use foam sponge brushes, cellulose sponges, or natural sponges to create designs. Printing with sponges is similar to printing with cookie cutters. In both activities, children apply paint to a printing tool and press it onto paper. The resulting print impression is directly related to the size and shape of the sponge or cookie cutter. The activities also differ significantly. Sponges soak up paint, while plastic cookie cutters do not. Cookie cutters have a rigid shape that makes a specific print; sponges, however, are more pliable, which allows children to print with both the flat surfaces and the edges.

Helpful Hints

Many fabric and craft stores sell sets of sponge brushes in different sizes.

Art Experiences

▲ exploring the technique of printing with a pliable tool
▲ experimenting with paint by pressing rather than stroking
▲ creating relationships between the shape of the sponge and the shape of the print it makes
▲ creating different intensities of color with the sponge, depending on how much paint is on the sponge and how recently it was applied
▲ exploring the placement and arrangement of forms
▲ observing and creating patterns and symmetrical designs

Materials

Easel

- ▲ newsprint paper, 18 by 24 inches
- ▲ purple paint
- ▲ small tray, to hold the paint (1 for each easel station)
- ▲ set of 2 sizes of sponge brushes (1 set for each easel station)
- ▲ smocks

Special Activity Table

- ▲ white construction or drawing paper, 9 by 12 inches
- ▲ 4 trays, to hold the paper
- ▲ purple paint
- ▲ small tray, to hold the paint (1 per child)
- ▲ set of 2 sizes of sponge brushes (1 set per child)
- ▲ smocks

Child's Level

This activity is appropriate for both preschool and kindergarten children.

What to Look For

Children will use the sponges to create prints and strokes.

Many children will stroke the sponge brush like an easel brush and make stripes of paint on the paper instead of printing.

Some children will randomly "hop" the sponge across the paper.

Some children will explore the effects of making several prints before adding more paint to the sponge.

Some children may repeat the sponge print around the perimeter of the paper.

Some children may experiment by printing with both the flat surface and the edge of the sponge.

Modifications

Vary the color of paint used with any of the sponge brushes, shape sponges, or natural sponges.

Select two colors of paint to use with two different varieties of sponges.

Combine two sizes of sponges with two different colors of paint.

Use a circular sponge in combination with paper cut into a large circle.

Comments & Questions to Extend Thinking

What did you do here to create such a faint print?

How did you make this print? I don't see a sponge in that shape.

What happens if you "hop" the sponge across the paper?

5.21 Fruit and Vegetable Prints

Special Activity

Description

Making prints with fruits and vegetables is a common activity in many early childhood programs. In this activity, children print with one-half of a fruit or vegetable, such as an orange, apple, or green pepper. Many fruits and vegetables are naturally symmetrical and create lovely prints. However, soft fruits, such as bananas and peaches, are too fragile for children to use. Teachers can experiment to find the best fruits and vegetables to select for this activity.

Helpful Hints

Cut fruits and vegetables across the middle rather than from the stem down.

Art Experiences

- ▲ exploring rotational symmetry in nature
- ▲ exploring patterns in nature
- ▲ experimenting with repetition of a shape or design

Materials

- ▲ white construction paper, 9 by 12 inches
- ▲ 4 large trays, to hold the paper
- ▲ 4 small trays, to hold the paint
- ▲ 2 oranges, cut in half (½ orange for each child)
- ▲ smocks

Child's Level

Printing with fruits and vegetables is most appropriate for older preschool and kindergarten children. Younger children may have difficulty holding onto many of the pieces. Teachers can observe their children and assess the appropriateness of this activity for their group.

What to Look For

Some children will notice the relationship between the design of the orange and the print it makes.

Some children will press the orange onto the paper, lift it, and press it again for several repetitions.

Some children will cover the paper with paint by rubbing the orange across the paper like a brush.

Some children will have difficulty holding onto the fruit or vegetable pieces.

Modifications

Plan this activity with any of the following fruits and vegetables:

- red, green, or golden peppers
- all varieties of onion (except tiny pearl onions)
- lemons and limes
- apples
- star fruit

Experiment with other fruits and vegetables to observe whether they have interesting designs children can explore in a printing activity.

Combine three different colors of apples or peppers in one activity. Children can observe similarities in the designs they each make.

Change the paper to 12 by 18 inches to provide more room for explorations.

Use white paint to print with apples on red paper.

Use white paint to print with oranges on orange paper.

Comments & Questions to Extend Thinking

What happens if you press the orange onto the paper many times without adding any paint?

Is there a way to make a lighter print with the orange?

I see many round shapes on top of each other on your paper.

5.22 Loofah Prints
Easel

Helpful Hints

Look for inexpensive loofahs in dollar stores.

Description

The loofah sponges in this activity are mounted to the end of a long handle. This presents quite a challenge to children printing at the easel. Children must solve the problem of how far back from the easel they should stand. They must also consider the best way to hold onto the implement in order to press the loofah sponge onto the paper.

Art Experiences

- ▲ printing with a natural material
- ▲ creating overlays of paint
- ▲ combining colors

Materials

- ▲ newsprint, 18 by 24 inches
- ▲ loofah attached to a long handle (2 for each child)
- ▲ disposable microwave trays to hold the paint (2 for each child)
- ▲ red and blue paint
- ▲ smocks

Child's Level

This activity is most appropriate for older preschool and kindergarten children. Younger children may have difficulty manipulating the long-handled implement.

What to Look For

Children will press the loofah onto the paper to see what kind of mark it makes.

Some children will stroke the loofah across the paper like a brush.

Some children will create overlapping prints with the red and blue paint.

Some children will combine the paint to produce purple.

Children will notice that if they do not re-dip the loofah in the paint, the marks become fainter.

Some children will press the loofah onto the paper in many places.

Some children may comment on the hard quality of the loofah.

Modifications

Use one loofah and black paint. The high contrast allows children to more easily observe the tiny holes in the loofah.

Plan this activity with any two primary colors of paint to help children observe the blending of colors.

Plan a printing activity with smaller pieces of loofah made by cutting the loofah into slices.

Combine a loofah sponge and a natural sponge with two colors of paint.

Comments & Questions to Extend Thinking

You made purple paint, but I only see red and blue paint in the trays. How did you do that?

Is there another way to make a print with the loofah?

5.23 Crumple Prints

Easel or Special Activity

Description

Children often crumple paper during their daily activities. Paper towels, tissues, and other papers in the classroom are crumpled before children dispose of them. These papers also form interesting designs when dipped into a small amount of paint and pressed onto paper. This is similar to the faux finish techniques designers suggest as home decorating possibilities.

Helpful Hints

Crumple the paper before the children arrive. Otherwise, they may be tempted to flatten it and re-crumple it during the activity.

Art Experiences

▲ exploring familiar materials in new ways
▲ creating overall designs with random movements
▲ observing different intensities of color within the overall design

Materials

Easel

▲ newsprint paper, 18 by 24 inches
▲ small trays, to hold the paint (1 for each easel station)
▲ blue paint
▲ several pieces of crumpled paper
▲ smocks

Special Activity Table

- ▲ white construction or drawing paper, 9 by 12 inches
- ▲ small trays, to hold the paint (1 per child)
- ▲ blue paint
- ▲ several pieces of crumpled paper
- ▲ smocks

Child's Level

This unusual printing activity is most appropriate for older preschool and kindergarten children. Younger children may be tempted to flatten the paper!

What to Look For

Some children will stroke the crumpled paper like a brush.

Some children will dab the crumpled paper in many places on the large piece of paper.

A few children may not want to use something they view as trash. The teacher can comment on the process as other children print with the crumpled paper. This may help children have a more positive attitude.

Modifications

Plan this activity with plastic wrap, cheesecloth, or other materials that can be crumpled.

Use a different color of paint along with one piece of crumpled paper per child each time you plan the activity.

Combine two pieces of crumpled paper for each child and two primary colors of paint, one for each paper.

Use smaller pieces of crumpled paper and one color of paint.

Combine a larger and a smaller piece of crumpled paper with one color of paint. This encourages children to think about patterns.

Plan this activity as a class mural. Children can select paper or other materials in various sizes and crumple them to use on the group project.

Comments & Questions to Extend Thinking

What happens when you print with red paint over the blue paint? (See *Modifications*.)

Is there a way to make a darker print?

I see a row of this flower-shaped mark on your paper.

5.24 Hand & Foot Prints

Special Activity

Helpful Hints

Do not add soap to the liquid paint if children will walk across the roll of shelf paper. Their feet may be slippery and cause them to fall.

Description

Creating handprints is easily implemented as a special activity. Making footprints, however, presents more of a management challenge. Teachers may want to plan foot painting as an outside activity in warm weather (activity 8.5). If desired, handprints and footprints can be made in the classroom on large paper or a roll of shelf paper. The paper for handprints can be taped to the wall, while the paper for footprints must be kept on the floor. Teachers can use a paintbrush to paint each child's hand or foot. This causes lots of giggles. Children can press their hands onto the paper to create a class mural. They can either step onto a large piece of paper or walk across a roll of shelf paper to create footprints.

Art Experiences

- ▲ printing with a body part
- ▲ enhancing self-concept by focusing on personal attributes
- ▲ comparing size

Materials

- ▲ newsprint, 18 by 24 inches, or a roll of white shelf paper
- ▲ paintbrush, for the teacher
- ▲ any color of paint
- ▲ bucket of water and towel, for cleaning feet

Child's Level

This activity is appropriate for both preschool and kindergarten children.

What to Look For

Children will press their hands and feet onto the paper and observe the prints they make.

Children will compare how their hands and feet look.

Some children will rub paint across the paper with their fingers or toes.

Some children may at first be a bit squeamish about getting paint on their feet.

Children may notice the tiny marks created by fingers and toes.

Modifications

Use two colors of paint, one for each hand. This may help children focus on left-right orientation.

Use black paint on white paper to produce high contrast.

Make handprints on 9- by 12-inch paper. They can be assembled into a class book with each child's photograph.

Comments & Questions to Extend Thinking

Your feet made a pattern as you walked across the paper—left-right, left-right.

Is there another way to move across the paper that creates a different pattern?

I see lots of different hands on this mural. It looks like we have a hundred children in our class!

5.25 Shoe Prints

Special Activity

Helpful Hints

Resale shops are a source for inexpensive baby shoes.

Description

In this activity, children create impressions with small shoes, such as doll shoes, shoes from key chains, and baby shoes. This is similar to printing with cookie cutters (activity 5.17) and sponges (activity 5.20). Children dip the shoes into a small amount of paint and press them onto paper to create an impression. Many of the shoes have designs on the bottom.

Art Experiences

- ▲ creating unusual impressions
- ▲ observing similarities and differences in prints
- ▲ comparing individual shoe prints

Materials

- ▲ white construction or drawing paper, 9 by 12 inches
- ▲ 4 trays, to hold the paper
- ▲ 1 large tray, to hold the paint
- ▲ 8 to 10 small shoes, as described above
- ▲ smocks

Child's Level

This activity is appropriate for both preschool and kindergarten children.

What to Look For

Children will dip the shoes in paint and observe the marks each one makes.

Some children will create a relationship between the design on the shoe and the print that it makes.

Some children will print with every shoe in the tray.

Some children will select one or two shoes and repeat the prints with only those shoes.

Some children will inspect the bottom of each shoe to observe the designs.

Some children may create a pattern with just one shoe, such as sideways–right-side-up, sideways–right-side-up.

Modifications

Vary the color of paint used in this activity.

Change some of the shoes in the activity.

Comments & Questions to Extend Thinking

Are there any shoes that make the same print as this one?

Is there a way to make only a heel print?

I can't see the middle of this print. How did that happen?

Sewing & Stringing

Carolene raced into the classroom with her quilt square tightly clenched in her hand. The teacher had sent home a piece of white felt with each child so that each family could contribute a square to the class family quilt. Carolene proudly showed her quilt square to the teacher. It was embroidered with beautiful Cambodian letters. "It say my name!" Carolene declared. A note attached to the square indicated that it also said, "Carolene loves school."

▲ ▲ ▲

Jeff climbed into the car and opened his book bag. He pulled out an amorphous burlap ball and told his mother resignedly, "We sewed today, but everything I try to sew turns into a ball." After they got home, Jeff's mother brought out an embroidery hoop. "Want to try to sew with this?" she asked. Jeff watched delightedly as his stitches appeared on the fabric, and the hoop kept his creation from turning into a ball.

▲ ▲ ▲

Working with fabric and fibers allows young children to explore and create using techniques and materials that are often new to them. Sewing on loosely-woven fabric; stringing materials that vary in size, weight, and shape; and joining fibers together to create new materials all engage children in the construction of new knowledge as they learn to manipulate and express their creativity through new media.

Teachers' Questions

How do young children benefit from sewing activities?

Sewing activities allow children to construct knowledge about fabrics and how they can be joined together. While young children have often had many opportunities to experiment with the use of glue, tape, or staples to hold materials together, they are frequently unfamiliar with the process of sewing. Sewing encourages them to think further about the unique properties of fabrics.

Sewing activities enable children to experiment with the creation of lines, shapes, and images through a process that is different from drawing or painting. As with any new material or technique, children first need the opportunity to experiment with fabric, sewing implements, and techniques. Once they understand the relationship between the placement of the needle and the size and position of the stitch, they can use this knowledge to create their own designs.

Sewing activities help children develop fine-motor skills and eye-hand coordination. They quickly learn the relationship between where they insert the needle and where it emerges on the other side of the fabric. Children must also judge how hard to pull the yarn to create a stitch tension that is not too loose or too tight. All of this exploration involves coordinating groups of muscles in new ways.

Can preschool children sew?

Yes, preschool children relish the opportunity to sew when given materials that are designed to meet their developmental needs. While small metal needles would be frustrating for young children to attempt to manipulate, large plastic needles enable them to experiment with sewing techniques while using a tool that is large enough for them to successfully handle. Loose-weave fabrics, such as burlap, are easy for young children to sew on since the needle easily penetrates the spaces between the fibers. Doubling the yarn by threading the needle and tying the loose ends together ensures that the yarn will not come out of the needle while children are attempting to sew. An embroidery hoop to hold the fabric is essential for successful sewing experiences for young children.

What kinds of sewing activities can teachers plan?

Teachers may start by having children sew on Styrofoam plates. Children can switch to burlap or another loose-weave fabric once they are accustomed to using the needle. Styrofoam plates make an ideal first sewing medium because children can easily insert their needle into the plate, and they do not have to worry about up-down orientation. When children switch to sewing on fabric, they must construct an understanding of the up-down pattern to sewing. Otherwise, the yarn wraps around the edge of the fabric and pulls it into a bunch. If the fabric is held by a hoop, the yarn winds around the hoop, which prevents removal of the hoop when the project is finished. With experience, children learn the up-and-down sequence incorporated in sewing.

As with other art experiences, young children are initially absorbed by the process rather than the product when they begin to sew. Later, they may plan the size, color, and placement of their stitches to achieve a specific result. Small burlap squares are appropriate for beginning sewing experiences. Older or more-experienced children may begin to actually sew two pieces of fabric together to create a serviceable item. Purses and bags are popular.

What materials do teachers need for sewing activities?

Colorful burlap, large plastic needles, yarn, and embroidery hoops are the essential supplies for sewing experiences. Burlap is inexpensive and comes in a wide variety of bright colors. Large plastic needles can often be found in the craft department of fabric stores or in craft stores. Yarn fits through the large hole in plastic needles and creates a wide, easily visible stitch. A 6- or 7-inch-diameter embroidery hoop is ideal for holding the fabric while children sew. Teachers may introduce large-hole beads, spangles, or colored pasta to add a new dimension to sewing.

How should teachers set up sewing activities?

Most teachers prefer to start with sewing as a special activity. Materials for up to three children can be placed at a special table with adult supervision. Children are usually very excited when they see sewing materials. A waiting list may be essential! Generally, one adult can adequately supervise and assist three children. Until children have had more experience, the adult will probably need to thread the needles for the children, remind them to alternate pushing the needle up and down, and help them backtrack and remove stitches that wrap around the hoop. Adults can also tie the ends of the yarn as children finish with each strand. Such close supervision allows the adult to monitor safety issues and provides many opportunities for commenting or asking questions about the sewing process. This helps children form relationships between their finger and arm movements and the length, placement, and tightness of their stitches.

How do sewing activities differ for kindergarten children?

While kindergarten children often use the same materials for sewing as preschool children, they may extend the process further and work more independently than preschool children. Initially, kindergarten children need opportunities to experiment with sewing materials under close adult supervision. However, once they have mastered the basics, kindergarten children may be able to work independently with sewing materials. This involves being able to mount the fabric on the embroidery hoop, cut the yarn, and thread the needle. Kindergarten children may wish to cut fabric into different shapes and sew pieces together. They may create items, such as doll clothes or puppets, once they have had many experiences with sewing.

How can sewing activities lend themselves to class projects?

Class quilts are a natural outgrowth of class sewing activities. They give children an opportunity to express themselves individually while contributing to a project that represents the entire group. Of course, children first need opportunities to explore the process of sewing, as well as samples of their sewing to take home, before they may be interested in contributing to a class project. Activities 6.4, 6.5, 6.6, and 6.7 describe class sewing projects.

Why are stringing activities important for young children?

Stringing activities combine a precise fine-motor activity with the opportunity for children to create using color and shape. Children are initially intrigued with the idea of inserting a string through objects with holes. Some children place an object on the string only to immediately remove it and put it on again. Subsequently, children often become interested in how materials can be aligned on a string. They may wish to add beads until the entire string is full. In the process, they become increasingly more adept at eye-hand coordination. Once children have mastered the process of stringing, they may become interested in exploring the mathematical and artistic relationships of pattern and symmetry. Teachers often notice that children's first explorations with pattern occur during stringing activities.

What kinds of stringing activities can teachers plan?

Teachers can design stringing activities that incorporate a wide variety of materials. Colored pasta, many types of beads, spangles, straw pieces, paper shapes with holes punched in them, shells with holes, lace pieces, cereal with holes, and nuts with holes drilled through them are some of the many materials available. Many teachers start with plastic lacing cord for stringing. It holds its shape during stringing activities, which makes it easier for children to manipulate. Yarn or cord can also be used for stringing. Teachers may wish to wrap a piece of masking tape around the tip of the yarn to stiffen it for threading.

How are stringing activities related to age and development?

Young children need larger materials with bigger holes to string; older children can usually string smaller materials with tinier holes. Rigatoni pasta, which can be colored with food coloring diluted with water, is perfect for young children since it has a large hole to thread the string through. Ditalini pasta, with its smaller hole, is preferable for older preschool or kindergarten children. Stiffer materials, such as pipe cleaners or plastic lacing cord, are easiest for young children to string with. Kindergarten children can use a wider variety of strings, including cord threaded through a large plastic needle.

What other activities are related to sewing and stringing?

Lacing and weaving also involve fabrics and fibers and utilize techniques related to sewing and stringing. While lacing is similar to sewing, the cord is inserted through specific holes in the material to produce a desired effect. Older children sometimes use lacing to create a border for other projects. Weaving involves maneuvering some type of yarn or string over and under cross-fibers to create a new fabric with its own distinctive design. Children can experiment with various patterns as they explore lacing and weaving activities.

What types of weaving activities can teachers plan?

Teachers can utilize preexisting structures, such as plastic produce baskets, for weaving activities. Teachers can also make simple weaving frames to use with a variety of materials. Children need many opportunities to explore the in-and-out and over-and-under relationships involved in weaving. Although teachers can suggest weaving patterns, such as over one thread and under one thread, they should expect and welcome random experimentation by children. An open-ended agenda allows children to explore how fibers look as they maneuver them over and under other fibers.

Where can teachers get materials for sewing and weaving activities?

Parents are an excellent source of donations for sewing and weaving activities. Yarn, ribbon, lace, and fabric scraps can all be utilized for sewing and weaving. Teachers can purchase burlap, large needles, and embroidery hoops at craft or fabric stores. Directions for making weaving frames are included in activity 6.14.

How can teachers assess children's use of sewing, stringing, and weaving materials?

Teachers can record children's progress in the use of sewing, stringing, and weaving materials by saving samples of their work, taking photographs, or writing anecdotal notes. As teachers assess children's development, they should take care to record the process rather than just focusing on a product. Children may wish to describe the process they used when creating with various materials. Their comments can be displayed along with either their actual artwork or a photograph of the artwork.

Sewing & Stringing Activities

6.1 Sewing on Styrofoam

Description

Sewing on Styrofoam is an easy first sewing experience since there is no fabric to "bunch up." Children use yarn with large plastic needles to sew on Styrofoam plates. Since there is no sewing frame or embroidery hoop to wrap the yarn around, children do not need to be concerned about the placement of the stitches.

Helpful Hints

After threading the needles, pull the yarn through to create a double strand and knot the loose ends. This will prevent the needles from unthreading as the children sew.

Art Experiences

- ▲ sewing
- ▲ creating lines with stitches
- ▲ experimenting with placement patterns

Materials

- ▲ Styrofoam plates
- ▲ several colors of yarn
- ▲ 3 large plastic children's needles

Child's Level

This activity is most appropriate for older preschool or kindergarten children.

What to Look For

Children will push the needle into the plate and look to see where it emerges on the other side.
Many children will make stitches randomly at first.
Children will notice designs that appear on their plates, such as stitches that cross to make an **X**.
Children may not understand how they created long or short stitches until they have had several experiences with sewing.
Children may need some direction on how tightly to pull the yarn. Some children may leave loose loops of yarn while others may pull so tightly that the yarn cuts the plate.

Modification

For children who are too young to use the plastic needles, poke holes in the plates. They can push plastic cord through the holes for a first sewing experience.

Comments & Questions to Extend Thinking

Where do you think the needle will come out if you push it in here?
Where do you have to put the needle to get a long stitch?
This part of your sewing looks like the letter **L**.
You have lines crisscrossing on all of the parts of your plate.

Integrated Curriculum Activities

Plan other art experiences that emphasize lines, such as working with string or wire.
Read books about sewing, such as *Something from Nothing*, by Phoebe Gilman (New York: Scholastic, 1992).
Include Styrofoam modeling as another art experience. Children can create sculptures by inserting pipe cleaners, toothpicks, and coffee stirrers into the Styrofoam (activity 7.1).

6.2 Sewing on Burlap

Description

This is a good follow-up experience to sewing on Styrofoam. For this activity, children sew on squares of colorful burlap that are held in place with 6-inch diameter embroidery hoops. The hoops keep the burlap from bunching up as the children sew. Children use yarn and large plastic needles for their sewing.

Helpful Hints

Fray the edges of the burlap by pulling off several threads from each side. This provides a nice edge for the squares and prevents more strands from pulling loose as the children sew.

Art Experiences

- ▲ sewing
- ▲ creating lines with stitches
- ▲ working with textures
- ▲ experimenting with placement patterns

Materials

- ▲ colorful burlap, cut in 8-inch squares
- ▲ yarn, in assorted colors
- ▲ three 6-inch embroidery hoops
- ▲ 3 large plastic children's needles

Child's Level

This activity is most appropriate for older preschool or kindergarten children.

What to Look For

Children will watch to see where the needle comes out after they insert it into the burlap.

Most children will wrap the yarn around the hoop several times before they master the up-and-down pattern to sewing.

Children will experiment with how tightly to pull the yarn.

Children will explore a variety of colors of yarn. Many children will want to use all of the colors.

With repeated experience, children will begin to learn where to place the stitches to achieve a desired effect.

Some children will create pictures or designs with their stitching.

Modifications

At a later time, introduce yarn of different thickness and various types of thread, such as embroidery floss. Children can observe how the thickness of the thread changes the look of their stitches.

Once children have become experienced with sewing on burlap, add beads to the activity (see activity 6.3).

Comments & Questions to Extend Thinking

What did you do to make this line cross this one?

You made a border of stitches around the edge of your burlap.

What happens when the yarn goes around the hoop?

Oops! I made a mistake on this one. I'll have to work backwards to fix it.

Integrated Curriculum Activities

Look for sewing samples from many cultures to include in the classroom. Import stores, craft stores, and festivals often have examples. Parents may also contribute.

Read books about sewing, such as *The Patchwork Quilt*, by Valerie Flourney (New York: Dial, 1985), and *The Quilt Story*, by Tony Johnston (New York: Scholastic, 1985).

Include an assortment of cut fabric in the art area for collage.

Place a variety of fabrics and materials in the sensory table with water. Children can explore the absorbency characteristics of each (see *More Than Magnets*, activity 4.15).

Assemble a collection of buttons for sorting and classifying (see *More Than Counting*, activity 3.2).

6.3 Sewing with Beads

Description

This activity is an extension of sewing on burlap (activity 6.2). It introduces large-hole beads and spangles to the sewing process. Children continue to sew on burlap squares held in place with embroidery hoops. In addition, they can thread beads and spangles onto their needles and add them to their stitches.

Helpful Hints

Pony beads are easy to sew and are usually inexpensive. Look for them in craft stores.

Art Experiences

▲ sewing
▲ creating lines with stitches
▲ working with textures
▲ stringing
▲ creating in three dimensions
▲ experimenting with placement patterns

Materials

▲ colorful burlap, cut in 8-inch squares
▲ yarn, in assorted colors
▲ three 6-inch embroidery hoops
▲ 3 large plastic children's needles
▲ assortment of plastic or wooden beads with large holes
▲ spangles

Child's Level

This activity is most appropriate for older preschool or kindergarten children.

What to Look For

Children will experiment by adding varying numbers of beads to their stitches.

Some children will notice that if they put several beads on their needle and take a small stitch, the beads make a little arc. They may attempt to reproduce this effect.

Some children will string long strands of beads before taking a stitch.

Some children will allot one bead to each stitch.

Some children will sew beads to the back of the fabric as well as the front.

Modification

Cut straws into small pieces for an inexpensive bead substitute.

Comments & Questions to Extend Thinking

You put the beads in the same color order on each one of your stitches.

How did you make that arc with the beads?

Jamie says his sewing looks like a roller coaster.

When the spangles are strung on top of each other, I can only see the spangle on the top. When the beads are strung on top of each other, I can still see all of the beads.

Integrated Curriculum Activities

Add a jewel collection to the math area for sorting and classifying (see *More Than Counting*, activity 3.11).

Read *Grandma's Jewelry Box*, by Linda Milstein (New York: Random House, 1992).

Put wooden or plastic beads in the manipulative area for stringing.

6.4 Class Sewing Frame

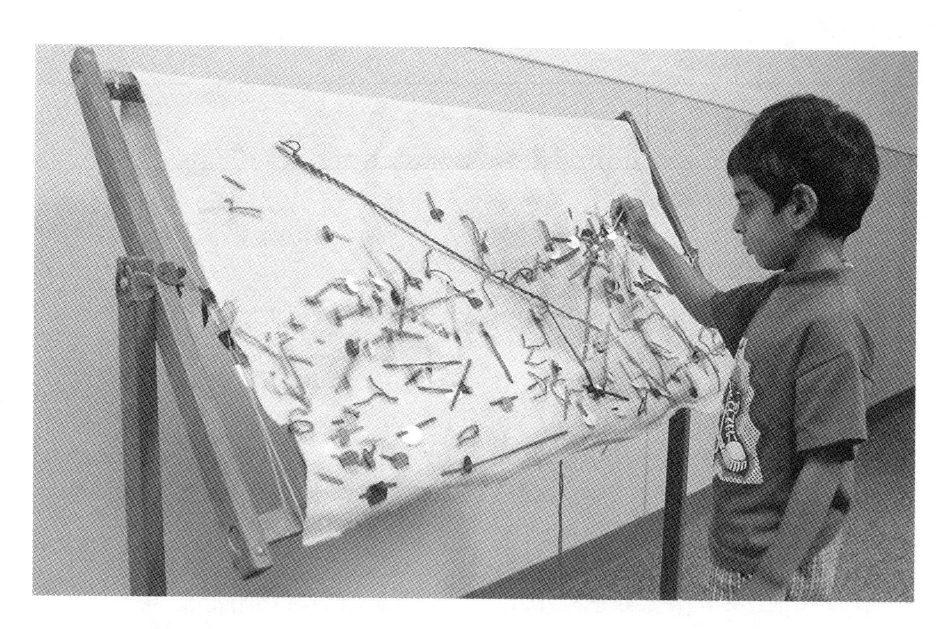

Description

For this activity, burlap is stretched over a large wooden frame for a group sewing project. Children often like to work in pairs on this activity. One child can push the needle into the fabric, and a partner on the other side of the frame can poke the needle back through to the front.

A variety of materials can be used to create a large sewing frame. Some teachers convert the class puppet theater into a frame by stretching the burlap across the window. An old window frame can also be used for a sewing frame. Attach two small pieces of wood to the sides of the frame at the bottom to keep the frame from falling over. Burlap can also be stretched between two pegboard room dividers for group sewing projects.

Teachers who want to make a frame can assemble two ¾-inch-diameter dowels, each 30 inches long, and two pieces of wood, each 2 by 24 inches. Drill a ¾-inch hole near the top and bottom of each strip of wood. Insert the dowels into the holes to create the frame, and wrap the burlap around the dowels. It can be unrolled as needed for sewing. To complete the frame, use wing nuts to attach the center of each side piece of wood to another strip of wood, 2 by 30 inches, to form the sides of the frame. Extend another piece of wood across the bottom of the frame between the two sides for support. Attach two wooden feet, approximately 3 by 12 inches, to the sides to keep the frame from tipping over. (See the photograph above.)

Helpful Hints

Thread a set of needles ahead of time. Then you won't have to keep coming over to thread needles for the sewing project. However, close supervision of the children's use of the needles is always necessary.

Art Experiences

- ▲ sewing
- ▲ creating lines with stitches
- ▲ creating a group mural
- ▲ experimenting with placement patterns

Materials

- ▲ large sewing frame
- ▲ large piece of burlap
- ▲ several colors of yarn
- ▲ 2 large plastic children's needles
- ▲ beads (optional)

Child's Level

This activity is most appropriate for older preschool or kindergarten children.

What to Look For

Children will be interested in seeing where their partner inserts the needle to return it to the other side.

Children will compare the needle placement with the size of the stitches.

Some children may plan together to create a specific effect.

Children will watch as the mural changes with each addition.

Modification

Try using a quilting hoop for a smaller group sewing frame.

Comments & Questions to Extend Thinking

Where would you put the needle to create a small stitch?

How do you think Riikka and Ben made this design?

There are beads on the left side, but no beads on the right side. Do you think it looks balanced?

Ask Mark if he'll push the needle through for you.

Integrated Curriculum Activities

Try making a class quilt (see activities 6.5, 6.6, and 6.7 for ideas).

At a later time, use the same frame for a group weaving project (activity 6.15).

6.5 Class Sampler Quilt

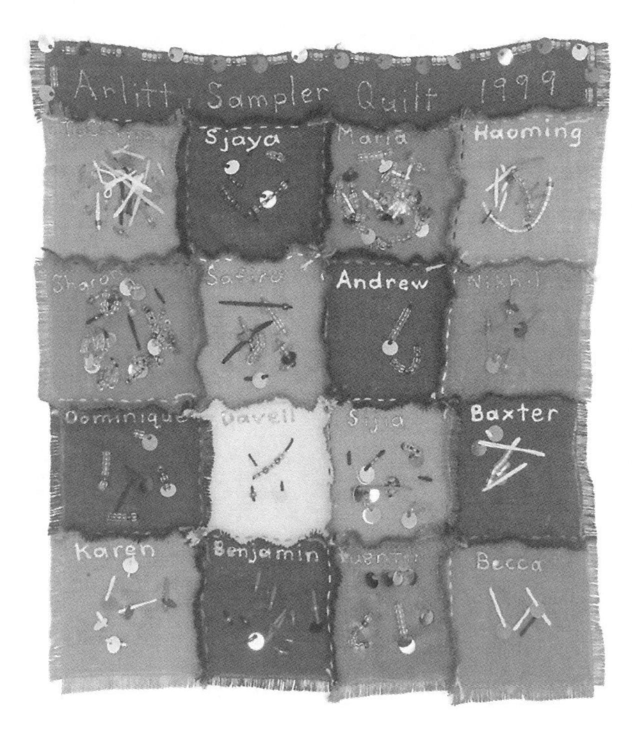

Description

Older preschool and kindergarten children often enjoy combining their artwork into a group project once they have made several individual creations. For this activity, each child stitches on a burlap square (see activities 6.2 and 6.3). Plastic beads and novelty beads are included in the sewing supplies. When each child has completed a square, the edges of each piece of burlap are frayed by pulling out several strands of burlap thread. The squares are then sewn together with the frayed edges facing upward to create a textured fringe border between each square. Individual names can be printed on each square with puffy paint. Teachers can document the process of making the quilt through photographs and children's dictations which can be mounted on poster board and laminated.

Helpful Hints

Look for novelty beads in craft stores. Be sure the large needle fits through the beads.

Art Experiences

- ▲ sewing
- ▲ stringing
- ▲ creating lines with stitches
- ▲ working with textures
- ▲ creating in three dimensions
- ▲ combining individual work into a group project

Materials

- ▲ colorful burlap, cut in 8-inch squares
- ▲ yarn, in assorted colors
- ▲ three 6-inch embroidery hoops
- ▲ 3 large plastic children's needles
- ▲ plastic pony beads, in bright colors
- ▲ novelty beads, such as fish, airplanes, trains, or animals

Child's Level

This activity is most appropriate for older preschool or kindergarten children.

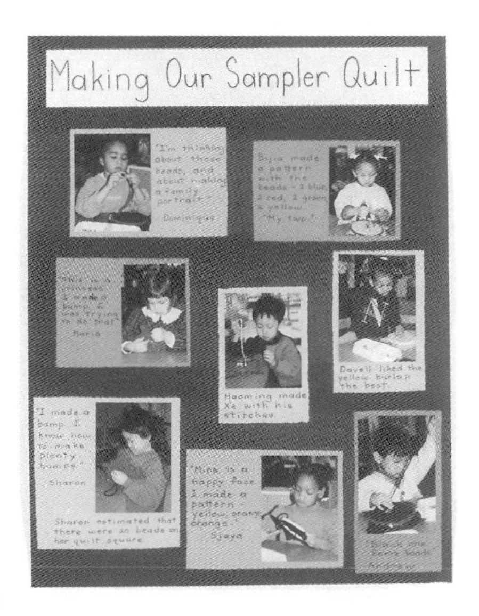

What to Look For

Children will compare colors of burlap and yarn as they work on their individual squares.

Children will talk about their creations with one another as they work.

Children will experiment with adding varying numbers of beads to their stitches.

Some children will notice that if they put several beads on their needle and take a small stitch, the beads make a little arc. They may attempt to reproduce this effect.

Some children will string long strands of beads before taking a stitch.

Some children will allot one bead to each stitch.

Modification

Kindergarten-age children may be able to help sew the quilt together by using long running stitches. Some classes may wish to continue adding squares to the quilt throughout the year.

Comments & Questions to Extend Thinking

Which color of square would look good next to this one?

Jane used lots of stitches and only a few beads; James used lots of beads and only a few stitches.

Tuukka has a story about what his airplane is doing on his quilt square.

What did you have to do to make a bridge for your train?

Integrated Curriculum Activities

Make other types of quilts with the children (activities 6.6 and 6.7).

Read quilt stories from many cultures. *Luka's Quilt*, by Georgia Guback (New York: Greenwillow, 1994), which is Hawaiian, and *The Quilt*, by Ann Jonas (New York: Greenwillow, 1984), which is African-American, are examples.

Include pictures of quilts, perhaps from a calendar, throughout the classroom.

Encourage children to share quilts or favorite blankets from home with the class.

Make a quilt math game by using quilt stickers for the grid boards and spools of thread for the counters (see *Much More Than Counting*, activity 6.11).

6.6 Class Story Quilt

Description

Traditional quilts from some cultures tell a story. For this group quilt, each child draws with fabric markers on a white cloth square. The squares are then sewn together, with colorful pieces of calico added between the white squares. Children love to revisit the story quilt and discuss their pictures with parents, guests, and one another. Some children may wish to dictate or write stories to accompany their quilt squares. The stories can be mounted along with photographs of the squares as further documentation of the process of making the quilt.

Story quilts have been made for many years by children at our school. Some children return years later and are delighted to once again be able to revisit their quilt.

Helpful Hints

Put a piece of paper under the cloth so the marker does not bleed through onto the table.

Art Experiences

- ▲ drawing on fabric
- ▲ combining individual work into a group project
- ▲ experimenting with color, line, shape, and form

Materials

- ▲ white cotton fabric, cut into 7-inch squares
- ▲ fabric markers, in assorted colors
- ▲ calico pieces, cut in 3½-inch squares
- ▲ calico rectangles, 7 by 3½ inches
- ▲ quilted fabric, for the back of the quilt
- ▲ quilt binding, to finish the edges

Child's Level

This activity is most appropriate for older preschool or kindergarten children.

What to Look For

Children will explore how the markers react on fabric as opposed to paper.
Children will tell stories as they draw.
Children will revisit their quilt to compare stories about their squares.

Modification

Younger children may also enjoy drawing on fabric. They require close supervision to ensure that they do not put the fabric markers in their mouths.

Comments & Questions to Extend Thinking

Is it easier to draw on cloth or paper?
Tell me about your quilt square.
Sharon says the person with dots has chicken pox.

Integrated Curriculum Activities

Read books that focus on the meaning behind some quilts. Examples are *Sweet Clara and the Keeping Quilt*, by Deborah Hopkinson (New York: Knopf, 1993), and *The Keeping Quilt*, by Patricia Polacco (New York: Simon & Schuster, 1988).
Put fabric in the art area for other types of activities. Children may wish to paint or glue on the fabric.
Add small quilts to the dramatic play area.
Design board games that have a quilt theme for the math area (see *Much More Than Counting*, activities 6.11, 7.11A, and 7.11B).

6.7 Class Family Quilt

Description

The idea for this quilt came from a parent. Each child is given a square of white felt to take home. The child and family work together to create a quilt square to bring back to school. They may choose to draw, paint, glue, or sew on the felt. The squares are then assembled into a class family quilt by spray mounting them onto quilted fabric. Ribbon scraps are scalloped around the edges of the squares and secured in place with a glue gun to provide a colorful border for each square. Finally, the name of each family is printed with puffy paint below the appropriate quilt square.

The class family quilt is a wonderful multicultural activity. Some families choose to include some aspect of their culture on their quilt square. Many families represent their family history or heritage. Examples that have appeared on our quilts include writing in other languages, African trade beads, Native American beadwork, and shells from the South Pacific.

Helpful Hints

Choose quilted fabric in a solid color for the background so that the quilt squares stand out.

Art Experiences

- ▲ creating on fabric
- ▲ working together to produce a group project
- ▲ family sharing

Materials

- ▲ white felt squares, 7 by 7 inches
- ▲ quilted fabric, large enough to hold all of the quilt squares mounted on it
- ▲ ribbon scraps, to use for borders around the squares
- ▲ spray mount
- ▲ glue gun
- ▲ puffy paint

Child's Level

This activity is appropriate for either preschool or kindergarten children.

What to Look For

Children will eagerly describe the squares they created with their families.

Children will discuss the different types of squares on the class quilt.

Children will return to the quilt again and again to look at their families' squares.

Modifications

Teachers may wish to invite families to share aspects of their cultures on the squares. This should always be presented as only one option. Families should never feel pressured into producing what the teacher wants.

If a family does not have any supplies at home to create a quilt square, the teacher might send markers or glue along with the quilt square for them to use if they choose.

Comments & Questions to Extend Thinking

How did your family produce these beautiful shades of paint?

How many different people worked on this square?

Erica's family found a way to draw and glue on her square.

Everyone started with a white square, but all of the squares look completely different from one another now.

Integrated Curriculum Activities

Read books about family quilts. *The Quilt*, by Ann Jonas (New York: Greenwillow, 1984), and *Before I Was Born*, by Harriet Ziefert (New York: Knopf, 1989), are good examples.

Put dollhouse furniture and small fabric samples in the block area.

Cut shapes from colored felt. Children can assemble them on a flannelboard to create quilt designs.

6.8 Stringing Pasta

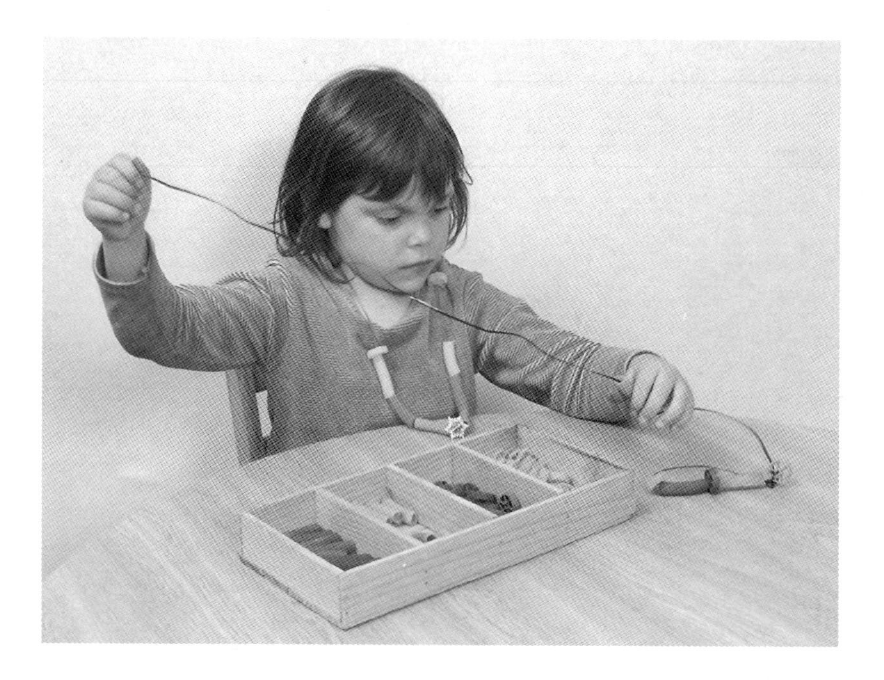

Description

Pasta with holes, such as rigatoni, penne rigate, ditalini, and wagon wheel, makes an interesting and inexpensive material for stringing activities. The pasta can be colored with food coloring diluted with water or alcohol. Teachers can vary the type of pasta depending on the ages and fine motor skills of their class. Rigatoni is large and easy to handle for young children. Wagon wheel pasta has lots of holes, which increases the success rate for young fingers trying to thread a cord through a hole. On the other hand, ditalini is much smaller and looks like beads. It provides a more challenging and appealing stringing medium for older preschool or kindergarten children. While penne rigate is long, it has a smaller hole than most rigatoni and is therefore more difficult for some children to string.

As with other art materials, children initially need time to explore stringing materials and develop competency in using them. Later, children often begin to create patterns and designs with the pasta as they explore its creative potential.

Helpful Hints

Tie a piece of pasta at the bottom of each string so that the pasta will not fall off the end of the cord as the children string.

Art Experiences

- ▲ stringing
- ▲ creating patterns and designs

Materials

- ▲ pasta shapes, colored with diluted food coloring
- ▲ plastic cord

Child's Level

This activity is appropriate for either preschool or kindergarten children, depending on the size of the pasta.

What to Look For

Children will place each type of pasta on the string to see how it looks.

Some children will select just one color of pasta to string.

Some children will have to learn the technique of pulling the string through the pasta and allowing the pasta to drop to the end of the string.

Some children will create patterns or symmetry with the colors or types of pasta.

Some young children will put the cord through the pasta and then pull it back out. They are curious about how the string moves in and out of the hole.

Modification

Vary the size of the pasta depending on the age of the class, as previously described.

Comments & Questions to Extend Thinking

Sahil put a group of red pasta together, then a group of blue pasta, and then a group of green pasta.

Where does the string come out?

Luke put a wheel, then a bead, then a wheel, then a bead. What do you think will come next?

Can you create a different pattern with these shapes?

Jessica's necklace is symmetrical. The colors on each side of the center bead are the same.

Integrated Curriculum Activities

Put beads for stringing in the manipulative area.

Use pasta and pipe cleaners for modeling on a Styrofoam base (activity 7.1).

Cook with pasta. Children can compare the texture of cooked and uncooked pasta.

6.9 Stringing Straws & Paper Shapes

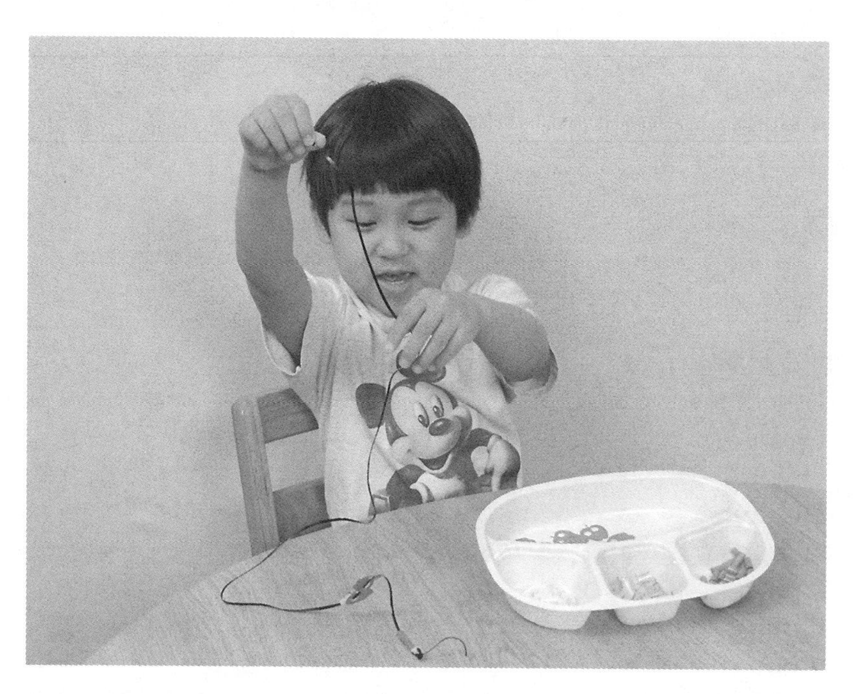

Description

Colored straws cut into small pieces provide an inexpensive but aesthetically pleasing stringing material. Children can combine the straw pieces with hearts or other shapes cut from paper. Two holes punched through the shapes allow them to hang flat when strung. Older children often create patterns with this activity.

Helpful Hints

You can quickly punch out many paper shapes using a design hole punch. They come in many varieties.

Art Experiences

- ▲ stringing
- ▲ creating patterns and designs

Materials

- ▲ colored straws, cut into small pieces
- ▲ shapes cut from paper, with two holes punched in each piece
- ▲ plastic cord

Child's Level

This activity is appropriate for either preschool or kindergarten children.

What to Look For

Some children will initially string the paper shapes through only one hole. This causes the shapes to bunch up rather than lie flat.

Some children will create alternating patterns with straws and paper shapes.

Modifications

Older children may wish to cut out their own paper shapes to use for stringing. They may also use design hole punches to create the shapes.

Teachers may wish to vary the paper shapes seasonally. Leaves, pumpkins, apples, snowflakes, and shells are some of the many shapes that can be easily cut with design hole punches.

Comments & Questions to Extend Thinking

What happens when you put the string through both holes on the heart?

How can you combine these straws and leaves?

Keith has two straws between each apple shape.

Integrated Curriculum Activities

Include design hole punches on the art shelf so children can create their own shapes.

Use sponges cut in various shapes for a painting activity (activity 5.20).

6.10 Stringing Buckeyes & Nuts

Description

Stringing nuts is a unique way of creatively exploring autumn materials. Teachers or parents can drill holes through the nuts with either an electric or hand drill. Children can then use the nuts for stringing.

Helpful Hints

Hold the nuts in a vise while drilling.

Art Experiences

- ▲ stringing
- ▲ creating patterns and designs
- ▲ creating with natural materials

Materials

- ▲ a variety of nuts, with holes drilled through them
- ▲ plastic cord

Child's Level

This activity is appropriate for either preschool or kindergarten children.

What to Look For

Children will compare the size, shape, color, and texture of the nuts as they string them.

Children will be surprised at how heavy nuts are when they wear their necklaces.

Some children will create patterns or designs with the nuts.

Modification

Some teachers may wish to combine the nuts with other stringing materials, such as natural-colored pasta. This helps extend the supply of nuts.

Comments & Questions to Extend Thinking

How does this nut feel?

Are there any other nuts that have circles on them like this buckeye?

Jamal alternated dark brown and light brown nuts on his necklace.

Adair put two small nuts after each large nut.

Integrated Curriculum Activities

Assemble a collection of nuts for sorting and classifying (see *More Than Counting*, activity 3.15).

Use nuts as counters for a math grid game (see *More Than Counting*, activity 4.5).

Include nuts and other natural materials on the art shelf for collage (activity 2.6).

Put nuts, buckets, and tongs on the sensory table.

Sing songs about nuts (see *More Than Singing*, activity 6.8).

6.11 Lacing Valentines

Description

Large hearts with holes punched around the edges provide a medium for lacing. Older children like to transfer sewing techniques to lacing around the edges of the hearts. Younger children may just like to thread ribbon in and out of holes randomly. The hearts can then be decorated with glitter, lace, or other materials from the art area of the classroom.

Helpful Hints

Tape a length of ribbon to each heart. This will keep the ribbon from unthreading as the children lace around the edges of the valentine.

Art Experiences

- ▲ lacing
- ▲ creating borders
- ▲ gluing

Materials

- ▲ large hearts, cut from wallpaper or construction paper, with holes punched around the edges
- ▲ ribbon, for lacing around the edges of the hearts
- ▲ 3 glue containers, with spreaders
- ▲ glitter, lace, sequins, and other collage materials

Child's Level

This activity is appropriate for either preschool or kindergarten children.

What to Look For

Some children will weave the ribbon in and out of the holes to create a border.
Some children will thread the ribbon up through each hole to create a whip-stitched border around the edge.
Some children will insert the ribbon randomly in the holes.
Children will decorate the hearts.

Modification

Some children may find the combination of lacing and gluing to be too complicated. For these children, substitute markers for the gluing portion of the activity.

Comments & Questions to Extend Thinking

I see two different lacing patterns. Annie went in and out of the holes, and Amit went up through each hole.
Can you use this ribbon to create a border?
What would you like to add to your valentine?

Integrated Curriculum Activities

Include hole punches and ribbon on the art shelf. Children may choose to create other lacing activities.
Use ribbon for weaving activities (activities 6.12, 6.13, 6.14, 6.15).
Include hearts for lacing on a valentine art shelf (activity 2.13).
Design heart or valentine math games (see *More Than Counting*, activities 4.10, 5.6, and 5.16).
Include books about mail delivery, such as *The Jolly Postman*, by Janet and Allan Ahlberg (New York: Little, Brown, 1986), and *A Letter to Amy*, by Ezra Jack Keats (New York: Harper Row, 1968), in the reading area.
Clap the word for friend in other languages as a rhythm activity (see *More Than Singing*, activity 3.3).

6.12 Weaving Plastic Baskets

Description

Plastic vegetable baskets make good frames for beginning weaving activities. There is no one correct way to weave with them. While older children may follow an in-and-out pattern as they thread ribbons or pipe cleaners through the baskets, younger children can maneuver the weaving materials in and out of the holes wherever they choose. Parents can save baskets for the class, thus providing a free resource.

Helpful Hints

Attach the pipe cleaners to the baskets for initial weaving experiences.

Art Experiences

- ▲ weaving
- ▲ creating in three dimensions

Materials

- ▲ plastic vegetable baskets
- ▲ pipe cleaners, in assorted colors
- ▲ narrow ribbon, about 12 inches long, in assorted colors

Child's Level

This activity is appropriate for either preschool or kindergarten children.

What to Look For

Some children will weave in and out of the holes on the baskets.

Some children will insert the pipe cleaners through the holes randomly.

Some children will hook the pipe cleaners onto the baskets at various angles to create sculptures.

Some children will create patterns with the pipe cleaners or ribbon.

Modification

Pipe cleaners are easy for young children to use. Older children may enjoy ribbons or yarn as weaving materials.

Comments & Questions to Extend Thinking

What can you do with these pipe cleaners and baskets?

Can you create a weaving pattern? In-and-out is one pattern. Here is a different pattern—over two, under one.

Integrated Curriculum Activities

Include vegetable baskets on the art shelf. Children can use them for weaving or modeling activities of their own design.

Look at a variety of types of woven fabrics.

6.13 Weaving with Potato Bags

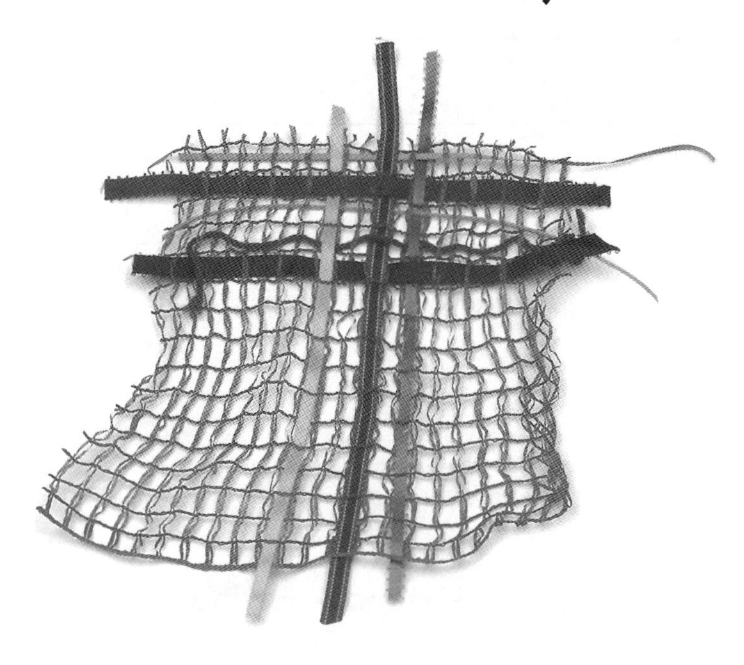

Helpful Hints

Ask parents and friends to save potato and onion bags.

Description

Net potato or vegetable bags provide a flat surface for children to use for weaving. The webbing has holes that are large enough for young children to easily thread ribbon, yarn, or colored cord through them. In addition, children can weave in two directions—horizontally or vertically.

Art Experiences

- ▲ weaving
- ▲ creating patterns and designs

Materials

- ▲ potato bags, cut in sections
- ▲ ribbon pieces, about 12 inches long
- ▲ yarn pieces, about 12 inches long
- ▲ colored cord, about 12 inches long

Child's Level

This activity is most appropriate for older preschool or kindergarten children.

What to Look For

Children will explore weaving the ribbon and yarn through the holes.

Some children will randomly insert the ribbon and yarn through the holes.

Some children will follow an in-and-out pattern as they weave with the materials.

Some children may develop other weaving patterns, such as over two, under one, especially if encouraged by the teacher.

Modification

Onion bags often have a tighter weave than potato bags. This may provide a more challenging weaving framework for older or more-experienced children.

Comments & Questions to Extend Thinking

Weave this yarn through the holes and see how it looks.

How did you decide which holes to put the ribbon through?

Audrey wove her green cord vertically and her red cord horizontally.

Can you think of another weaving pattern to try?

Can you go over two, under two? How do you like the way that looks?

Integrated Curriculum Activities

Read books about weaving, such as *Abuela's Weave*, by Omar S. Castaneda (New York: Lee & Low, 1993), and *Charlie Needs a Cloak*, by Tony Johnston and Tomie de Paola (New York: Putnam, 1985).

Set up a large weaving frame in the classroom for group weaving projects (activity 6.15).

Try weaving through the bars of the playground fence (activity 8.7).

6.14 Weaving Frames

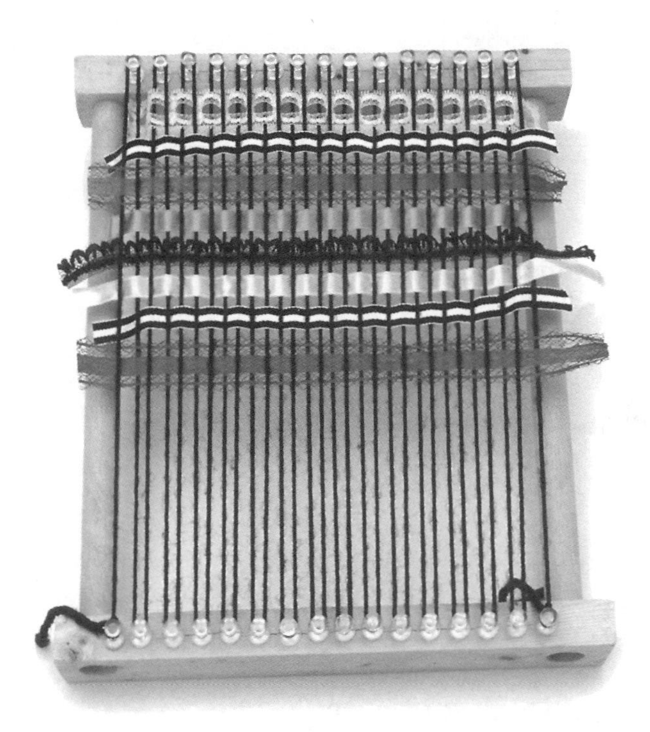

Helpful Hints

Ask parents to save ribbon scraps, lace pieces, and yarn. They are all good for weaving activities.

Description

Small wooden weaving frames are easy and inexpensive to make. Each frame consists of two strips of wood (9 by 1¼ inches) and two dowels (⅝-inch-diameter and 10 inches long). Drill a ⅝-inch hole near each end of the two strips of wood. Glue the dowels into the holes to form a rectangle, as pictured. Tap push tacks into the top edge of each wood strip at ½-inch intervals. Wind string around the tacks to form the warp threads for the weaving frame. Children can weave in and out of the strings to form the woof strands. The strings can be cut and tied as each child finishes his or her weaving.

Art Experiences

- ▲ weaving
- ▲ creating patterns and designs
- ▲ working with fibers

Materials

- ▲ 2 or 3 small wooden frames, as described above
- ▲ ribbon pieces, about 12 inches long
- ▲ yarn pieces, about 12 inches long
- ▲ colored cord, about 12 inches long

Child's Level

This activity is most appropriate for older preschool or kindergarten children.

What to Look For

Children will explore weaving the ribbon and yarn through the strings.

Some children will randomly insert the ribbon and yarn over and under the strings.

Some children will follow an in-and-out pattern as they weave with the materials.

Some children may develop other weaving patterns, such as over two-under one, especially if encouraged by the teacher.

Some children will be ready to learn weaving techniques such as reversing the over-under pattern on each row to produce a stronger weave.

Modification

For young children, start with wider materials to weave since they are easier to manipulate. Wide ribbon, thick yarn, and paper strips are possibilities. For older or more-experienced children, switch to narrower yarn, thin ribbon, or colored cord.

Comments & Questions to Extend Thinking

You can use these materials to make the cross strands of the weaving.

Can you make this red ribbon go over the strings that the blue ribbon went under?

Can you create a pattern with these three colors of yarn?

Integrated Curriculum Activities

Look at examples of weavings from various cultures with the children. The library may have books with good examples. Museums may have weavings on display.

Read books about weaving, such as *Abuela's Weave*, by Omar S. Castaneda (New York: Lee & Low, 1993), and *Charlie Needs a Cloak*, by Tony Johnston and Tomie de Paola (New York: Putnam, 1985).

Take a field trip to visit a weaver, if possible.

6.15 Group Weaving Frame

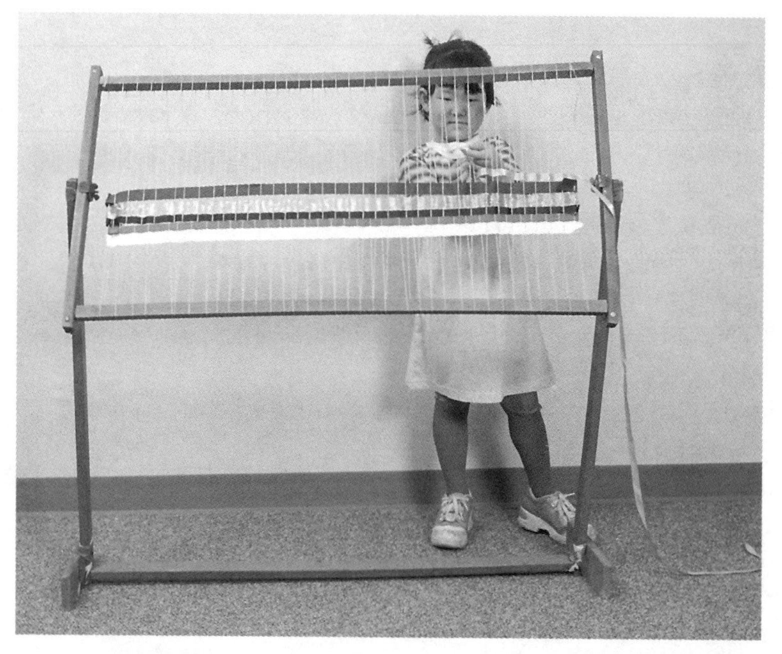

Description

For this project, a large wooden frame strung with string is left out in the classroom with a variety of weaving materials—yarn, ribbon, paper strips, fabric strips, lace, etc. Children can take turns adding to the group weaving in their own way. The frame is the same one described in activity 6.4. Instead of burlap, string is wrapped around the dowels to create the warp threads for the weaving.

Helpful Hints

When the weaving is finished, cut and tie the strings. The weaving can then be displayed.

Art Experiences

- ▲ weaving
- ▲ creating with fibers and textures
- ▲ creating patterns and designs
- ▲ working together on a group project

Materials

- ▲ large frame, as described above and in activity 6.4
- ▲ yarn, in assorted colors and thickness
- ▲ various types of ribbon
- ▲ long fabric strips
- ▲ lace

Child's Level

This activity is most appropriate for older preschool or kindergarten children.

What to Look For

Children will add to the group weaving in many different ways, depending on their level of development and their own creativity.

Children will discuss weaving patterns and techniques with one another.

Children will compare colors and textures in the group weaving.

Modification

Teachers may wish to limit the choices of weaving materials at first so that children are not overwhelmed. Additional materials can be added at intervals to stimulate renewed interest.

Comments & Questions to Extend Thinking

If Pat's yarn starts by going over the first string and under the second string, how should this next row start?

What color order should we use with this yarn?

Where would be a good place on the weaving for this special piece of lace?

We have a lot of wide strips at the bottom of the weaving. The strips get thinner near the top.

Integrated Curriculum Activities

Take photographs of the children weaving. Children can describe the weaving process, and the photos and comments can be displayed along with the weaving.

Put pieces of various types of woven fabric on the art shelf. Children can use them for gluing or for mixed-media creations.

6.16 School Quilt

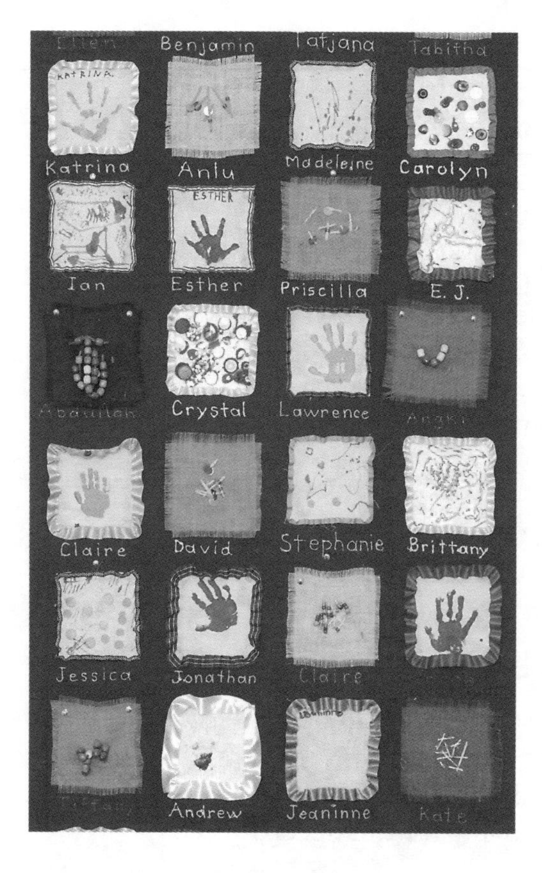

Description

Children who have seen class quilts hanging throughout their school may wish to combine their creativity in a school quilt. For this project, each classroom that wishes to participate selects a medium for expression—sewing, drawing on fabric, handprints, gluing, or painting. The squares are mounted on a large, navy blue sheet with spray mount. Ribbon pieces are scalloped around the edges of the squares and secured with a glue gun. Each child's name, color-coded by classroom, appears below the appropriate square. The school quilt makes a dramatic piece when hung in an entryway, a stairway, or on a large wall. Children revisiting the school for years to come will see their quilt.

Helpful Hints

Each child's name can be printed on the sheet with puffy paint.

Art Experiences

- ▲ drawing, painting, sewing, or gluing
- ▲ combining artistic creations to produce a large group project

Materials

- ▲ white cotton fabric, cut into 7-inch squares (for classes that choose to draw)
- ▲ white felt, cut into 7-inch squares (for classes that choose to glue)
- ▲ colored burlap, cut into 7-inch squares (for classes that choose to sew)
- ▲ see activity 6.5 for additional sewing materials
- ▲ see activity 6.6 for additional drawing materials
- ▲ one or more large navy blue sheets
- ▲ spray mount
- ▲ ribbon scraps
- ▲ glue gun

Child's Level

This activity is appropriate for preschool, kindergarten, and primary children. Each class can select a type of artwork appropriate for the developmental levels of the children.

What to Look For

Children will be amazed at the huge size of the school quilt.
Children will show their quilt squares to their families.
Children will talk with one another about their squares.

Modification

One sheet may not be large enough to hold all of the squares. Use as many sheets as necessary. The school could have a family celebration when the quilt is unveiled.

Comments & Questions to Extend Thinking

Can you tell which squares our class made?
How did Monica's class make their squares?
How many squares do you think there are on the quilt?
This quilt is as tall as the ceiling!

Integrated Curriculum Activities

Consider a field trip to a museum to look at other quilts.
Have a quilt party. Each child can bring his or her favorite quilt or blanket.

CHAPTER 7

Three-Dimensional Art

Peter was busy rolling note cards into tubes and taping them so that they would hold their shape. No one knew what he was up to, but he obviously had some master plan in mind as he diligently worked at his project. Soon he began to cut paper into various shapes, folding and bending it when necessary, and using prodigious amounts of masking tape. At last, he carefully taped the small cardboard tubes onto his creation. He then took his project to the block area and began flying it around to the admiration of his friends. He had made an almost exact replica of a Star Wars *spaceship.*

▲ ▲ ▲

Art is not limited to two dimensions. In order to fully explore their own creative potentials, children need materials and opportunities to create in three dimensions. As they explore the possibilities, children construct relationships about the relative strength of materials and how to adhere them in various positions. For example, glue holds cardboard together relatively easily on a flat, horizontal surface, but as Peter had already discovered in the above anecdote, tape works much better for vertical construction.

Some children create more naturally in three dimensions than in two. Thus, teachers may notice that some children construct elaborate block structures long before they can draw representationally. Other children may create complex drawings but seldom build. When teachers include three-dimensional art activities in their planning, all children have the opportunity to create in unique ways.

Teachers' Questions

What are three-dimensional art activities?

Three-dimensional art activities are activities that enable children to explore length, width, and depth. Many typical art activities are two-dimensional. Children draw, paint, or glue on a flat surface. Three-dimensional art activities extend the creative process beyond the flat surface through materials and techniques that allow spatial representations. Modeling with clay or playdough, manipulating wire and pipe cleaners, working with boxes and tubes, and creating mobiles are some of the three-dimensional art activities that children can explore.

Why is it important to encourage children to create in three dimensions?

Extending art beyond two dimensions opens new possibilities for creative expression. Some children seem to create naturally in three dimensions. They respond quickly to the possibilities presented by modeling or building materials. Other children may be more accustomed to drawing or painting. Creating with alternative types of art media extends their thinking as they experiment with the materials and attempt symbolic representations with them.

Three-dimensional art activities also encourage children to construct new knowledge about the properties of materials. Clay, playdough, silly putty, and wire all respond differently to children's manipulations. While glue easily holds paper on a flat surface, it may prove inadequate for a project that includes boxes, tubes, corks, and plastic containers. Working with different types of art materials encourages children to ponder new approaches to solve creative problems.

How do children's explorations of three-dimensional art possibilities change with development?

As with other art materials, children start by experimenting with the materials and observing how they react. The process of interacting with the materials takes precedence over attempting to create a specific form with them. Children who have reached the developmental stage of creating representational forms with art or building materials may begin to produce recognizable products once they have developed sufficient skill in using the materials. Some children may name their creations after they have already made them because the form or shape of the creation reminds them of something. This is similar to children naming their scribbles before they reach the stage of actually setting out to draw a specific object.

What types of three-dimensional art activities can young children explore?

Children can model with materials such as clay or playdough; create sculptures with wire or other bendable materials; explore movement and balance through mobiles; construct with boxes and a variety of found materials; and transform existing materials, such as melting plastic cups into unique configurations. Clay and playdough activities encourage children to use their hands to manipulate and mold the materials and to experiment with particular tools and techniques unique to each substance. Work with wire challenges children to create interlocking lines and forms with materials that are only straight lines to begin with. Experimenting with mobiles encourages children to think about balance, spacing, and movement. Using boxes and other found materials as art media allows children to build unique structures and preserve their creations. Transforming familiar materials, such as layering colored salt in jars or melting plastic cups, enables children to view traditional materials in new ways. Each type of activity enhances learning and creativity in its own way.

Why is working with clay important?

Clay provides tactile stimulation for young children, strengthens their finger and hand muscles, and lends itself to a range of creative endeavors. Young children are naturally drawn to the sensory stimulation of clay. It satisfies the urge to play with something that is messy yet can be controlled. The cool, damp plasticity of clay is calming to many children. Clay provides a firmer resistance to touch than playdough and requires children to exert pressure from many different muscles as they manipulate it, thus helping to strengthen their fingers, hands, and arms. The unique ability of clay to hold the form imposed on it encourages many children to sculpt with it.

What type of clay should teachers purchase?

Teachers can either purchase clay that has to be fired in order to preserve the artwork or self-hardening clay. Clay that is not self-hardening is labeled by its firing temperature. Clay labeled 06-04 is considered desirable for use by children. This clay is inexpensive and responsive to modeling but must be heated at very high temperatures in a kiln in order to preserve the product. Fired clay can be glazed and then fired again. Self-hardening clay does not have to be heated, but is more expensive. It can be painted with watercolors. Teachers who do not have access to a kiln may choose to use regular clay for daily modeling activities that will not be saved and self-hardening clay for special projects that will be kept. Approximately one pound of clay is needed per child.

What types of clay activities should teachers begin with?

Teachers should begin with activities that encourage children to manipulate the clay with their hands. A lump of malleable clay on a tray is an ideal first encounter. As children poke and prod the clay, they discover the properties of clay. They can focus on how the clay feels and responds to their touch. Children may experiment with a variety of types of movements and watch how the clay reacts to pressure from different body parts, such as an elbow, a forearm, a fist, or a finger. These beginning experiences allow children to construct essential knowledge about clay, which they can refine later when they begin to use tools with clay.

What techniques are unique to working with clay?

Coiling, creating pinch pots, and using slip are the three standard techniques used in working with clay. Knowledge of these techniques is helpful for young children as it increases their ability to create with clay. *Coiling* involves rolling pieces of clay between the palms of the hands or across a flat surface to create long "worms." The coils can be layered to create pots or other structures. This traditional clay technique has been used for thousands of years in many cultures. Another clay technique involves forming a *pinch pot*. A lump of clay is held in the hand while the thumb pokes a hole in it. The clay is squeezed and rotated to the desired size and shape. Pinch pots can form the base of a variety of forms, from animals to bowls to people. A final technique involves the use of *slip*, or very wet clay, to hold pieces of clay together at the connections. Teachers can model these techniques and allow children to experiment with them. Children can use the techniques to produce their own unique creations with clay.

What tools are appropriate to use with clay?

Many common objects make useful tools to use with clay. A piece of fishing line works well to cut clay. Dowels or small rolling pins can be used to flatten clay. Toothpicks, wooden craft sticks, combs, and coffee stirrers make useful devices for carving clay. Many objects can be used to make imprints on clay. Leaves, beads, pastry wheels, shells, and lace are some of the many possibilities. Potato mashers cut clay into interesting shapes, while garlic presses transform it into long tendrils, like hair.

How can teachers keep clay from drying out?

Store clay along with a moist sponge in a tightly sealed plastic bag. The moisture from the sponge keeps the clay from drying out without becoming too wet and sticky. Clay may begin to dry out as children are working with it. This frustrates children because the clay becomes hard to manipulate and breaks apart. To keep clay moist while children are using it, supply moist paper towels that children can use sparingly to dab the clay. Bowls of water should be avoided. Children cannot resist adding more and more water to the clay, and the clay quickly dissolves.

What other types of modeling media should children use?

Playdough and silly putty are interesting modeling media for children. Clay, playdough, and silly putty are all very different from one another. Playdough is much easier to manipulate than clay. While it holds its form better than silly putty, it is not as strong as clay for modeling and sculpting. However, playdough works well with molds and cookie cutters and is interesting to use with tools such as potato mashers and garlic presses. Silly putty, on the other hand, stretches and flows but does not retain its shape. It is fascinating to watch as it assumes the shape of its container. Children like to watch silly putty ooze and snip it with scissors. Activities for clay, playdough, and silly putty are included in this chapter.

Why should teachers include wire as an art material?

Wire allows children to focus on the use of line in art as they explore the properties of metal. Modeling with wire also increases children's finger dexterity. With the possible exception of pipe cleaners, wire has traditionally not been used as an art material with young children in the United States. However, educators are impressed with the way children create with wire in the Reggio Emilia schools in Italy. Their success has encouraged early childhood teachers in other countries to also incorporate wire into the art curriculum.

What types of wire should teachers use for art experiences with children?

Many types and gauges of wire are appropriate for art experiences. Brass, copper, and steel wire are all readily available at hardware, building supply, and craft stores. Plastic-wrapped wire is also interesting for children to explore. Wire gauge is determined by the thickness of the wire; the higher the number of the gauge, the thinner the wire. Wire gauges of 14 to 28 are appropriate for young children to manipulate. Children quickly discover that thicker wire, such as 14 gauge, is harder to bend than thinner wire. Activities 7.1, 7.2, 7.3, 7.4, and 7.5 incorporate wire.

Where can teachers find materials for three-dimensional art activities?

Teachers can use found objects, natural materials, and parent donations. Boxes, tubes, film containers, spools, lids, bottle caps, and Styrofoam packing material provide excellent raw material for children's creations. Leaves, pine cones, sticks, nuts, stones, and shells make interesting impressions in modeling substances. Parents can contribute many of the materials teachers need for implementing three-dimensional art activities. A request list posted on the classroom door keeps the wished-for items fresh in parents' minds.

What is the teacher's role in implementing three-dimensional art activities?

The teacher's role is to ask leading questions that encourage children to experiment, discover, and create. Children are natural explorers, so they are typically eager to experiment with new art materials. However, the teacher's questions may help children construct relationships between what they are doing with a material and how the material is responding. For example, children may not notice that glue sticks to a plastic film container while paint does not. The teacher's questions may encourage children to try colored glue on places where paint does not work.

Teachers may also occasionally model techniques for working with special materials, such as clay. Demonstrating a technique is very different from modeling the creation of a product and may serve to scaffold a child's introduction to a new material. Rather than limiting the child's experience, it may supply the knowledge needed for the child to proceed with unique applications and creations.

How can teachers assess children's use of three-dimensional art materials?

Teachers can document the process, as well as any products created, through anecdotal notes, photographs, and children's comments. Photographs, along with children's comments, can be preserved in a memory book of each child's school experiences. They can also be mounted on poster board and displayed in the classroom or hallway. This is a good way to document the art process.

Three-Dimensional Art Activities

7.1 Styrofoam Sculptures

Description

Children use Styrofoam sheets as a base for these fanciful sculptures. They can insert toothpicks; coffee stirrers; pipe cleaners; and wire, twisted and bent into myriad shapes, into the Styrofoam. Children can add a wide array of other objects to their designs: pasta with holes, pieces of tissue paper, lace, and beads, to name a few. All of these materials are held in place by the wires and toothpicks. While some children delight in experimenting with colors and shapes, others may create towns, amusement parks, or imagined scenes from outer space.

Helpful Hints

Styrofoam sheets can be purchased in craft stores. Or ask parents to save Styrofoam packing material. Styrofoam plates are not thick enough to serve as a base.

Art Experiences

- ▲ creating three-dimensional designs
- ▲ working with wire
- ▲ experimenting with color, form, and shape

Materials

- ▲ Styrofoam sheets or blocks, for bases
- ▲ colored toothpicks
- ▲ copper, brass, or steel wire, in various gauges
- ▲ pipe cleaners, in various colors
- ▲ colored pasta

- ▲ beads
- ▲ lace
- ▲ tissue paper, cut or torn into pieces

Child's Level

This activity is most appropriate for older preschool or kindergarten children.

What to Look For

Children will experiment with bending the wire and pipe cleaners and poking them into the Styrofoam.

At first, some children will not realize that both ends of the wire or pipe cleaners can go into the Styrofoam.

Children will gain ideas for their creations by experimenting and by watching others.

Children will discuss their designs and create stories about them as they work.

Modification

For younger children, eliminate the toothpicks and wire as a safety precaution. Select larger objects that they can easily fit onto the pipe cleaners.

Comments & Questions to Extend Thinking

How can you secure these beads to the Styrofoam using just the materials we have here?

What other shapes can you make with the wire?

John put all of his toothpicks in one area of his Styrofoam.

Molly says she made a rainbow with the pipe cleaners.

Integrated Curriculum Activities

Add large Styrofoam pieces and pipe cleaners to the block area. Children can add imaginative designs to their block structures.

Include pipe cleaners and colored pasta as a woodworking accessory. Children may choose to wrap pipe cleaners around the nails they hammer.

7.2 Basket Sculptures

Description

In this activity, children can bend or weave pipe cleaners and wire through the webbing of plastic vegetable or fruit baskets. Additional materials with holes, such as spools, beads, pasta, or lace, are included. The baskets create a three-dimensional base for the creations. Imaginations can run wild with this activity.

Helpful Hints

Grocery stores may be willing to donate vegetable baskets or sell them at a nominal price. Parents can save them for your class.

Art Experiences

- ▲ working with wire
- ▲ creating in three dimensions
- ▲ experimenting with line, shape, and form

Materials

- ▲ plastic vegetable baskets
- ▲ pipe cleaners, in various colors
- ▲ copper, brass, or steel wire, in various gauges
- ▲ spools
- ▲ beads
- ▲ pasta
- ▲ lace

Child's Level

This activity is most appropriate for older preschool or kindergarten children.

What to Look For

Children will experiment with bending the wire and pipe cleaners.

Some children may initially stick the pipe cleaners through the holes without bending them. Leading questions may help them discover properties of wire that enable them to use it more creatively.

Some children may use the pipe cleaners to make handles for their baskets and then decorate the baskets.

Modification

To simplify the activity, start with just pipe cleaners. Various types of wire can be added later.

Comments & Questions to Extend Thinking

How can you attach the pipe cleaners to the basket?

Can you change the shape of the pipe cleaner?

Where do you want these beads to go on your sculpture?

Show Charlie how to keep his pasta wheel from falling off.

Joshua made a bead maze with a different kind of bead on each path.

Integrated Curriculum Activities

Put bead mazes in the manipulative area. They may encourage children to create their own mazes with the beads and pipe cleaners.

Add vegetable baskets and pipe cleaners to the art area after children have used them as a special activity.

7.3 Wire Explorations

Description

This activity introduces children to wire modeling. It includes a variety of types of wire for children to explore. Although wire has not been one of the traditional materials used with young children in the United States, it has gained prominence as an art medium for children through its incorporation in the Reggio Emilia schools in Italy. The beginning explorations of wire in this activity form the basis for later sculpturing with wire (activity 7.4).

Helpful Hints

Look for wire in hardware or building supply stores. Ask parents to bring in extra pieces of wire, such as cords from broken appliances.

Art Experiences

- ▲ creating with wire
- ▲ experimenting with line and shape
- ▲ creating new forms

Materials

- ▲ copper, brass, and steel wire (in assorted lengths, but not longer than 12 inches)
- ▲ plastic-wrapped wire (not longer than 12 inches)
- ▲ wire in various gauges (14–28 gauge)

Child's Level
This activity is most appropriate for older preschool or kindergarten children.

What to Look For
Children will experiment with bending the wire into various shapes.
Children will compare how easily various types of wire bend.
Some children will create specific forms with the wire.
Children will discover how to join pieces of wire together.

Modification
Start with relatively short pieces of wire (no longer than 12 inches). Longer pieces may easily become tangled and frustrate inexperienced children. Later, wire of varying lengths can be added.

Comments & Questions to Extend Thinking
Which wire is the easiest to bend?
Does the coated wire bend?
Can you make a circle with the wire? A square?
How can you attach two pieces of wire together?
This green piece of wire doesn't seem to stay bent as well as this copper piece.

Integrated Curriculum Activities
Put a lap harp in the music area. Children can pluck the metal strings (see *More Than Singing*, activity 5.16).
Add wire to the woodworking area. Children can bend the wire around nails after they hammer them into the wood.

7.4 Wire Sculptures

Description

After children have had some experience exploring wire, they may begin to create with it. This activity includes a variety of types of wire, but also incorporates dowel pieces for children to bend the wire around to create coils. Other metallic objects are available to add to the sculptures.

Art Experiences

▲ creating with wire
▲ experimenting with line, form, and shape
▲ working with three-dimensional forms

Helpful Hints

If the wire is sharp after it has been cut, quickly sand the ends with sandpaper.

Materials

▲ copper, brass, and steel wire (in assorted lengths, but not longer than 12 inches)
▲ plastic wrapped wire (not longer than 12 inches)
▲ wire in various gauges (14–28 gauge)
▲ springs
▲ steel wool
▲ metal washers and nuts
▲ flip tops
▲ paper clips
▲ short dowel pieces or spools, in several diameters
▲ wire cutters (for the teacher's use)

Child's Level

This activity is most appropriate for older preschool or kindergarten children.

What to Look For

Children will explore the characteristics of the various types of wire.
Children will experiment with wrapping the wire around dowel pieces or spools to create coils.
Some children will be challenged to create wire sculptures without the use of a base plate (as in activity 7.1).
Some children will attempt to create representational forms with the materials.
Some children will use the wire to make jewelry.

Modification

Use shorter pieces of wire for children who have not had many experiences creating with wire. Shorter pieces are easier to manipulate.

Comments & Questions to Extend Thinking

Show Takuo how to twist the pieces of wire together to make a longer piece.
Connie wants to use steel wool for hair. Does anyone have any ideas about how she can attach the steel wool to her wire circle?
How can you make the flip top stay in one place and not slide down the wire?

Integrated Curriculum Activities

Read the book *Galimoto*, by Karen Lynn Williams (New York: Lothrop, 1991), to the class. A young boy makes marvelous toys out of wire.
Use wire for other art activities (activities 7.1, 7.2, 7.3, and 7.5).
Use Slinkies as a rhythm instrument. Children can play the beats of a song on the Slinkies by stretching them apart and then clicking them back together (see *More Than Singing*, activity 6.5).

7.5 Modeling Goop Creations

Description

Modeling goop provides a secure base for this modeling activity. Children bend wire pieces and pipe cleaners into fanciful shapes and insert the ends into a lump of teacher-made goop. Children can also add tubular pasta, straw pieces, and sequins to their creations. The goop hardens as it dries to preserve the sculptures.

Modeling Goop Recipe
1 ½ cups cold water
2 cups salt
1 cup cornstarch

Boil ⅔ cup water and salt. Mix cornstarch and remaining water (⅓ cup plus ½ cup). Stir well until a smooth liquid forms. Add salt mixture to cornstarch mixture and stir. Return to pan and heat at a moderate temperature until the mixture clumps together. Cool slightly and knead. Keep covered. Mixture will harden in several hours.

Helpful Hints

The recipe makes enough modeling goop for about eight children.

Art Experiences

▲ creating with wire
▲ working in three dimensions
▲ experimenting with line, shape, and form

Materials

▲ modeling goop base
▲ 3 trays to work on (1 per child)
▲ pipe cleaners
▲ wire pieces, cut from copper, brass, and steel wire (14–28 gauge)
▲ tubular or circular pasta (colored with food coloring, diluted with water)
▲ straws, cut into small pieces
▲ sequins

Child's Level

This activity is appropriate for either preschool or kindergarten children.

What to Look For

At first, children will explore sticking the pipe cleaners into the goop.
Children will experiment with bending the wire and pipe cleaners to create new shapes.
Children will add a variety of auxiliary pieces to their creations.
Some children will group the pasta by color on the pipe cleaners.
Some children will create patterns with the pasta and straw pieces.
Children will be excited to see the goop harden.

Modification

For young children, use just pipe cleaners and pasta at first since they are easier to handle.

Comments & Questions to Extend Thinking

Will these sequins fit on the pipe cleaners?
What materials do you want to use on your sculpture?
We're going to leave the sculptures on the shelf overnight and see how they look and feel tomorrow.
Rachel put all wheel-shaped pasta on this pipe cleaner.
The straw pieces can move across the arc made by this wire.

Integrated Curriculum Activities

Ask children for suggestions for other materials to use on their sculptures.
Write down the children's comments about their sculptures. These can be mounted and displayed along with photographs that illustrate the process of creating the sculptures.

7.6 Tubes & Boxes

Description

This activity includes a variety of small boxes and cardboard tubes for children to glue or tape onto a cardboard base. A collection of found objects, such as spools, film containers, bottle caps, and tape dispenser rings, fuels eager imaginations. Children can paint their creations when they finish.

Helpful Hints

Shallow cardboard boxes left behind when soda pop machines are filled are perfect for the bases.

Art Experiences

- ▲ designing three-dimensional structures
- ▲ gluing and taping
- ▲ experimenting with form and shape

Materials

- ▲ heavy cardboard, for the bases
- ▲ small boxes
- ▲ paper tubes
- ▲ film containers
- ▲ spools
- ▲ corks
- ▲ bottle caps and lids
- ▲ 3 glue containers, with spreaders
- ▲ tape
- ▲ tempera paint (optional)

Child's Level

This activity is appropriate for either preschool or kindergarten children.

What to Look For

Children will build using the boxes and tubes like blocks.
Some children will randomly place items on the base.
Some children will plan specific structures.
Some children will tell or write stories to accompany their creations.
Children will discover that some of the materials balance while others do not.
Children will learn that some things have to be held with tape rather than glue.

Modification

For younger children, use materials that can be held in place with glue. Combining both glue and tape in the same activity may be overwhelming at first.

Comments & Questions to Extend Thinking

What can you do with all these things?
How did you get this box to balance on top of this tube?
David says he's making a town.
If the glue won't hold your film container in that position, do you see anything else that might?

Integrated Curriculum Activities

Encourage interested children to write or dictate stories about their creations.
Let interested children take their structures to the block area after they have dried. They may wish to incorporate them into their block play.
Put large boxes in the gross-motor area for building.
Sing a song about building, and add each child's name and type of box structure to the song (see *More Than Singing,* activity 7.1).

7.7 Painting Pumpkins

Description

Small gourd pumpkins provide an interesting three-dimensional surface for children to decorate with acrylic paint. Many children are accustomed to carving pumpkins. Painting pumpkins is a different way to explore them creatively.

Helpful Hints

Buy several extra pumpkins. Usually at least one pumpkin rots before it can be used.

Art Experiences

- ▲ painting
- ▲ working on a three-dimensional surface
- ▲ creating with natural materials

Materials

- ▲ 1 small pumpkin or gourd pumpkin per child
- ▲ several colors of acrylic paint
- ▲ small portion cups, to hold the paint
- ▲ small watercolor or cosmetic brushes
- ▲ 3 trays to work on (1 per child)
- ▲ smocks

Child's Level

This activity is appropriate for either preschool or kindergarten children. However, since acrylic paint is permanent, an alternative paint choice may be appropriate for younger children.

What to Look For

Some children will paint stripes on the pumpkins to correspond to the grooves.
Some children will paint stripes in patterns.
Some children will paint faces or other shapes on the pumpkins.
Many children will want to cover the entire surface of their pumpkin with paint.

Modification

Acrylic paint is used in this activity because it is permanent and will adhere to the pumpkins. For young preschoolers, mix 1 part sugar to 2 parts liquid tempera paint to create a washable paint that will not crack and fall off the pumpkins when it dries.

Comments & Questions to Extend Thinking

Is the pumpkin smooth or bumpy?
This pumpkin has stripes—red-green-black, red-green-black. What color do you think will come next?

Integrated Curriculum Activities

Put pumpkins and gourds in the water table. Children can scrub them with small brushes.
Set up a produce market in the dramatic play area.
Take a trip to a pumpkin farm to see how pumpkins grow. Make a graph with the children's predictions before the trip (see *More Than Counting*, activity 6.6).
Estimate the number of grooves on a pumpkin (see *Much More Than Counting*, activity 3.4).
Read books about pumpkins. *Pumpkin, Pumpkin*, by Jeanne Titherington (New York: Greenwillow, 1986), is a good choice.

7.8 Painting Flowerpots

Description

Just as painting pumpkins is interesting and apropos in autumn, so is painting clay flowerpots in the spring. Children can paint the pots with acrylic paint. They can then add dried flower arrangements or bedding plants to the pots. Children can also plant seeds in the pots.

Helpful Hints

Be sure the paint has dried thoroughly before children add flowers or seeds to the pots.

Art Experiences

▲ painting
▲ working on a three-dimensional surface
▲ creating with natural materials

Materials

▲ 1 small clay flowerpot per child
▲ several colors of acrylic paint
▲ small portion cups, to hold the paint
▲ small watercolor or cosmetic brushes
▲ 3 trays to work on (1 per child)
▲ smocks
▲ dried flowers, bedding plants, or soil and seeds

Child's Level
This activity is appropriate for either preschool or kindergarten children. However, since acrylic paint is permanent, an alternative paint choice may be appropriate for younger children.

What to Look For
Some children will paint randomly on the pots.
Some children will paint designs or specific figures on the pots.
Some children will want to cover their entire pot with paint.

Modification
Acrylic paint is used in this activity because it is permanent and will adhere to the clay pots. For young preschoolers, mix 1 part sugar to 2 parts liquid tempera paint to create a washable paint that will not crack and fall off the pots when it dries.

Comments & Questions to Extend Thinking
Is the pot rough or smooth?
How does it feel to paint on clay?
I see a purple border around the top of this pot.

Integrated Curriculum Activities
Plant several types of seeds and compare how they grow.
Read books about flowers. *Flower Garden*, by Eve Bunting (New York: Harcourt, 1994), is a good choice.
Make a flower garden math manipulative game. Use tiny wooden flowerpots and plastic flowers for the counters (see *Much More Than Counting*, activity 5.7).
Put dried flower petals or potpourri on the art shelf for collage.

7.9 Playdough Explorations

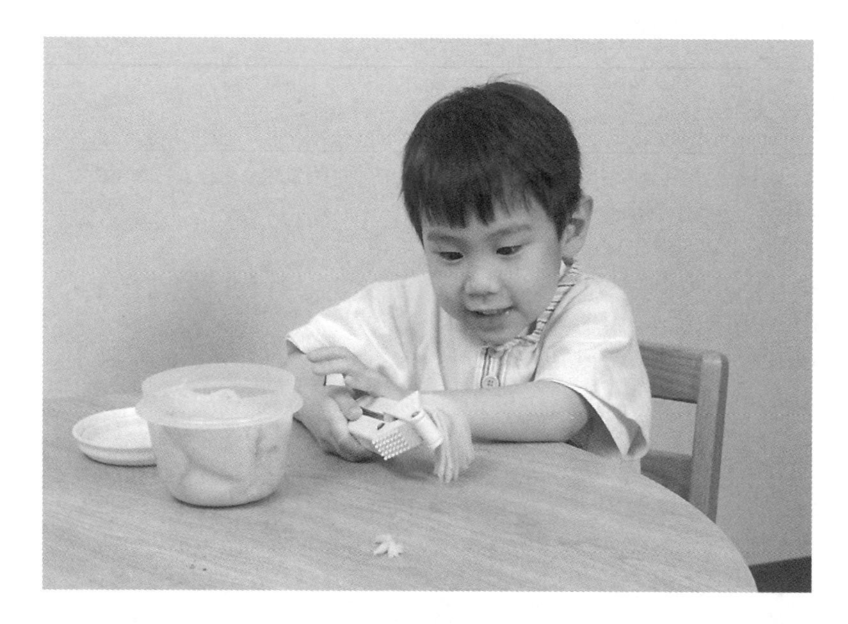

Description

As with all art materials, children need opportunities to explore a medium before they create with it. This playdough activity shows a variety of tools that children can use to experiment with playdough. Garlic presses, potato mashers, pastry wheels, and rollers are some of the possibilities.

Helpful Hints

Playdough can be easily colored with food coloring. Add food coloring to the water before mixing the ingredients.

This playdough does not need to be refrigerated.

Playdough Recipe
2 cups flour
2 cups water
1 cup salt
3 tablespoons cream of tartar
2 tablespoons oil

Mix all ingredients and cook over medium heat until the batter clumps together. Cool the playdough and knead.

Art Experiences

- ▲ modeling
- ▲ using tools with a modeling medium
- ▲ creating in three dimensions
- ▲ making imprints

Materials

- ▲ 4 trays (1 per child)
- ▲ 4 containers of playdough
- ▲ 4 rollers (small rolling pins or dowels)
- ▲ 4 pastry wheels, garlic presses, or potato mashers

Child's Level

This activity is appropriate for either preschool or kindergarten children.

What to Look For

Children will manipulate the playdough with their fingers.

Children will experiment to discover how each implement affects the playdough.

Children will describe what is happening with the playdough and create stories as they play.

Modification

Do not use all of the tools at once. Start with the rollers and gradually add new tools as the children become accustomed to each of the implements.

Comments & Questions to Extend Thinking

What does the roller do to the playdough?

How can you make the playdough into a ball?

How did you make the playdough look like spaghetti?

What do you think will happen if you push on the playdough with this potato masher?

I wonder how Greg made all of these triangular shapes look exactly alike.

Integrated Curriculum Activities

Use some of the same tools, such as pastry wheels and potato mashers, as painting or printing implements.

Use the potato mashers to mash potatoes for a cooking activity.

7.10 Playdough Molds & Impressions

Description

Playdough is an ideal medium to use with molds. It holds its shape when cut with cookie cutters or pressed into containers. Children derive endless satisfaction from rolling the dough, cutting it into shapes, or molding it to fit a container. Children can create designs and patterns on the playdough by making impressions with straws, wooden craft sticks, golf tees, buttons, shells, and an endless assortment of small objects.

Helpful Hints

Store the playdough in tightly covered plastic containers. It does not need to be refrigerated.

Art Experiences

- ▲ modeling
- ▲ using molds
- ▲ creating imprints

Materials

- ▲ 4 containers of playdough (see activity 7.9 for the recipe)
- ▲ 4 trays (1 per child)
- ▲ 4 rollers (small rolling pins or dowels)
- ▲ cookie cutters, small molds, or small containers
- ▲ straws, craft sticks, golf tees, buttons, or shells, to create imprints

Child's Level

This activity is appropriate for either preschool or kindergarten children.

What to Look For

Children will roll out the playdough and cut it into shapes with the cookie cutters.

Inexperienced children may try to cut the playdough with the cookie cutters before they roll it flat.

Children will experiment to see if the playdough holds its shape after they remove it from a mold.

Children will use the various implements to create impressions in the playdough. In the process, they will construct the relationship between the shape of the tool and the impression it makes in the playdough.

Modifications

Do not use all of the materials at once. Start with the rollers and cookie cutters and switch to molds on another day.

Introduce objects to create impressions sparingly so children can construct the relationship between each individual object and the shape it makes in the playdough.

Comments & Questions to Extend Thinking

What do you think will happen to the playdough if you pull it out of the star mold?

Bill used the straw to put little circles on his playdough.

What kind of mark do you think the golf tee will make in the playdough?

Can you tell which shell made this impression?

Integrated Curriculum Activities

Use the cookie cutters to bake cookies.

Put a bakery in the dramatic play area.

Use cookie cutters as printing tools with paint (activity 5.17).

Put molds with wet sand on the sensory table.

7.11 Clay Explorations

Description

Children need opportunities to explore clay with their hands before they use tools with it. Otherwise, they tend to focus on the tools rather than the clay. This activity introduces children to two traditional techniques used in clay modeling. Teachers can describe and demonstrate these techniques while children experiment on their own. The first technique, *coiling,* involves rolling the clay between the palms of the hands or against a flat surface to produce "worms." These coils can be layered to create pots or larger structures. In the *pinch pot* technique, a ball of clay is held in one hand while the thumb of the other hand pushes a hole into it. The clay can be rotated and pinched to create a larger hole. Children can use these two techniques later when they begin to sculpt with clay.

Helpful Hints

If the clay starts to dry out and becomes hard to work with, dab it with a moist paper towel. Don't allow children to add water to the clay as it will quickly dissolve.

Store clay in a heavy plastic bag with a wet sponge. Squeeze out the air before sealing.

Art Experiences

- ▲ modeling with clay
- ▲ creating in three dimensions
- ▲ exploring a tactile medium

Materials

- ▲ 4 lumps of clay (about 1 pound per child)
- ▲ 4 trays
- ▲ smocks
- ▲ moist paper towels, to dab the clay if it begins to dry out

Child's Level

This activity is appropriate for either preschool or kindergarten children.

What to Look For

Children will push and pull the clay with their hands.
Children will create impressions in the clay with their fingers, knuckles, elbows, and arms.
Children will talk about the way the clay feels.
Some children will create representations with the clay.
Children will experiment with creating coils and pinch pots.

Modification

Young children may need additional time to experiment with the clay before coiling and pinch pot techniques are introduced.

Comments & Questions to Extend Thinking

Andy says he made a snake.
How does the clay feel?
What happens to the clay when you roll it between your hands?
Can you make a ball and put your thumb into it? How do you make the hole bigger?
What can you do to the clay to make it flat?

Integrated Curriculum Activities

If possible, visit a potter so the children can see how artists work with clay.
Include *Earth Daughter*, by Joseph Ancona (New York: Simon & Schuster, 1995), in the reading area. Vivid photographs show an Acoma Pueblo girl working clay with her hands.

7.12 Clay Sculptures

Description

Children naturally begin to sculpt with clay once they have had some experiences with it. This activity introduces some standard tools useful in working with clay: toothpicks, craft sticks, small combs, and fishing line for cutting the clay. Teachers who have access to a kiln can fire the sculptures, closely supervise children while they glaze them, and fire the sculptures again. Children whose clay will be fired will need some instruction on using *slip* to hold the parts of their sculpture together. Slip is very wet clay. The points of connection must be scratched with a toothpick and brushed with water (creating slip) to adhere the parts together. Children who use self-hardening clay can paint it with watercolors once the clay has thoroughly dried.

Art Experiences

- ▲ modeling with clay
- ▲ using tools with clay
- ▲ painting
- ▲ exploring a tactile medium
- ▲ working in three dimensions

Materials

- ▲ firing clay (06-04) or self-hardening clay
- ▲ 4 trays
- ▲ smocks
- ▲ toothpicks

Helpful Hints

If you don't have access to a kiln, check with a local high school, recreation center, or potter to see if they would be willing to fire the children's clay.

Let clay dry at least a week before firing.

Store clay in a heavy plastic bag with a wet sponge. Squeeze out the air before sealing.

- ▲ craft sticks
- ▲ small combs
- ▲ fishing line

Child's Level

This activity is most appropriate for older preschool or kindergarten children.

What to Look For

Children will experiment with manipulating the clay.
Some children will create representational forms with the clay.
Children will use the available tools to cut, score, or make impressions in the clay.
Some children's clay will not hold together when fired. Additional experience will be necessary.

Modification

A wide assortment of objects can be used with clay. Introduce new implements periodically. Pastry wheels, pizza wheels, pieces of chain, beads, pieces of screen, garlic presses, and jewelry are some of the many materials that can be used to cut clay or create imprints.

Comments & Questions to Extend Thinking

What happens to the clay when you push this screen down on it?
Julie wants to use a garlic press to make hair for her person.
What do you have to do to make long strands come out of the garlic press?
Do you want to attach this handle to the basket? Scratch the ends with a toothpick and mush it together with slip.

Integrated Curriculum Activities

Let children press clay onto a variety of surfaces to see what impressions they will make.
Take photographs of the children working with clay to document the process.
Bring samples of various types of soil into the classroom for children to compare tactilely. Sand, potting soil, and clay all feel very different.

7.13 Clay Tiles

Description

Children can apply their experiences in working with clay to creating clay tiles. An endless variety of styles is possible. Children start by smoothing the clay flat with a roller. They can then add patterns and designs to the clay by pressing various objects into it. Leaves and shells make interesting impressions, as do lace, beads, chains, and many more found objects. The edges of the clay can be cut to create tiles of the desired shape: rectangular, square, hexagonal, etc. The teacher may need to help with this. The clay can then be allowed to dry. It can be fired if it is not self-hardening clay. Depending on the type of clay, children can either paint or glaze their tiles.

Helpful Hints

Teachers may wish to cut out the center of the tiles before the clay is fired or hardens to create picture frames. Be sure the clay is not too thin after it is rolled out or it may easily crack. Don't roll the clay all the way to the edge.

Art Experiences

- ▲ working with clay
- ▲ creating impressions in clay
- ▲ experimenting with a tactile medium

Materials

▲ firing clay (06-04) or self-hardening clay
▲ 4 trays
▲ smocks
▲ rollers (small rolling pins or dowels)
▲ objects to create impressions (as described above)
▲ glaze or paint (optional)

Child's Level

This activity is most appropriate for older preschool or kindergarten children.

What to Look For

Children will smooth the clay with the rollers.
Children will experiment with the variety of impressions they can make in the clay.
Some children will create patterns or designs in the clay.
Some children will mold the clay with their hands rather than trying to create tiles.

Modification

Plan many opportunities for children to experiment with making impressions in clay before creating tiles.

Comments & Questions to Extend Thinking

Can you make the clay flat and smooth with the roller?
What impressions do you want to put in the clay?
Sanjay used a chain to make a border around his tile.
What shape do you think this strand of beads will make in the clay?

Integrated Curriculum Activities

Consider a field trip to a tile store. Children can look at the many different kinds of tiles.
Children may wish to combine their tiles to cover part of a wall.

7.14 Silly Putty Sensations

Description

Silly putty behaves very differently as a modeling substance when compared to either playdough or clay. Since silly putty does not retain its shape, it is not useful for sculpting. On the other hand, it is a fascinating tactile material. Children love to snip it with scissors, try to smash it down, watch it stretch into long tendrils, and observe it as it oozes into molds or across a tray.

Helpful Hints

Try to keep the silly putty off the children's clothes and hair. Dab liquid starch on the silly putty to remove it from clothes or hair.

Silly Putty Recipe
1 cup liquid starch
2 cups Elmers glue (regular, not school glue)

Gradually add the glue to the starch, and knead. If the silly putty is too sticky, add a little more starch. Refrigerate when not in use.

Art Experiences

- ▲ exploring tactile materials
- ▲ cutting
- ▲ using molds

Materials

- ▲ 4 containers of silly putty
- ▲ 4 trays
- ▲ smocks
- ▲ 4 pairs of scissors
- ▲ various types of molds

Child's Level

This activity is appropriate for either preschool or kindergarten children.

What to Look For

Children will stretch the silly putty.

Children will discover that the silly putty is easy to snip with scissors.

Children will experiment with putting silly putty into molds.

Children will discover that although silly putty takes the shape of the container it is in, it does not retain the shape when removed from the mold.

Modification

Start with just silly putty, scissors, and molds. Later, add marbles or other materials to create impressions in the silly putty. Children will notice that the silly putty does not retain the impression once the object is removed.

Comments & Questions to Extend Thinking

Look what happens to the silly putty when you hold it and let part of it drop.

What happens to the silly putty when you take it out of the mold?

Your silly putty is oozing off the tray.

How does the silly putty feel?

Integrated Curriculum Activity

Use some of the implements with silly putty that children have already used with playdough. They can compare how the two substances react.

7.15 Fiberfill Modeling

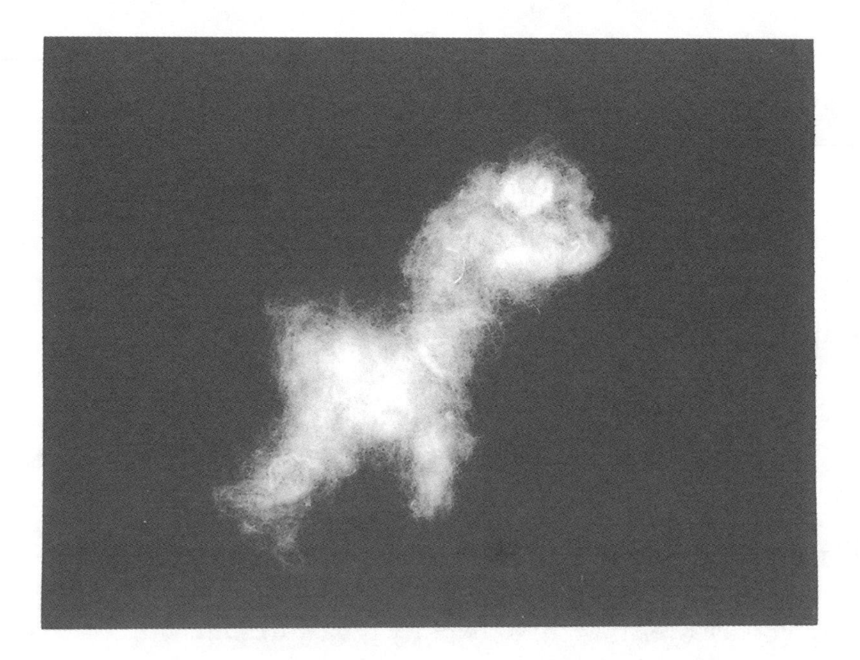

Description

Many children delight in the book *It Looked Like Spilt Milk*, by Charles G. Shaw, and the many forms clouds can take. In this activity, children can form and reform fiberfill into a variety of shapes and then glue it to dark construction paper to preserve the shapes.

Helpful Hints

Inexpensive fiberfill is available at fabric and craft stores.

Art Experiences

- ▲ modeling
- ▲ creating with three-dimensional materials
- ▲ gluing

Materials

- ▲ bag of fiberfill
- ▲ dark construction paper
- ▲ 4 glue containers, with spreaders
- ▲ 4 trays

Child's Level

This activity is most appropriate for older preschool or kindergarten children.

What to Look For

Children will pull the fiberfill and watch how it reacts.
Some children will attempt to form shapes with the fiberfill.
Some children will name the shapes they make with the fiberfill after they see what they look like.

Modification

Younger children may want to use the fiberfill as a collage material. It is soft and feels very different from many of the materials they typically use with glue.

Comments & Questions to Extend Thinking

What shapes can you make with the fiberfill?
Sometimes it looked like a _______.
How can you preserve the shape of the fiberfill?

Integrated Curriculum Activities

Read *It Looked Like Spilt Milk,* by Charles G. Shaw (New York: Harper, 1947), to the class.
Put white pom-poms in blue water in the sensory table. Children can fish them out with tongs.
Make cloud pictures by putting white paint on dark blue construction paper and letting the children blow the paint with straws (activity 5.13).
Sing songs about clouds (see *More Than Singing,* activity 2.8).

7.16 Pasta Mobiles

Description

Mobiles are three-dimensional art forms that move. For this activity, children use dowels, wire, and colored pasta to create mobiles. They can experiment with balance as they add pieces to their creations.

Helpful Hints

Invest in wire clippers. Although scissors will cut the wire, they will soon become damaged.

Art Experiences

▲ creating mobiles
▲ experimenting with shape, color, and balance
▲ creating with wire
▲ exploring movement

Materials

▲ 1-inch-diameter dowels, cut in 4-inch lengths, with two ¼-inch holes drilled through them so that the holes are perpendicular to each other (1 dowel piece per child)
▲ two 12-inch lengths of ¼-inch-diameter dowel inserted through the holes on each 1-inch-diameter dowel
▲ thin-gauge wire (22–26 gauge)
▲ colored pasta in a variety of shapes (rigatoni, penne rigate, rotelle, wagon wheel), colored with a mixture of food coloring and water
▲ screw eyes or cup hooks to attach to the top of each mobile

Child's Level

This activity is most appropriate for older preschool or kindergarten children.

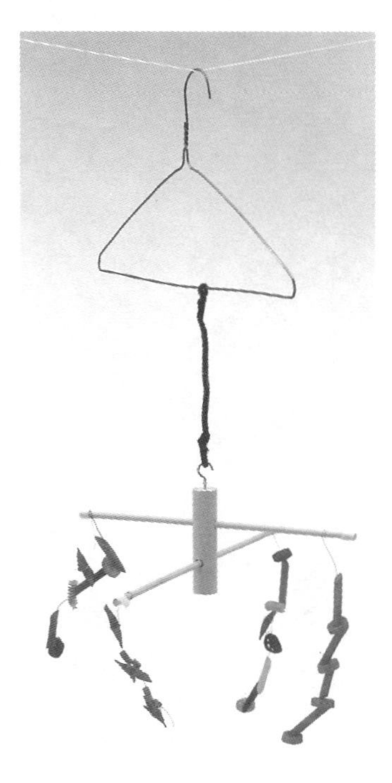

What to Look For

Children will string the pasta or bend the wire around the pasta to hold it.

Children will attach strands of pasta to the dowels.

Children will experiment with the positioning of the dowels and pasta to see how they affect the balance of the mobile.

Some children will create patterns with the pasta.

Modifications

Use large pasta and pipe cleaners for younger children if they have trouble manipulating the wire.

Older children can attach additional pieces of dowel to their mobiles with wire to create more complex mobiles.

Comments & Questions to Extend Thinking

How will you decide where to put the different kinds of pasta on your mobile?

If you hang more pasta on this side, will it still balance?

What happens if you move the dowel?

When the door opened, your mobile moved. Why do you think that happened?

Integrated Curriculum Activities

Put a balance scale in the science area along with a basket of nuts. Children can see what happens as they add or subtract nuts from the two sides of the scale (see *More Than Magnets*, activity 3.9).

Put wind chimes in the music area. Children can use a fan or bellows to make them move.

7.17 Layered Salt Jars

Description

In this activity, children first color salt or white sand on paper plates by rubbing colored chalk across it. As they finish with each color, they pour the salt into clear jars and observe the layers, lines, and patterns that emerge.

Helpful Hints

Ask parents to save baby food jars or other types of jars for this activity.

Art Experiences

- ▲ creating in three dimensions
- ▲ experimenting with lines and layers
- ▲ creating colors

Materials

- ▲ 4 trays (1 per child)
- ▲ salt or white sand
- ▲ colored chalk
- ▲ clear jars, with screw-on lids (baby food, olive, or peanut butter jars)
- ▲ paper plates

Child's Level

This activity is most appropriate for older preschool or kindergarten children.

What to Look For

Children will be surprised to see the salt or sand change color as they rub it with chalk.

Children will notice layers developing each time they add another color of sand to their jar.

Some children will comment on the lines created between each layer.

Some children will shake their jars so that all the sand blends together!

Modification

After children have had an initial experience creating layered salt or sand, provide jars of various sizes and shapes. Children can watch how the layers unfold in jars of varying dimensions.

Comments & Questions to Extend Thinking

What is happening to your salt as you rub it with chalk?

What color would you like to use next?

Is the line straight or crooked between the layers?

What would you have to do to make a thin layer?

There is more purple sand on this side of the jar, but more green sand on the other side of the jar.

Integrated Curriculum Activities

Use colored salt for a gluing activity. Children can shake it from salt shakers or apply it with tiny spoons (activity 4.8).

Make maracas out of clear plastic jars for the music area. Use three different fillers (sand, rice, and beans) so children can compare how the different fillers affect the sound (see *More Than Singing*, activity 5.4).

Put sand and iron filings on the sensory table. Children can search for the filings with magnetic wands (see *More Than Magnets*, activity 2.15).

7.18 Light Catchers

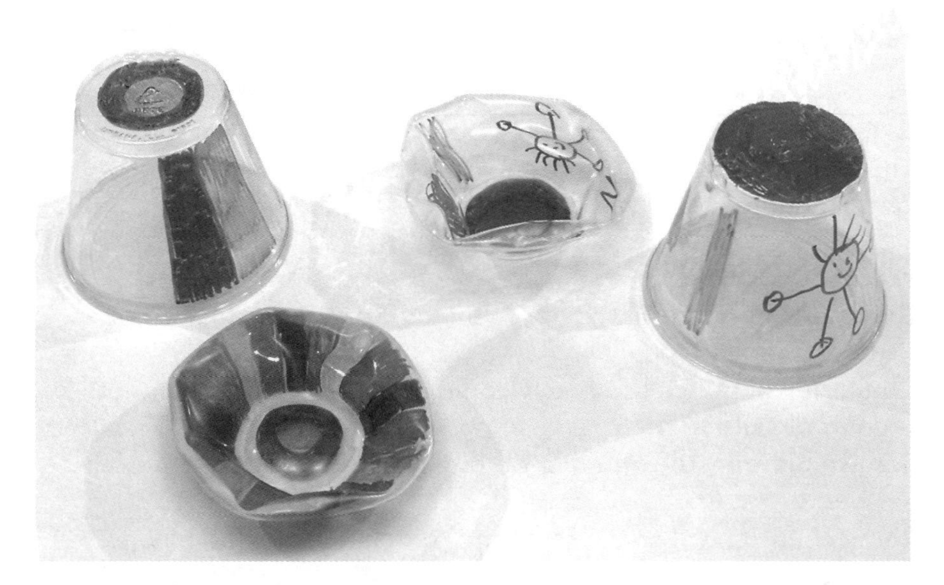

Description

This activity allows children to observe the changes that occur when heat is applied to clear plastic cups. Children start by decorating the cups with permanent markers. Then the teacher melts the cups in a toaster oven. The resulting shapes are quite interesting. The light catchers can be hung in windows to capture the light.

Helpful Hints

Use a hole punch to poke a hole in each cup before it is melted. The hole provides a means for hanging the light catcher.

Art Experiences

- ▲ creating with color
- ▲ observing the effects of heat on shape and dimension

Materials

- ▲ 4 trays
- ▲ clear plastic cups
- ▲ several colors of permanent marker
- ▲ smocks
- ▲ toaster oven
- ▲ aluminum foil (to cover the grill in the oven)
- ▲ tongs (helpful when removing the melted cups from the oven)

Child's Level

This activity is appropriate for either preschool or kindergarten children, with close adult supervision.

What to Look For

Children will decorate the cups in a variety of ways.

Children will be amazed at the unusual shapes the cups take as they melt.

Children will comment on the changes in the placement of their colors and designs on the melted cups.

Modification

Young children can use regular watercolor markers, but the colors will not be permanent even after the cups have been melted.

Comments & Questions to Extend Thinking

I wonder where this red circle on the top of your cup will be after we heat it.

What is happening to the cup?

How do you think this flower you drew will look after the cup melts?

What shape does the cup have now?

How do you like the way the colors on your light catcher look when the light shines through it?

Integrated Curriculum Activities

Explore colors in other ways. Children can glue colored cellophane onto clear cellophane and hang their creations in the windows.

Put color paddles in the science area.

Let children build with transparent colored Duplos. Set their creations near a window so they can watch the light come through them.

Read books about color-mixing, such as *Color Dance*, by Ann Jonas (New York: Greenwillow, 1989).

Sing a song about colors as children dance with colored scarves (see *More Than Singing*, activity 6.14).

Outdoor Art

A large sheet of white paper stretched across the fence of the outdoor playground. Lined up in front of it, children in paint smocks sprayed colored water onto the paper and watched the colors make trails down the paper. As children eagerly traded bottles of red, yellow, and blue water, they watched their group creation constantly change color and hue. Some children excitedly pointed out to one another that they had changed blue into purple or yellow into green. One little girl said that she had made the sunrise. Other children just squirted and squirted and squirted.

▲ ▲ ▲

The outdoor area allows children to explore art materials in ways that would be impossible inside. Management issues, such as dripping water or tracking paint, cause less concern. Art activities that require a large amount of space, such as pendulum art or large group murals, are much easier to organize outside. The art area also allows children to create in an environment that is aesthetically very different from the typical indoor environment. Children can watch the clouds, feel the breeze, or bask in the sun as they create. They have much more freedom of movement. Introducing art into the outdoor area also gives children more choices for using their outside time.

Teachers' Questions

Why should teachers encourage art in outdoor areas?

Outdoor art activities often attract children who are less likely to participate in art activities indoors. Children who gravitate towards more active areas of the classroom and seldom initiate art activities are sometimes the first to be attracted to art activities outside. By introducing art into areas where more active children feel comfortable, teachers help engage them in a greater variety of activities. The opportunity for children to participate in a type of activity they often avoid, while in an area of the environment where they feel comfortable, may translate into future use of the art area inside.

Planning art activities for the outside area increases the variety of experiences that children can have in that environment. Unfortunately, planning for outside experiences often becomes sterile. Activities may become relegated to the same tricycles, climber, and sandbox. By introducing activities into the outdoor area that are typically planned for indoors, teachers may spark renewed interest in the art activities and generate more possibilities for outside play.

The outdoors has a unique ambiance that may stimulate creativity in children. They may translate the feel of the sun or wind into their artwork. At the very least, children notice the effect that the elements have on their art materials. The breeze quickly dries paint while the sun softens the crayons.

What types of art activities are especially suited for outdoors?

Art activities that require more freedom of movement, and therefore more space, are ideal for outside areas. Experiences that encourage more interaction with nature are also well suited to outdoor environments. Some activities are much easier to supervise outside. Foot painting, spraying colored water, and making bubble prints are examples of art activities that are relaxing and enjoyable in an outside environment but may be difficult to manage inside. Art activities with strong tie-ins to nature, such as coloring the snow or painting with natural paintbrushes, are well suited to the outdoors. Children may find additional materials in nature to contribute to their creations, such as new items to use as painting tools.

Should traditional indoor activities ever be moved outside?

Art activities that are typically set up in the classroom often acquire new interest when moved outdoors. Common materials, such as markers and paper, seem to take on a new life outside. Children often gather in bunches to draw and may explore new themes, such as depicting children on climbers or tricycles. Watercolors, crayons, chalk, and glue all seem to spark children's interest when relocated to the outside area.

What outside spaces work best for outdoor art activities?

Areas that are removed from high-traffic areas work best. A small table in a shady part of the playground is a nice addition. A standard easel can be located in a corner of the outside area. Some easels attach to the fence. Large paper for murals can be clipped to a fence or taped to the side of the building. Natural elements quickly erase any stray traces of paint or chalk. Children often become hot and uncomfortable sitting in the sun, so shady areas are ideal.

How do children respond to outside art activities?

Children are usually excited and eager to participate. Some art activities are highly unusual, so children are naturally intrigued. While children may have experimented with ramps and pendulums indoors, in the outside area they can paint with them. Children can draw on the pavement with sidewalk chalk, while they can never write on the floor indoors. On certain days, they may dip their feet in paint and hop around on paper to make tracks. There is a certain freedom to art in the outdoors that is often not possible inside.

What should teachers consider when setting up outside art activities?

Teachers should have all the materials ready ahead of time, perhaps in bins or on trays, so that they can be easily transported outside. Sometimes art activities can be set up outside before the children arrive. Paper may need to be taped to the table or weighted down so that it doesn't blow away. Teachers should plan ahead for a water source. If there is no water available outside, it can be carried out in buckets. Finally, teachers should decide where to hang the finished art projects while they dry. Some teachers may move a drying rack to the outside area, while others may decide to tape finished pictures to the fence. As with all activities involving young children, outdoor art activities progress much more smoothly if careful preparation is made ahead of time.

How often should teachers plan activities for outside areas?

Some teachers plan art activities for the outside area several times a week during nice weather. Art activities do not need to be elaborate. Teachers can transfer a special activity to the outside area or take a few materials from the art shelf outside. On special occasions during the winter, such as after a fresh snowfall, art activities may be planned for the outside. Spraying the snow with colored water or sculpting with snow are natural outgrowths of a snowy day.

How can teachers assess children's use of outside art materials?

Outdoor art activities may provide teachers with the opportunity to document the art experiences of children who do not typically engage in art activities in the classroom. As with other art experiences, teachers can take anecdotal notes that specifically record children's use of materials, including hand preference, type of hand grasp, and stage of drawing or representation. Teachers can further document art experiences through photographs. Children may wish to comment on the activity when they see the photograph, or write or dictate their thoughts about the artwork.

Outdoor Art Activities

8.1 Spray Bottle Painting

Description

Children are fascinated with watching colors combine to produce new colors. In this activity, children spray a large piece of paper with bottles of water tinted with red, blue, or yellow food coloring. The paper is attached to the fence. As the colors overlap, new colors emerge. Children can also observe the movement of the water down the paper. They can work individually on a section of the mural or team up to combine their colors.

Helpful Hints

Have extra water and food coloring ready to refill the bottles. Children go through the water quickly.

Art Experiences

- ▲ spray painting
- ▲ combining primary colors
- ▲ working together on a group project

Materials

- ▲ large piece of paper, attached to a fence or wall
- ▲ 3 to 6 spray bottles, filled with water tinted red, blue, or yellow with food coloring
- ▲ smocks

Child's Level

This activity is appropriate for either preschool or kindergarten children.

What to Look For

Children will initially be fascinated with watching the water come out of the bottle.
Children will watch the colors combine to produce new colors.
Some children will alter the spray mechanism on the bottles to change from mist to a stream.
Children will discuss with one another the way the colors look.
Some children will remember the colors produced by various color combinations.

Modification

Substitute easel paper for mural paper if children wish to have a picture to take home.

Comments & Questions to Extend Thinking

How can you make the water come out of this bottle?
What happened when the yellow went on top of the blue?
What would you have to do to make purple?
I see orange where that red stream of water went over the yellow section, and purple where it went over the blue part.
This part reminds me of sunrise.

Integrated Curriculum Activities

Use tiny spray bottles to repeat the experience at the inside easel.
Let children draw with crayons and then spray colored water over the picture (activity 3.14).
Create a bottle scale for the music area by filling bottles to varying depths with colored water (see *More Than Singing*, activity 5.15).
Add basters and small balls to the water table. Children can squirt the balls with water to make them move (see *More Than Magnets*, activity 4.10).
Read books about color-mixing, such as *Mouse Paint*, by Ellen Stoll Walsh (New York: Harcourt, 1989).

8.2 Natural Paintbrushes

Description

Painting outdoors provides an ideal opportunity to explore natural materials used as painting tools. Although the teacher should have some materials already planned, children may find others to experiment with. The objects used for painting tools may include thistles, pine bows, sticks, and long grass. Each makes a unique brush stroke. Children can paint at an easel or attach their paper to the side of the building. Initially, only one color of paint should be used so that the children can focus on the type of mark made by each implement rather than on the colors of paint.

Helpful Hints

Tape around the stem of the thistle so that children don't prick their fingers.

Art Experiences

- ▲ painting
- ▲ experimenting with unique brushes

Materials

- ▲ 4 jars of tempera paint (1 color)
- ▲ dishes or trays, to hold the paint (1 for each painting station)
- ▲ thistles, pine bows, sticks, and long grass (or other natural materials), to use as painting tools
- ▲ smocks (one for each painting station)

Child's Level

This activity is appropriate for either preschool or kindergarten children.

What to Look For

Children will experiment with the natural painting tools.
Children will comment on the various strokes or imprints made by each material.
Some children will begin to use specific materials to create particular effects once they have had experience using them.
Children may find additional items to use as painting tools.

Modification

Using only one color of paint helps children focus on the strokes made by each implement. Switch to a variety of colors of paint for subsequent experiences.

Comments & Questions to Extend Thinking

What kind of mark does the thistle make?
What could you use to create a thick line?
The pine branch made lots of lines at once.

Integrated Curriculum Activities

Use natural paintbrushes to create a group mural.
Put natural maracas in the music area. Dried gourds, lotus pods, and locust pods make interesting maracas (see *More Than Magnets*, activity 6.10).
Take a nature walk to find natural materials for the art shelf. Children may find materials to use for collages as well as new painting tools.

8.3 Weed Painting Mural

Description

Children use a variety of types of weeds to paint this group mural. The painting is done on a horizontal surface (either the ground or a large table) so that the children can more easily examine the tracings made by the various types of weeds.

Helpful Hints

Have an extra supply of weeds handy. They may get soggy in the paint and need to be replaced.

Art Experiences

- ▲ painting
- ▲ experimenting with natural materials as paintbrushes
- ▲ working together on a group project
- ▲ combining colors to make new colors

Materials

- ▲ large piece of paper
- ▲ red and yellow paint
- ▲ weeds, to use as paintbrushes
- ▲ smocks

Child's Level

This activity is appropriate for either preschool or kindergarten children.

What to Look For

Children will carefully examine the marks made by the various weeds.

Children will notice that the yellow and red paint combine to create orange where they overlap.

Children will experiment with the materials and comment on the results.

Modification

Red and yellow were selected as paint choices because they combine to produce a new color. For subsequent experiences, switch to other primary colors, such as yellow and blue, or red and blue.

Comments & Questions to Extend Thinking

Which weed makes a wide mark?

What should I use to make a thin line?

How did you get orange on the paper? There's no orange paint!

Integrated Curriculum Activities

Let children experiment with color-mixing in ice cube trays. They can use eyedroppers to combine red, yellow, and blue water.

Read *We're Going on a Bear Hunt*, by Michael Rosen (New York: Simon & Schuster, 1989). Children will enjoy the description of moving through weeds.

Put weeds at the easel to use as painting tools so that children can also make individual pictures.

8.4 Feather Duster Mural

Description

In contrast to the mural painted with weeds in activity 8.3, this project is painted on a vertical surface. Children use feather dusters dipped in paint to create the mural. The use of feather dusters on a vertical surface encourages large arm movements. The paint choices are black and white, used on a light blue paper. Children can observe how the black and white paint combine to create shades of gray.

Helpful Hints

Look for feather dusters in dollar stores or discount stores.

Art Experiences

- ▲ painting with large movements
- ▲ using feather dusters as brushes
- ▲ combining black and white paint
- ▲ working together on a group project

Materials

- ▲ 6 feather dusters (3 children can paint at a time)
- ▲ 3 bowls each of black and white tempera paint (1 set per child)
- ▲ large piece of light blue paper, clipped to a fence or taped to a wall
- ▲ smocks

Child's Level

This activity is appropriate for either preschool or kindergarten children.

What to Look For

Children will notice the unique marks created by the feather dusters.

Children will use large arm movements.

Children will observe the shades of gray produced when the black and white paint combine.

Modification

On subsequent occasions, use white paint with another color of paint. Children can observe the shades created when white is mixed with other colors.

Comments & Questions to Extend Thinking

What marks will these feather dusters make with the paint?

Is there any way to make just one line with the feather duster?

What happens when the white and black mix on the paper?

I see dark gray on this part of the paper, and light gray over here. How did you make the different shades?

Integrated Curriculum Activities

Let children experiment with white and gray in other art materials, such as chalk or crayons.

Take photographs of the classroom using black and white film. Children can look for shades of gray in the photos.

Explore shadows with children. They can look for light and dark areas.

Put feathers on the art shelf for collage.

Watch feathers float in the air. Then encourage the children to move like feathers.

8.5 Tracks

Helpful Hints

Have a bucket of water and washrags ready next to the paint area to clean children's feet.

Description

Children are fascinated with making footprints, and this activity gives them the opportunity to experiment with the various marks they can create. The teacher paints the bottom of each child's feet, one child at a time, so that they can walk across a long strip of paper and observe their footprints. Then they move to a large sheet of paper, where they can hop, tiptoe, glide, jump, or dance as they mingle their tracks. Children can step into a tray of paint to recoat their feet when necessary.

Art Experiences

- ▲ making tracks
- ▲ painting with feet
- ▲ working together to create a group project

Materials

- ▲ long strips of paper, for making tracks
- ▲ large sheet of mural paper, for dancing feet
- ▲ jar of tempera paint and paintbrush

- ▲ small chair, for children to sit in as their feet are painted
- ▲ tray with tempera paint spread across the bottom

Child's Level

This activity is appropriate for either preschool or kindergarten children.

What to Look For

Children will be excited about the tactile feeling of the paint on their feet.

Children will examine the marks created by their feet.

Children will notice that the paint gets fainter as they walk across the paper.

Some children will try to paint with particular parts of their feet, such as a toe or their heel.

Modification

On another day, children can sit on chairs and paint with their toes.

Comments & Questions to Extend Thinking

What parts of your foot do you see on the paper?

Why is there a place with no paint in the middle of each footprint?

What kind of mark can you make with your heel?

I see more toes than any other type of mark on your mural.

Your footprints make a pattern—right-left, right-left.

Integrated Curriculum Activities

Place a tray of moist sand and an assortment of small novelty shoes in the science area. Children can observe the imprints made by each type of shoe (see *More Than Magnets*, activity 2.14).

Read books about footprints, such as *Footprints in the Snow*, by Cynthia Benjamin (New York: Scholastic, 1994).

Assemble a collection of tiny novelty shoes for sorting and classifying (see *More Than Counting*, activity 3.3).

Use the children's shoes for a patterning activity (see *Much More Than Counting*, activity 2.19).

8.6 Snow Rainbow

Description

For this activity, children spray the snow with colored water. It is exciting to watch the snow take on the colors of the water. Some children combine colors to create new colors, while others draw large pictures with the spray bottles. Children are usually eager to see if their colors and pictures last from day to day. A camera can capture the creations before they melt.

Art Experiences

- ▲ spray bottle painting
- ▲ painting on an unusual surface

Materials

- ▲ snowy outside area
- ▲ spray bottles, filled with colored water (red, blue, and yellow)
- ▲ camera

Helpful Hints

Have a set of old gloves available, or ask parents to send old gloves or mittens, as the food coloring may stain the children's gloves.

Water can be quickly colored with a few drops of food coloring.

Child's Level

This activity is appropriate for either preschool or kindergarten children.

What to Look For

Children will watch eagerly as the snow turns colors.
Children will combine colors of water on the snow to produce new colors.
Some children will create pictures with the spray bottles on the snow.
Children will watch to see if their creations change from day to day.

Modification

After they have had some initial experiences with spraying the snow different colors, children may wish to create sculptures with the snow and then spray them with colored water.

Comments & Questions to Extend Thinking

How did you make purple snow without having purple water?
Can you use the spray bottle to make a picture?
Look. Someone made a red circle and colored it in with blue.

Integrated Curriculum Activities

Color ice cubes by adding a drop of food coloring to the water before freezing (activity 3.13). Children can draw with them.
Put snow in the water table. Children can color it with tiny spray bottles of colored water and observe how the colors look as they melt.
Put colored ice cubes in the water table. Children can watch the colors change as they melt and mix together.

8.7 Fence Weaving

Description

Most playgrounds are fenced for safety, and the fence makes a large, natural loom for weaving. Children can use strips of paper, yarn, crepe paper streamers, or wallpaper border strips to transform their fence into a group weaving.

Helpful Hints

Attach the paper strips to the fence with tape so that they don't pull all the way through when the children start to weave them.

Art Experiences

- ▲ weaving
- ▲ working together to create a group project
- ▲ creating in large dimensions
- ▲ patterning

Materials

- ▲ fence
- ▲ paper strips
- ▲ crepe paper streamers
- ▲ yarn

Child's Level

This activity is most appropriate for older preschool or kindergarten children.

What to Look For

Children will weave the paper strips in and out of the fence.
Some children will follow a pattern when weaving, such as over one bar and under one bar.
Children will discuss weaving strategies with each other.
Some children will move the paper strips randomly over and under bars on the fence.
Some children will perceive the weaving patterns more easily if they are chanted rhythmically.
Children will admire the total effect of the large weaving on the fence.

Modification

Crepe paper streamers may be easier for children to observe when they first try weaving the fence. Yarn can be introduced later.

Comments & Questions to Extend Thinking

How do you think the fence will look if we weave these streamers through the bars?
Can you make the red streamer go over the bars that the blue streamer goes under?
I see a different pattern here. The streamer goes over two bars and under one.
What color do you think we should use next?
Can we create a pattern with the colors we choose?

Integrated Curriculum Activities

Plan weaving activities for the classroom (activities 6.12, 6.13, 6.14, and 6.15).
Take photographs of the fence so children can remember the various ways they have decorated it.

8.8 Decorating the Sidewalk

Helpful Hints

Take photographs of the sidewalk drawings so children can compare how they look before and after they are sprayed with water.

Description

The sidewalk provides a large surface for children to decorate with colored chalk. It has a rougher texture than they are accustomed to working on. After children have drawn on the sidewalk with chalk, they can spray their creations with water and watch the changes.

Art Experiences

▲ drawing with chalk
▲ working on unusual surfaces

Materials

▲ colored chalk
▲ spray bottles of water

Child's Level

This activity is appropriate for either preschool or kindergarten children.

What to Look For

Children will experiment with the chalk on the pavement.
Some children will draw pictures with the chalk.
Children will notice how quickly the chalk wears away when they draw with it on the pavement.
Children will notice how the colors of the chalk darken when they spray it with water.

Modification

Some children may find it easier to draw on the pavement with large pieces of chalk. Start with wide sidewalk chalk and introduce smaller pieces of chalk later.

Comments & Questions to Extend Thinking

How does the pavement feel when you move the chalk across it?
What is happening to the chalk?
How do you think the chalk will look if you spray water on it?
The blue chalk looks light blue when it's dry and dark blue when it's wet.

Integrated Curriculum Activities

Plan chalk activities for indoors as well as outdoors.
Let children compare the effects of chalk dipped in water with dry chalk.
Use chalk to color sand or salt and use the colors to make layered sand jars (activity 7.17).

8.9 Wall Rubbings

Description

For this activity, children place paper against the wall of the building or on various ground surfaces and rub over the paper with the side of a crayon. Different textures and patterns emerge.

Helpful Hints

Ask parents of school-age children to donate their used school crayons at the end of the year. You'll have a supply all ready for the next year's art activities.

Art Experiences

▲ creating rubbings
▲ working with various surfaces

Materials

▲ thin white paper, such as newsprint or photocopy paper
▲ crayons, with the paper removed
▲ various wall and ground surfaces

Child's Level

This activity is most appropriate for older preschool and kindergarten children.

What to Look For

Children will watch patterns and textures emerge as they rub over the surfaces.

Children will experiment with creating rubbings on a variety of surfaces.

Some children will construct the relationship between the way the rubbing looks and the surface that is under the paper.

Some children will use the tip of the crayon instead of the side because that is what they are used to.

Some children will have trouble holding the paper still while they rub over it.

Modification

Tape the paper to the surface for children who have trouble holding the paper while they rub over it.

Comments & Questions to Extend Thinking

Where did this design come from?

Do all of the walls make the same pattern?

What do you think the brick will look like if we rub over it?

Look at this rubbing and see if you can find out where it was made.

Integrated Curriculum Activities

Bring textures into the classroom for children to use as materials for rubbings. Sandpaper, linoleum tiles, rocks with fossils, and textured wallpaper are possibilities.

Create rubbings of items from nature, such as leaves.

Put various objects in a box with a hole large enough for a child's hand. Children can guess what is in the box by feeling the materials.

8.10 Giant Pendulum Designs

Helpful Hints

Experiment ahead of time with the thickness of the paint. It may have to be thinned with water so that it will drip from the bottle.

Description

Teachers can create a large pendulum outside by suspending an inverted bottle from an A-frame or a large climber. Drill or poke a hole in the bottom of the bottle so that it can be suspended by a string. Children can create giant pendulum designs by dripping paint from the bottle onto a large paper as they swing the pendulum.

Art Experiences

▲ painting with a pendulum
▲ creating patterns and symmetry

Materials

▲ large pendulum, as described above
▲ tempera paint
▲ large sheets of paper

Child's Level

This activity is most appropriate for older preschool and kindergarten children.

What to Look For

Children will observe the designs created by the pendulum.
Children will watch for extended periods of time while others use the pendulum.
Some children will want to grab the pendulum rather than letting it swing freely.
Children will see elliptical patterns emerge.

Modification

Colored sand can also be used to create pendulum pictures. Cover the paper with a thin coating of glue or media mix and let sand drip from the bottle.

Comments & Questions to Extend Thinking

What kinds of lines is the pendulum making?
The pendulum is making an elliptical shape all by itself.
What did you have to do to make the design?
This half of the painting looks the same as this half.

Integrated Curriculum Activities

Plan pendulum activities for the science area (see *More Than Magnets*, activities 3.17, 3.18, and 3.19).
On another day, let the children use the pendulum to knock over 1-liter bottles.
Suspend a tire from a large A-frame. Children can swing on it and experience the feeling of being on a pendulum.

8.11 Giant Ramp Painting

Description

For this activity, paper is taped to a large outdoor ramp. The ramp could be a wide slide or a large piece of wood or heavy cardboard that is elevated at one end. Children can dip a variety of objects in paint and roll them down the ramp to create this group picture.

Helpful Hints

Place a box at the bottom of the ramp to catch the objects so they don't roll all over the playground.

Art Experiences

- ▲ painting on an incline
- ▲ using a variety of objects as painting tools
- ▲ working together to produce a group project

Materials

- ▲ large incline, as described above
- ▲ large piece of paper
- ▲ plastic tub or tray, filled with tempera paint
- ▲ objects to roll down the ramp (pine cone, car, golf ball, block, spool, etc.)
- ▲ tempera paint (1 color)

Child's Level

This activity is appropriate for either preschool or kindergarten children.

What to Look For

Children will watch to see the tracks made by various objects.
Some children will construct the relationship between the characteristics of a particular object and the track it makes on the paper.
Some children will select particular objects to create specific effects.
Children will talk with each other about the types of marks they create.

Modification

Start with one color of paint so that children can focus on the marks created by the various objects rather than on the colors of the paint. Later, introduce different colors of paint.

Comments & Questions to Extend Thinking

How did you make two trails with just one spool?
What kind of trail did the pine cone make?
Will any of these things make a wide mark?
I see lots of marks going down but no tracks going across the paper.

Integrated Curriculum Activities

Put a small ramp in the science area. Children can experiment with rolling a variety of objects down it (see *More Than Magnets*, activity 3.1).
Dip marbles in paint and create pictures by rolling them across paper in the bottom of a box (activity 5.14).
Construct a ramp out of hollow wooden blocks for children to use with tricycles.

8.12 Bubble Prints

Description

For this activity, food coloring is added to a bubble mixture. When the bubbles burst on paper, they create interesting prints. Children are fascinated with the designs they can make with bubbles. This is an ideal outdoor project. It seems to work best when the paper is placed on a horizontal surface, such as a table or the ground.

Helpful Hints

The bubbles splatter when they hit the paper. Children may want to wear woodworking goggles to keep the bubbles out of their eyes.

Bubble Mixture
1 tablespoon glycerin (check the lotion department of pharmacies)
1 cup Dawn or Joy dishwashing liquid
Water, enough to make 1 gallon

Art Experiences

▲ creating designs with bubbles
▲ exploring circular designs

Materials

▲ bubble mixture, with a small amount of food coloring added
▲ bubble blowers
▲ easel paper
▲ smocks

Child's Level

This activity is most appropriate for older preschool and kindergarten children.

What to Look For

Children will watch the prints created by the bubbles as they burst on the paper.
Children will compare the sizes and colors of the prints.
Some children will notice that large bubbles make bigger prints.
Some children will compare the spherical shape of the bubbles to the circular mark they produce on the paper.

Modification

Many materials can be used to create bubbles. Plastic vegetable baskets, spools, slotted spoons, and funnels are some of them. Let children experiment with a variety of bubble-makers and see what kind of prints they make.

Comments & Questions to Extend Thinking

What does the bubble look like when it hits the paper?
Do all the bubbles look alike?
What made this big circle?
What did you use to create a cluster of circles?
I wonder why all the marks are round.

Integrated Curriculum Activities

Remove the tops and bottoms of two soup cans and tape the ends of the cans together. This long tube produces a giant bubble blower.
Make a bubble path game for math. Use bubble shapes for the path. Children can decide what should happen if they land on a popped bubble (see *More Than Counting*, activity 5.23).
Plan a variety of bubble activities. For ideas, see *Bubble Festival*, by Jacqueline Barber and Carolyn Willard (GEMS, Lawrence Hall of Science, University of California–Berkeley, 94720).

Also from Redleaf Press

More Than Counting – Math is so easy that children can do it, if we let them! Over 100 ideas for unusual and new manipulatives, collections, grid games, path games, graphing, and gross-motor play that combine to make a complete math experience. A teacher-friendly resource.

More Than Magnets – More than 100 activities engage children in interactive science in many areas of the classroom. Prepares teachers and caregivers to ask and answer questions. Includes life science, physics, and chemistry activities.

More Than Singing – Over 100 activities and ideas for songs, instrument making, music centers, and extensions into language, science, and math. Clear directions and musical notations guide you. The cassette contains songs accompanied by guitar or Autoharp. Includes original songs and songs for movement and transitions.

Much More Than Counting – Contains more than 100 activities that will make math more fun for children. This book addresses those questions most asked by teachers, providers, and parents, as well as questions about toddlers, children with disabilities, estimation, and patterning—topics that often are forgotten in an early math curriculum. Each of the activities is accompanied by a photograph and a detailed explanation of how to set up the activity or construct materials.